COOKING AT HOME

COOKING
AT HOME

REVISED
EDITION

with The CULINARY INSTITUTE of AMERICA

Houghton Mifflin Harcourt
Boston • New York • 2013

THE CULINARY INSTITUTE OF AMERICA

President	Dr. Tim Ryan '77, CMC
Provost	Mark Erickson '77, CMC
Dean, Academic Support Services	Carolyn Tragni
Director of Publishing	Nathalie Fischer
Editorial Project Managers	Lisa Lahey '00
	Margaret Wheeler '00
Editorial Project Coordinator	Erin Jeanne McDowell '08
Editorial Assistant	Laura Monroe '12

For information about permission to reproduce selections from this book,
write to Permissions, Houghton Mifflin Harcourt Publishing Company,
215 Park Avenue South, New York, New York 10003.

www.hmhbooks.com

LIBRARY OF CONGRESS CATALOGING-IN-PUBLICATION DATA
Cooking at home / The Culinary Institute of America ; photography by Ben Fink.
pages cm
ISBN 978-0-470-58781-2
1. Cooking, American. I. Culinary Institute of America.
TX715.C783155 2013
641.5973—dc23
2013019221

PRINTED IN CHINA
TOP 10 9 8 7 6 5 4 3 2 1

CONTENTS

INTRODUCTION

The primary focus of this book is education, which is not surprising considering that it is authored by The Culinary Institute of America, the world's preeminent culinary college. The fundamentals of the key cooking techniques are thoroughly covered here in a well-organized, easy-to-understand way. They have been taught in the Institute's kitchens for decades, and it is well understood that they are the secret to working through and even improving the recipes you use to cook your daily meals. The techniques are written so they are instantly accessible to readers at all skill levels, and the information contained will inspire you to get into the kitchen. The photos that accompany each technique illustrate their key points so they can be executed successfully. These techniques can be used to make a vast number of dishes, and the recipes included can be altered to incorporate seasonal ingredients to create myriad variations. This knowledge should serve as the foundation upon which to build your expertise through experience cooking in your home. The basic lessons of cooking are the same whether you prepare food for yourself or for family and friends. Therefore, we hope that those who look to cooking for a creative outlet will come to regard this book as a valuable tool.

Preparation prior to the ultimate stage of cooking is the most important step that any home cook must embrace, especially when you are trying to put a meal on the table within an allotted amount of time. Good cooking is the result of carefully developing the best possible flavor and most perfect texture in any dish. Basic flavoring and aromatic combinations constitute the flavor base, and effective preparation prior to cooking is essential whether you are an aspiring home cook or a seasoned professional. With some advance planning, smart shopping, an organized kitchen, and time-saving techniques, healthy, exciting meals can become the norm rather than the exception in your household. You may also grow to enjoy the innovative expression it provides as well as the satisfaction of a delicious, home-cooked meal spent with your family.

STOCKS, SOUPS, AND SAUCES

Stocks, soups, and sauces are all considered basic kitchen preparations. The major distinction between stocks and soups is that soups can be served as is, whereas stocks are used in the production of other dishes, including soups. Sauces are often considered one of the greatest reflections of the skill of a chef, displaying both skill and depth of understanding of the food in both preparation and in the ability to pair a sauce with a particular dish.

Basic Preparations

Sachet d'épices (spice sachet) and bouquet garni (bundle of herbs) are bundles of spices and/or herbs that are used to add flavor to a simmering broth, soup, or stew. A basic sachet or bouquet will flavor 2½ to 3 quarts of liquid.

SACHET D'ÉPICES. To make a sachet, cut a small square of cheesecloth and a short length of kitchen twine. Place 5 to 6 peppercorns, 3 to 4 parsley stems, 1 sprig thyme (or ½ teaspoon dried thyme), and 1 bay leaf in the center. If desired, a garlic clove can be added. Bring the corners of the cheesecloth up to the center and twist them to form a bundle. Tie the top of the sachet with the twine to secure. If desired, the twine can be left long and tied to the pot handle during cooking for easy removal. Remove the sachet at the end of cooking and discard.

BOUQUET GARNI. To make a bouquet garni, gather together 1 sprig thyme, 3 to 4 parsley stems, and 1 bay leaf. Wrap the herbs in 1 or 2 leek leaves or 1 celery stalk, and then tie together with a short length of kitchen twine. Remove the bouquet garni at the end of cooking and discard.

STOCKS

A STOCK IS MADE BY SIMMERING meat bones, poultry bones, seafood bones or shells, or vegetables in water with aromatics. You can purchase bones for making stock, but it is also a great way to make use of any bones that you may have left over from other preparations. (If you purchase the bones frozen, thaw them before using.) Leave any meat trim on the bones to boost the flavor of the stock. Rinse the bones thoroughly, to remove any blood or impurities, and then cut the bones into pieces about 3 inches long before putting them into the stockpot.

As the stock simmers, you will need to use a ladle or skimmer to periodically skim off any fat and debris, usually called "scum," that accumulates on the surface. For this reason, it is important to start with cold water in the pot. The cold start allows for larger pieces of protein and fat to coagulate at the surface, which makes for easier skimming and a clearer finished stock (or broth). Once the stock is done, strain it to remove the bones and vegetables. The finished stock can be used right away or refrigerated or frozen for later use.

EXPERT tips

THE FLAVOR OF THE STOCK can be changed or deepened depending on the ingredients used. Some stocks include vegetables, sachet d'épices, or bouquet garni. Because the stock will eventually be strained, some chefs do not tie up the sachet or bouquet ingredients. However, tying makes it easy to remove the aromatics if their flavor becomes too strong.

COOKING WITH STOCK is an excellent way to infuse flavor into a dish without adding fat or excess calories. In addition to using it as a base for soups and sauces, use it to cook grains, vegetables, meats, and poultry.

1. Place the rinsed bones in a stockpot and add enough cold water to cover by 2 inches. Slowly bring the water to a simmer and adjust the heat to maintain a gentle simmer.

2. Simmer, skimming the surface of the stock as necessary. The cooking time will vary depending on the type of stock; vegetable and fish stocks require less time than those made with chicken or beef.

3. Add the vegetables to the stock.

4. About 45 minutes before the stock has finished simmering, add a sachet d'épices (opposite page) or bouquet garni (opposite page).

5. Strain the stock to remove the bones and vegetables: Pour or ladle the stock out of the pot through a cheesecloth, sieve, or colander and into a heatproof bowl.

6. If you're not going to be using the stock right away, quickly cool it over an ice bath. Skim off any fat that rises to the surface, and refrigerate or freeze the stock until ready to use.

Basic Equipment for Making Stock

STOCKPOTS. Pots used to make stock are typically taller than they are wide. This type of pot creates a small surface area so that less liquid evaporates while the stock simmers. Look for heavy-bottomed stockpots, which will help avoid hot spots during cooking.

SKIMMERS. Any tool that will effectively skim the scum off of the surface of the stock will work, including ladles, slotted spoons, and spiders.

TASTING SPOONS. Stock should be tasted frequently during cooking to monitor flavor and seasoning.

STRAINERS. Cheesecloth, sieves, and colanders can all be used to separate the bones and vegetables from the finished stock.

STORAGE CONTAINERS. Storage containers are useful for properly cooling and holding stocks that are made in advance.

SOUPS

SOUP IS ONE OF THE MOST VERSATILE FOODS in any cook's repertoire—it can be simple or complex, warm or chilled, light or hearty. Depending on the occasion, soups can make for excellent starters to a larger meal, or they can be the main course—flanked by good bread and a simple green salad. They can be made in advance and generally store well. Ever flexible, soups are an excellent way to showcase seasonal ingredients and can be made with nearly anything.

In addition, soups are an ideal foundation for learning some of the most important culinary lessons, such as flavor development and seasoning. A good soup is balanced—with the elements of aroma, texture, taste, and temperature all working together to make a delicious end product.

When making a soup, add the vegetables at staggered intervals according to the specific recipe. Stir the soup from time to time throughout the cooking process to prevent starchy ingredients from sticking to the bottom of the pot, and to maintain the best flavor, texture, and appearance. When the flavor is fully developed and all of the ingredients are tender, the soup may be finished or garnished and served right away, or cooled and refrigerated or frozen. Although some soups develop a more rounded, mellow flavor if served the day after they are prepared, no soup benefits from hours on the stove. Not only will the flavor become dull and flat, but the nutritional value will be greatly diminished as well.

As a rule, cream soups and bisques are about as thick as cold heavy cream and liquid enough to pour from a ladle into a bowl. Purées are somewhat thicker. Add a small amount of water or broth to thin soups to the desired texture. Thick soups, especially those made with starchy vegetables or dried beans, may continue to thicken during cooling, storage, and reheating or while keeping warm. For a soup that is too thin, a small amount of pure starch slurry (page 210) may be added. Have the soup at a simmer or slow boil when the slurry is added, then stir constantly and continue to simmer for 2 to 3 minutes.

Soups should be seasoned throughout the cooking process. Chopped fresh herbs, a few drops of lemon juice, Tabasco, Worcestershire sauce, or grated citrus zest may be added to brighten a soup's flavor.

Garnishes may provide contrasts of flavor and texture, or they may introduce a complementary flavor. They may also provide additional or contrasting color.

Shape large garnishes such as dumplings, filled pastas, or wontons to a size that does not allow them to overwhelm the soup cup or plate. It is equally important that they not be too difficult for the guest to eat. They should be soft enough to cut through with the edge of a soup spoon.

The five basic styles of soup addressed in this cookbook are: broths, hearty broths, cream soups, purée soups, and bisques.

Basic Equipment for Making Soups

POTS. Large pots that are taller than they are wide are ideal for cooking soups. Some soup preparations may require that the pot have a tight-fitting lid. Look for pots with heavy bottoms, which will help avoid scorching and developing hot spots during cooking.

SKIMMERS. Any tool that will effectively skim the scum off of the surface of the soup will work, including slotted spoons and spiders.

WOODEN SPOONS. These are the ideal tool for stirring a soup during preparation due to their ability to effectively withstand high temperatures.

TASTING SPOONS. Soups should be tasted frequently during cooking to monitor flavor and seasoning.

LADLES. Having a few ladles of different sizes will aid in the serving of a finished soup as well as in the adding of liquid ingredients during cooking.

FOOD MILL. Use for purée and cream soups to achieve a coarser finished texture.

FOOD PROCESSOR OR IMMERSION BLENDER. Use for purée and cream soups to achieve a velvety smooth consistency.

STRAINERS. Some soups require straining to obtain a smoother texture. Cheesecloth may also be recommended for an even smoother end result.

STORAGE CONTAINERS. Storage containers are useful for properly cooling and holding soups that are made in advance.

BROTHS

Broth is made with meat, poultry, fish, or vegetables, which may be roasted or seared prior to preparing the broth. The ingredients are slowly simmered in water, along with aromatic vegetables, spices, and herbs, to produce a clear and flavorful liquid.

MEAT AND POULTRY BROTHS. For meat and poultry broths, it is best to use the more exercised parts of the animal, as these will create fuller, more pronounced flavors. The meat and poultry can sometimes be reserved and used for other purposes, including garnishing the finished broth.

FISH BROTH. For fish broths, it is best to use lean white-fleshed fish (such as sole, flounder, halibut, or cod). Shellfish and crustaceans cooked in the shell in a small amount of liquid produce an excellent broth. It must then be strained very carefully to remove any traces of grit or sand.

VEGETABLE BROTH. Nearly any vegetable can be used to make vegetable broth. More commonly, a combination of vegetables (or vegetable trimmings) is used. Consider the strength of the vegetable's flavor and how that might affect the broth's balance. Some vegetables, such as cabbage and cauliflower, can become overwhelmingly strong when simmered for long periods. Additional ingredients can be added to lend flavor, aroma, and color to a broth. Some of the most common additions are a sachet d'épices or bouquet garni.

Chef's Lesson
BROTH

1. Combine the major flavoring ingredients, seasonings, and enough cold water to cover the ingredients completely. Gently bring the liquid to a simmer, skimming as necessary. Gentle simmering extracts maximum flavor and establishes a natural clarification process that encourages impurities (fat and scum) to collect on the surface, where they can be easily skimmed away. Add the remaining ingredients and aromatics at appropriate intervals. Sachet d'épices and bouquet garni ingredients release their flavors quickly and are added near the end of the cooking time.

2. Simmer until the flavor, color, and body of the broth are fully developed, skimming the surface as necessary. Since the cooking times for broths vary widely, consult specific recipes for guidance. Meat and poultry should be cooked until fork-tender. Fish, shellfish, and crustaceans should be simmered briefly until just cooked through. Vegetables should be extremely soft but not cooked to shreds.

3. To keep the broth clear, lift the meat or chicken and vegetables from the broth before straining. Line a sieve or colander with rinsed, doubled cheesecloth. A fine-mesh sieve or a paper filter can also be used. Then ladle, don't pour, the broth out of the pot. The broth can now be served or stored for later use. A properly cooked broth is clear, golden in color, rich tasting, and aromatic—with good flavor and noticeable body, typically indicated by a few droplets of fat on the surface.

HEARTY BROTHS

Hearty broths are made by adding additional ingredients to a broth to intensify flavor, texture, and body. Vegetables are added and simmered in the broth until tender, and other ingredients such as meat, grains, or pasta are added as well. These soups lack the clarity of regular broths because the additional ingredients are cooked directly in the broth. Hearty broths can also be made from a single vegetable (such as Onion Soup Gratinée, page 42).

Hearty broths are made using vegetables that are chosen both for their own flavors as well as their aromatic qualities. Prepare them by trimming, peeling,

EXPERT tips

ADDITIONS TO THE BROTH during the cooking process contribute flavor and texture to the finished soups.

MEAT, POULTRY, AND FISH. Cuts of meat that are more mature and less tender should be added to the soup early in the cooking process so that they will flavor the broth properly and finish cooking at the same time as the other ingredients. Add fish or shellfish to hearty broths close to the end of the cooking time to prevent overcooking.

GRAINS AND PASTA. Allow grains and pasta a little more time than would be necessary to cook in boiling salted water.

LEGUMES. Add lentils and black-eyed peas to the soup along with the stock to cook fully. Other beans may need to be cooked separately.

DENSE OR STARCHY VEGETABLES. Roots and tubers cut to small dice typically require 30 to 45 minutes to cook fully.

GREEN VEGETABLES. Add peas, green beans, and leafy vegetables such as spinach or kale during the final 15 to 20 minutes of the simmering time for the soup.

TOMATOES. In some cases, tomatoes may be added at the beginning of the cooking time, along with the aromatic ingredients, to act as a broth flavoring. A tomato garnish may be added during the final 5 to 10 minutes of simmering time.

HERBS AND SPICES. Add dried herbs and most spices to the soup along with the aromatics to flavor the broth throughout the cooking time. Fresh and dried herbs and spices may also be added in the form of a sachet or bouquet during the final 15 to 20 minutes of simmering time, or before serving for the freshest flavor.

GARNISHING A HEARTY BROTH is another way to introduce and influence flavor. Add garnishing ingredients, such as any of the following, at the very end of the cooking process:

Meat, poultry, or fish

Grains or pasta

Vegetables

Fresh herbs, or herb pastes such as pesto

Croutons

Cheese

Plain or flavored oils

Fortified wines, or others as desired

and cutting into even pieces so that they cook uniformly (see page 18 for more information about preparing vegetables). Some hearty broths also include meat, poultry, or fish. Trim and cut meat, poultry, or fish to suit the style of soup you are preparing. After cooking in the soup, these ingredients are often diced or julienned and returned to the soup just before it is finished. Other ingredients might include beans, whole grains, or pasta. For a relatively clear soup, cook these starchy ingredients separately and add them to the soup as a garnish. A more rustic approach calls for these ingredients to be cooked in the broth as part of the soup-making process. Such soups tend to have more body and are sometimes referred to as hearty vegetable soups.

Chef's Lesson
HEARTY BROTH

1. Cut the vegetables so that they are uniform in shape and size. Cook the vegetables in fat to the desired stage. If using more than one type of vegetable, add them at intervals to develop the best flavor, texture, and color.

2. Cooking vegetables such as onions to a deep golden brown will develop a richer flavor in the finished broth. Tender vegetables, such as broccoli florets and asparagus, should not be sweated with the aromatic vegetables. They are added at staggered intervals, according to individual cooking times. Consult recipes for specific instructions on cooking vegetables.

Add the broth and bring to a simmer, stirring, skimming, and adjusting the seasoning throughout the cooking time. Add the main flavoring ingredients at the appropriate intervals. Depending upon the flavor of the broth, appropriate seasoning may also be added at this point. Bear in mind that the soup will simmer for about 30 minutes longer. A slow simmer is the best cooking speed for most soups. Skim the surface as needed throughout preparation. Taste the soup frequently as it cooks, and make adjustments as necessary. The hearty broth can now be served or stored for later use.

3. The finished hearty broth should have a rich color, flavor, and aroma. Vegetables should be extremely soft but not cooked to shreds. Meat, poultry, fish, and starchy ingredients, such as potatoes and beans, should hold their shape but have a very soft texture.

CREAM SOUPS

Cream soups can be made a variety of ways. Classically, cream soups were based on a béchamel or velouté sauce (see page 31) and finished with heavy cream or a liaison (see page 30) of heavy cream and egg yolks. Today, a cream soup can simply mean a purée soup finished with heavy cream.

The main flavoring for some cream soups is often a single ingredient, such as broccoli, asparagus, chicken, or fish. When simmering poultry or fish in the soup to give flavor and body, be sure to trim, truss, or cut those ingredients as appropriate. Vegetables, whether used as main flavoring ingredients or as aromatics, should be peeled, trimmed, and cut into even pieces so they cook uniformly.

Use a well-seasoned, full-bodied broth as the base of the soup. Bring the liquid up to a simmer, along with seasonings, aromatics, or other ingredients meant to provide flavor. Refer to specific recipes for guidance. Thickeners including prepared roux (page 16), flour, potatoes, or the natural thickening of the puréed main ingredient give cream soups their texture.

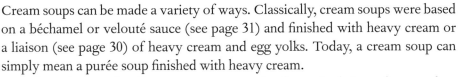

Chef's Lesson
CREAM SOUP

1. Cook the aromatic vegetables in fat to develop a good flavor base. White mirepoix (equal parts onion, celery, parsnip, and leek) is a common aromatic combination for cream soups.

2. Add the main flavoring ingredient(s) in the first stages of cooking. Cook gently over low heat until the vegetables are tender and translucent and begin to release their juices.

Prepare the thickening agent for the soup. This may be a prepared velouté or béchamel sauce, or it may be a roux or potatoes. Consult individual recipes for specific instructions on when to add ingredients. Add the thickening ingredients and the liquid (broth), and bring the soup just up to a simmer, stirring frequently.

Simmer until the main ingredient is fully cooked and tender and the soup has a good flavor, stirring, skimming, and adjusting the seasoning throughout the cooking time. Cream soups usually need 30 to 45 minutes of simmering time to develop flavor and thicken properly. Taste the soup frequently as it cooks and make adjustments as necessary. Stir frequently to prevent scorching. Skim the surface as needed throughout preparation.

3. Purée the soup (if necessary) with a food mill, food processor, or immersion blender and strain it. Vegetable soups must be strained, and any solids remaining in the strainer should be discarded. After that, the soup base should be added back to the pot and simmered until the desired consistency is achieved.

Cream soups based upon meat, poultry, or fish, are not necessarily puréed. The goal is to have a smooth, creamy finished texture.

4. For a hot cream soup, return the soup to a simmer over medium heat. Simmer the soup, checking for flavor, consistency, and seasoning before adding the cream. Add enough hot cream to enrich the soup, without overwhelming the main ingredient's flavor. The soup can now be served or stored for later use.

5. Good cream soups have a rich flavor, velvety texture, and a lightly thickened consistency, similar to heavy cream. If garnishing the hot soup, the garnishes must be very hot when added. Cook the garnish fully and season it well.

3

4

5

EXPERT tips

GARNISH THE SOUP with diced or julienned vegetables, or minced herbs, at the very end of the cooking process.

FOR A HEALTHIER OPTION, use puréed vegetables (especially those high in starch) to thicken the soup in place of roux, velouté, or flour. Replace cream with evaporated skim milk to reduce calories and fat.

PURÉE SOUPS

Purée soups are slightly thicker than cream soups and have a somewhat coarser texture. Often based on dried legumes, potatoes, or starchy vegetables, purée soups are usually entirely puréed, though occasionally some of the solids are left whole for an alternate finished texture. Purée soups are often garnished with croutons or a sprinkling of a complementary meat, fresh herbs, or a vegetable.

Many purée soups are based on dried beans: Great Northern, navy, or black beans, lentils, and split peas, for example. Beans other than lentils and split peas should be soaked for several hours before cooking (see page 257). The beans absorb some liquid, the overall cooking time is shortened, and the beans cook more evenly and absorb less liquid during the cooking process.

Relatively starchy vegetables such as potatoes, squash, or celery root are often the base for other purée soups. These have to be peeled and diced or sliced. Even though these ingredients are puréed, relative uniformity of cut size is necessary for the ingredients to cook evenly.

Water and broth are the most frequently used base liquids. Aromatic ingredients such as onions, garlic, carrots, and celery are often found in purée soups. Vegetables may be roasted or grilled beforehand for extra flavor.

Many purée soups based on a legume call for a bit of rendered salt pork, smoked ham, bacon, or other cured pork products. In some instances, these ingredients should be blanched first to remove any excess salt: cover them with cool water, bring the water to a simmer, and then drain and rinse. Consult individual recipes for specific instructions regarding ingredients.

1

Chef's Lesson
PURÉE SOUP

1. If the recipe calls for minced salt pork or bacon, render it over low heat to release the fat. You can also use butter or oil for a meatless soup. Lightly brown the aromatic vegetables: Cook over low to medium heat, stirring from time to time, until a rich aroma develops or until they take on a rich golden hue, 20 to 30 minutes. Add the main flavoring ingredient.

2. Add the broth and bring the soup to a simmer. Simmer until the main flavoring ingredient is tender. Add the remaining ingredients at the appropriate intervals. Add dry, dense, tough, fibrous, or starchy ingredients (dry beans, root vegetables, or winter squash, for instance) at the beginning of the cooking time, usually as soon as the stock or broth has reached a simmer. Simmer until the soup is well flavored and all the ingredients are very tender, 25 to 30 minutes for soups made with starchy vegetables or potatoes or 45 minutes to 1 hour for soup made with dried legumes. Taste the soup frequently as it cooks and make adjustments as necessary. Skim the surface as needed throughout the cooking time. Gently stir the soup frequently as it cooks to prevent starchy ingredients from sticking to the bottom of the pot.

3. Strain out a small portion of the cooking liquid and reserve for adjusting the final consistency of the soup. Purée the remaining solids and liquid with a food mill, food processor, or immersion blender, and adjust the seasoning and consistency. Different types of puréeing equipment will produce different textures in the finished soup. Rustic purées may be relatively coarse and may even simply rely upon the starch in the main ingredient to give the soup its thickened texture. A food mill fitted with a coarse disk can also be used for a textured purée. Food processors and immersion blenders produce very smooth soups with a very fine consistency. Return the soup to the pot and simmer until the desired consistency is achieved, adjusting with the reserved cooking liquid, if necessary. The soup can now be served or stored for later use.

4. The finished purée soup is thick in texture with a nice complexity of flavor. Purée soups are somewhat thicker and have a slightly coarser texture than other thick soups, but they should still be liquid enough to pour easily from a ladle into a bowl, with a consistency similar to heavy cream.

BISQUES

Traditionally, bisques were based on crustaceans, such as shrimp, lobster, or crayfish, and thickened with rice, rice flour, or bread. The crustacean shells are usually pulverized along with the other ingredients before a final straining. The end result is a soup with a consistency like that of a cream soup.

Today, bisques may be based on ingredients other than crustaceans and may rely on a vegetable purée or roux as the thickener. A vegetable-based bisque is prepared in the same manner as a purée soup. If the main vegetable does not contain enough starch to act as a thickener, then rice, roux, or a starchy vegetable such as potato may be used to provide additional thickness. When the vegetables are tender, the soup is puréed until smooth.

Crustacean shells for bisque should be rinsed well, then coarsely chopped. Shellfish should be scrubbed clean. Peel, trim, and chop any vegetables to be used in the bisque. Other ingredients frequently used to add flavor and color include tomato paste, sweet paprika, brandy, and wine. Cream and sherry are finishing ingredients for most bisques. Diced cooked pieces of the main flavoring ingredient commonly garnish a bisque.

Chef's Lesson
BISQUE

1. Traditional bisques get their color and flavor from shrimp, lobster, crab, or crayfish shells. Use one type of crustacean or a combination. Rinse and dry the shells well. Chop larger shells, such as crab or lobster, after rinsing. Cook the shells in fat, stirring frequently, until they turn a bright pink or red. Remove them from the pan.

2. Add the aromatic vegetables and cook until tender and beginning to brown, 20 to 30 minutes. Add tomato paste and cook until it has a sweet aroma and a deep rust color. Add spices such as paprika and other aromatics to cook in the fat.

3. Return the shells to the pan and cook, stirring well to combine. Add a prepared roux to the shells and cook long enough to soften the roux. Whisk in the liquid to form a velouté. Alternatively, a prepared velouté may be used in place of the roux and broth. A more traditional rice-thickened stock may also be used as the base for the bisque. In that case, there is no need to add either flour or a prepared roux. At this point, add wine and additional herbs or aromatics, such as a sachet d'épices or bouquet garni. Consult individual recipes for specific instructions.

4. Add the broth and bring to a simmer. A bisque takes 45 minutes to 1 hour to cook properly. Taste the soup frequently as it cooks and make seasoning adjustments as necessary. Skim the surface as needed throughout preparation. Stir the soup frequently as it cooks to prevent starchy ingredients from sticking to the bottom of the pot. After the correct cooking time, all of the ingredients (except, obviously, the shells) should be relatively tender, so they will purée easily. Use a food processor or immersion blender to purée the bisque to a fairly smooth and even consistency. Pulverizing the shells and puréeing the aromatic vegetables helps to release more flavor into the bisque.

5. Strain the bisque through a cheesecloth-lined strainer: First, set a fine-mesh sieve or colander in a clean pot. Drape the rinsed cheesecloth in the sieve and pour the bisque through it. Most of the bisque will pass through the cheesecloth. Press the contents in the strainer to help release the last drops of the bisque. The bisque can now be served or stored for later use.

6. The finished bisque will be slightly coarse, with a consistency similar to heavy cream. A good bisque reflects the flavor of the main ingredient. A crustacean bisque ranges from pale pink or red to ivory in color and a vegetable bisque, is a paler shade of the main vegetable.

4

5

6

EXPERT tips

TO THICKEN, any one of the following may be used depending on the desired results:

Velouté

Blonde roux

Flour

Rice or rice flour

GARNISHING A BISQUE is yet another way to introduce and influence flavors. Garnishing ingredients cut to the appropriate size and desired shape are added at the very end of the cooking process or just before serving. Any of the following may be used:

Heavy cream

Sherry

Diced cooked shrimp, lobster, or crab

FOR A HEALTHIER OPTION, use puréed vegetables (especially those high in starch) to thicken the soup in place of roux, velouté, or flour. Replace the cream with evaporated skim milk to reduce calories and fat.

ROUX

Roux thickens sauces, soups, and stews and lends those dishes a special flavor. Cooking flour in fat before using to thicken renders inactive an enzyme that, if not destroyed by high heat, interferes with the flour's thickening ability. Cooking flour also changes the flour's raw cereal taste to a toasty or nutty flavor. Both the flavor and the color become deeper the longer the roux cooks.

In addition to thickening a dish, roux will change the color of a sauce and, if a dark roux is used, lend it a nutty or toasted flavor. For example, dark roux is particularly important in Creole and Cajun cuisines, where it gives gumbos and stews their unique character. Another advantage of using roux is that the starches present in the flour do not break down as easily as some others, creating a more stable thickened sauce.

Roux can be prepared with any type of white wheat flour; however, the most desirable is all-purpose flour due to its starch content. Roux called for in this book was tested using all-purpose flour.

Chowders

CLASSICALLY, CHOWDERS WERE MADE FROM SEAFOOD AND INCLUDED PORK, POTATOES, AND ONIONS, though it is not uncommon for any thick, rich, and chunky soup to be called a chowder. There is also a group of chowders, of which Manhattan Clam Chowder (page 57) may be the most widely known, that is prepared more like a hearty broth.

The main flavoring ingredients for chowder are often shellfish, fish, or vegetables, such as corn.

Thickeners, including flour and potatoes, give chowders their texture. Traditionally, chowder is made employing a method in which the flour for thickening is cooked with the aromatic vegetables, but for more control over the finished product and ease of preparation, a velouté-based soup can be made. Because the roux will be hot, make sure the liquid to be added is cool or at room temperature; otherwise the roux will become lumpy. Add the liquid slowly while stirring constantly to further ensure that the finished liquid for the chowder will be smooth.

Clarified butter is the most common fat used for making roux, but whole butter, vegetable oils, rendered chicken fat, or other rendered fats may also be used. Each fat will influence the finished dish's flavor.

Heat the fat over medium heat and add the flour, stirring to combine. The basic formula for a roux is 60 percent flour to 40 percent fat (by weight). The roux should be very smooth and moist, with a glossy sheen—not dry or greasy. It should look like "sand at low tide." Adjust the roux's texture by adding more flour or fat. Stir the roux as it cooks to keep it from scorching, and continue to cook it to the desired color. To reduce the chances of scorching, large quantities of roux may be placed in a moderate oven (350° to 375°F) to complete cooking.

The four basic colors of roux are white (barely colored or chalky), blond (golden straw color with a slightly nutty aroma), brown (deep brown with a strong nutty aroma), and dark (dark brown with a pronounced nutty flavor and aroma). Once the roux is cooked to its desired doneness, it is ready to use, or it may be cooled and stored for later use.

Roux can be combined with liquid in three ways. Cool roux may be added to hot liquid, cool liquid may be added to hot roux, or warm roux may be added to liquid of the same temperature. For any approach, though, follow these general guidelines:

- Avoid temperature extremes to prevent lumping.

- Cool or room temperature roux can be incorporated into hot liquid more easily than ice-cold roux because the fat is not as solid.

- Very cold liquid should not be used, as it will initially cause the roux to harden.

- Extremely hot roux should be avoided, because it may spatter when combined with a liquid and cause serious burns.

The full thickening action of the roux becomes evident when the liquid has reached approximately 200°F. Long-cooking sauces and soups are further thickened through reduction.

Fabricating Fresh Vegetables

FROM TRIMMING AND PEELING TO SLICING AND DICING, many vegetables and herbs need advance preparation before they are ready to serve or to use as an ingredient in a recipe. Presenting perfectly cooked, aesthetically beautiful dishes begins with the mastery of these fabrication techniques.

The best dishes begin with the best-quality produce. Handle fresh produce carefully to maintain its flavor, color, and nutritional value. One key to preserving quality in produce is to perform all cutting tasks as close as possible to cooking time. Another important factor is the ability to select the right tool for the job and keep it in proper working condition. A steel should be on hand whenever you are cutting any food to periodically hone your knife blade as you work. Regardless of the vegetables being prepared, always try to make the cuts a uniform size to ensure even doneness in cooking.

Basic Equipment for Fabricating Vegetables

SWIVEL-BLADED PEELER. A swivel-bladed peeler can remove the skins from fruits and vegetables in a thin layer, because the swivel blade is able to follow the irregular contours of the food.

CHEF'S KNIFE. A chef's knife can be used for a wide variety of cutting tasks, from chopping onions to mincing herbs to slicing mushrooms.

PARING KNIFE. The 2- to 4-inch blades of paring knives are perfectly designed for peeling and trimming vegetables.

TONGS. Use a pair of tongs to safely hold a pepper or chile over the open flame when charring the skin.

KITCHEN SHEARS. Kitchen shears are the perfect tool for snipping the barbs off of an artichoke's leaves.

PEELING VEGETABLES

All fresh produce, even if it will be peeled before cutting, should be washed well. Washing removes surface dirt and other contaminants that might otherwise come in contact with cut surfaces by way of the knife or peeler. For the best shelf life, wash vegetables as close to preparation time as possible.

Not all vegetables require peeling before cooking, but when it is necessary, use a tool that will remove the skin evenly and neatly without taking off too much of the edible flesh. Chef's knives are better for larger vegetables or those with very tough rinds, such as celeriac or winter squash. Remove fibrous or tough skins from broccoli and similar vegetables by using a paring knife or swivel-bladed peeler to trim away the skin.

Some vegetables and fruits have relatively thin skins or peels. Examples include carrots, parsnips, asparagus, apples, pears, and potatoes. Peel these with a swivel-bladed peeler. These peelers can be used in both directions, so that the skin or peel is removed on both the downward and upward strokes. A paring knife can be used in place of a peeler in some instances. Hold the blade's edge at a 20-degree angle to the vegetable's surface, and shave the blade just under the surface to remove a thin layer.

CUTTING VEGETABLES

Gather herbs into a tight ball, then use a straight, downward cutting motion to chop them into coarse pieces.

When cutting vegetables into precise cuts, such as a dice and julienne, it is important to use the "slice" technique. To do this, the knife should be held firmly with a balanced grip and the wrist should be stable. Do not press the knife straight down or grip the knife with a loose wrist. The slicing motion should move either forward or backward and have a slight rocking motion.

CHOPPING. Chopping is done with a straight, downward cutting motion. Trim the root and stem ends, and peel the vegetables as necessary. Slice or chop through vegetables or herbs at nearly regular intervals until the cuts are relatively uniform (photo, right). This need not be a perfectly neat cut, but all the pieces should be roughly the same size.

To chop herbs, gather the herbs into a tight ball using your guiding hand to hold them in place, and slice through them to form coarse pieces. Once the herbs are coarsely chopped, use the fingertips of your guiding hand to hold the tip of the chef's knife in contact with the cutting board. Keeping the tip of the blade against the cutting board, lower the knife firmly and rapidly, repeatedly cutting through the herbs.

MINCING. Mincing is a very fine cut that can be used for many vegetables and herbs. Onions, garlic, and shallots are often minced. Finely mince vegetables and herbs by continuing to cut until the desired fineness is attained (photo 1). Green onions and chives are minced differently; rather than cutting them repeatedly, simply slice them very thinly. Mincing an onion is shown on page 23.

CHIFFONADE/SHREDDING. The chiffonade cut is used for leafy vegetables and herbs, and the result is a fine ribbon, often used as a garnish. For vegetables like radicchio, remove the leaves from the core and stack them. Make parallel lengthwise cuts to produce a shred. For greens with large leaves, such as romaine, roll individual leaves into cylinders before cutting them crosswise. Stack smaller leaves, such as basil, one on top of the other, then roll them into cylinders and cut. Use a chef's knife to make very fine, parallel cuts to produce shreds, or ribbons (photo 2).

BELOW, LEFT:

Mince herbs by continuing to cut until the pieces reach the desired fineness.

BELOW, RIGHT:

Leafy vegetables and herbs are often cut into a fine shred, called a chiffonade. Stack or roll the leaves together, and use a chef's knife to make parallel cuts to produce fine ribbons.

CLOCKWISE FROM BOTTOM LEFT:
Large dice, medium dice, small dice, brunoise, julienne, bâtonnet

JULIENNE AND BÂTONNET. Julienne and bâtonnet are long, rectangular cuts. The difference between these cuts is the size. Julienne are narrower than bâtonnet. Trim and square off the vegetable by cutting a slice to make four straight sides (photo 1, page 22). Cut both ends to even off the block. These initial slices make it easier to produce even cuts. The trimmings can be used for stocks, soups, purées, or other preparations where the shape is not important.

After squaring off the vegetable, slice the vegetable lengthwise, making parallel cuts of even thickness (photo 2, page 22). Stack the cut slices, aligning the edges, and make even parallel cuts of the same thickness for a bâtonnet (photo 3, page 22). Thinner slices in both directions make julienne.

DICING. Dicing produces cube shapes. Different preparations require different sizes of dice. From smallest to largest, the names given to the dices are brunoise and small, medium, and large dice. To begin, trim and square the vegetable as for julienne or bâtonnet. Gather the julienne or bâtonnet pieces and cut through them crosswise at evenly spaced intervals (photo 4, page 22).

1

2

3

4

ABOVE, LEFT:
For julienne and bâtonnet cuts, trim the vegetable as needed, and square it off by cutting slices to create four straight sides; cut off the ends to make an even block.

ABOVE, CENTER:
After squaring off the vegetable, slice it lengthwise, making parallel cuts of even thickness.

ABOVE, RIGHT:
Stack the cut slices, aligning the edges, and make even parallel cuts of the same thickness for bâtonnet. Thinner slices in both directions make julienne.

LEFT:
Gather the bâtonnet or julienne pieces and cut through them crosswise at evenly spaced intervals to create brunoise, small-dice, medium-dice, or large-dice cubes.

Onions are diced and minced using a different method. Peel the onion, taking off as few layers as possible: Use a paring knife to cut thin slices away from the stem and root ends of the bulb. Catch the peel between the pad of your thumb and the flat side of your knife blade and pull away the peel. Trim away any brown spots if necessary. Cut the onion in half through the root and stem ends. To dice or mince an onion half, lay it cut side down on a cutting board. Use a chef's knife to make a series of evenly spaced, parallel lengthwise cuts with the tip of the knife, leaving the root end intact (photo 1). Cuts spaced ¼ inch apart will make small dice; cuts spaced ½ inch or ¾ inch apart will produce medium or large dice. To mince the onion, space the cuts ⅛ inch apart. While gently holding the vertical cuts together, make two or three horizontal cuts parallel to the work surface from the stem end toward the root end, but do not cut all the way through (photo 2). To complete the dice, make even, crosswise cuts working from the stem end up to the root end, cutting through all layers of the onion (photo 3).

BELOW, LEFT:
Make a series of evenly spaced, parallel lengthwise cuts through the peeled onion half, leaving the root end intact.

BELOW, CENTER:
Hold the vertical cuts together and make two or three horizontal cuts parallel to the cutting board from stem toward the root end.

BELOW, RIGHT:
To complete the dice, make even, crosswise cuts working from the stem end up to the root end.

1 2 3

TOMATO CONCASSÉ

Tomato concassé—tomatoes that have been peeled, seeded, and chopped—is a basic preparation that is used in many different dishes. To prepare tomato concassé, score an X into the bottom of each tomato, but be sure not to cut too deeply. Remove the stem core. Bring a pot of water to a rolling boil. Prepare a bowl of ice water to shock the tomatoes after cooking. Drop the tomatoes into the boiling water and cook for 10 to 15 seconds, depending on their ripeness, and then remove them with a slotted spoon or spider and shock them in the ice water (photo 1, opposite). Once they are cool, use a paring knife to peel away the tomatoes' skin (photo 2, opposite). If a tomato was cooked properly, none of the flesh will pull away with the skin.

The true definition of a concassé calls for the peeled tomato to be roughly chopped, but the tomatoes can be cut as desired for a specific recipe. To roughly chop, first halve the tomato crosswise at its widest point, and gently squeeze out the seeds. (Cut plum tomatoes lengthwise to seed them more easily.) The seeds and juices of the tomato may be preserved for other preparations.

For more precise cuts, quarter the peeled tomatoes instead of halving them, and cut away the seeds and any membranes using a paring knife (photo 3, opposite). Cut the flesh into julienne, dice, or other desired shapes (photo 4, opposite).

Prepare a pot of boiling water and a bowl of
ice water. Drop the tomatoes into the boiling
water, and cook for 10 to 15 seconds. Remove the
tomatoes and immediately drop into the ice water.

ABOVE, CENTER:

Use a paring knife to peel away the skin.
If the tomato was properly cooked, none of
the flesh will be removed with the skin.

ABOVE, RIGHT:

Halve the tomato crosswise at its widest
point, and gently squeeze out the seeds. Or
quarter the tomato, and remove the seeds and
membranes with a paring knife, as shown.

LEFT:

Cut the tomato concassé as desired.

FRESH PEPPERS AND CHILES

Peppers and chiles are often roasted and peeled before they are used in a dish. They can be charred in a flame, broiled, grilled, or roasted to make them easier to peel and to give them a deep, rich flavor. To roast and peel fresh peppers and chiles, hold the pepper with tongs over a medium flame of a gas burner (photo 1, opposite), or place the pepper on a grill. Turn the pepper and roast it until the surface is evenly charred. Place the pepper in a stainless steel bowl covered with plastic wrap or in a paper bag and let stand for at least 30 minutes to steam the skin loose. When the pepper is cool enough to handle, use a paring knife or your hands to remove the charred skin (photo 2, opposite). Have a bowl of water nearby to rinse the charred skin off of your knife as you work. Rub the pepper lightly with a clean kitchen towel to remove any small bits of charred skin that may remain on the pepper. If you're preparing a large number of peppers or chiles, roast them in a hot oven or under a broiler, rather than charring them individually over a flame. Cut the peppers in half, remove the stems, seeds, and ribs if desired, and place the peppers cut side down on an oiled baking pan. Roast or broil until the exteriors are evenly charred. Remove from the oven and cover the peppers with an inverted baking sheet. Let stand for 30 minutes to steam the skin loose. Remove the skin as previously described.

To cut and seed fresh peppers and chiles, first cut through the pepper from top to bottom. If the pepper is especially large, you can cut it into quarters. Use the tip of a paring knife to cut away the stem and seeds. Much of a chile's heat is in the seeds, ribs, and blossom end, so you can control the degree of heat by adjusting how much, if any, of these parts you add to a dish.

You can make precise cuts out of the pepper by removing the seeds and ribs before starting to cut it. Cut away the top and bottom of the pepper to create an even rectangle. Roll the pepper away from the knife as you cut the seeds and ribs away to create a long rectangle of pepper (photo 3, opposite). Peel away the skin, if desired, and then cut the flesh into julienne or dice (photo 4, opposite). For an even more precise preparation, use a chef's knife to cut away a thin layer of the interior flesh to make a completely flat surface before cutting into julienne or dice.

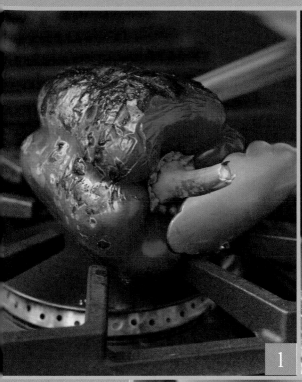 **1**

 **2** **3**

 **4**

ABOVE, LEFT:
*Cook the pepper over an open flame
until evenly charred on all sides.*

ABOVE, CENTER:
*Transfer the charred pepper to a stainless
steel bowl and cover with plastic wrap.
Let the pepper steam for at least 30
minutes, then peel the skin away.*

ABOVE, RIGHT:
*Cut away the top and bottom of the pepper. Roll
the pepper away from the knife as you cut the seeds
and ribs away to create a long rectangle of pepper.*

LEFT:
*Thinly and evenly slice the pepper. The
pepper can be cut again to create a dice.*

ARTICHOKES

Artichoke leaves have sharp barbs, like thorns. The edible meat of the artichoke is found at the base of each leaf, which grows from a stem, as well as at the fleshy base of the vegetable, known as the heart. Artichokes have a purple, feathery center—the choke—that is inedible in mature artichokes, although the choke in baby artichokes may be tender enough to eat.

To prepare a whole artichoke, first cut away part or all of the stem. The amount of stem removed is determined by how the artichoke is going to be presented, as well as by how tender or tough the stem is. Peel any remaining stem with a paring knife. Cut off the upper part of the top of the artichoke, and snip the barbs from each leaf with kitchen scissors. Rub the cut surfaces with lemon juice to prevent browning, or hold the trimmed artichoke in a bowl of water mixed with a small amount of lemon juice. To prepare artichoke bottoms, cut off the top half of each artichoke (photo 1). Remove the tough outer leaves with a paring knife (photo 2). To remove the choke, spread the leaves of the artichoke open and scoop the choke out with a spoon (photo 3).

BELOW, LEFT:
To prepare artichoke bottoms, make a cut through each artichoke at its widest point.

BELOW, CENTER:
Use a paring knife to trim the tough outer leaves away from the artichoke bottoms.

BELOW, RIGHT:
Scoop out the center of the artichoke bottom, known as the choke.

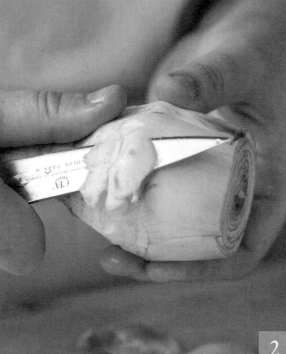

1

2

3

SAUCES

SAUCES CAN BE USED TO ADD MOISTURE, add visual interest, introduce complementary flavors, and adjust the texture of a dish. When it comes to serving sauces, first you must consider the texture of the food being served and decide how the sauce would be best presented. If the food has a crisp or other interesting texture, it might be best to pool the sauce beneath the food, spreading it in a layer directly on the plate. If the food could benefit from a little cover or if the sauce has an especially appealing look, you might choose to spoon or ladle the sauce directly over the food. Temperature is another important consideration when serving a sauce. Be sure to check not only the temperature of the sauce itself, but the temperature of the food being sauced and of the plate. Lastly, it is important to serve an appropriate portion of the sauce. There should be enough sauce for every bite of the food but not so much that the dish looks swamped.

The five basic sauces addressed in this cookbook are velouté, béchamel, tomato sauce, hollandaise, and beurre blanc. With seasoning and creativity, these preparations can then be used to make countless variations. There are, however, many sauces that do not fall within these five basic sauces, such as pestos, salsas, moles, chutneys and compotes, and other condiments, recipes for many of which also appear in this book.

Basic Equipment for Making Sauces

POT. Most sauces are prepared in a pot. Be sure to use a pot that is the appropriate size for the amount of sauce that you are preparing, and look for pots with heavy bottoms, which will help avoid scorching and developing hot spots during cooking.

SAUCEPAN. Sauces that start with a reduction, such as hollandaise and beurre blanc, should be prepared in a saucepan rather than a pot in order to allow the quick evaporation of the liquid.

WOODEN SPOONS. Wooden spoons are an ideal tool for stirring a sauce during preparation due to their ability to effectively withstand high temperatures. The back of a wooden spoon can also be used to test the consistency of a sauce (see page 31).

A VARIETY OF SEASONINGS can be added to velouté to create different flavors. Besides sachet d'épices or bouquet garni, vegetable trim from mushrooms or onions, lemon juice, white wine, roasted tomatoes, and grated cheese can be excellent additions. When experimenting with flavors, it is important to add the ingredients at the appropriate time:

VEGETABLES should be added at the beginning of the cooking process.

AROMATICS, such as sachet d'épices, should be added during the last 30 minutes of cooking.

CHEESE should be stirred in at the very end of cooking, after the sauce has been thickened.

WHITE SAUCES SCORCH EASILY, and they can take on a grayish cast if prepared in an aluminum pan. For the best results, choose a heavy nonreactive pot with a perfectly flat bottom when making béchamel, and simmer over a low, even heat.

WHISK/WHIP. A whisk or whip can be used to blend the sauce ingredients into a homogenous mixture. Gently whipping a sauce can also help achieve a smooth texture by dispersing any lumps that have formed. In a sauce containing egg yolks, such as hollandaise, the motion of whipping also causes the sauce to increase in volume.

TASTING SPOONS. Sauces should be tasted during cooking to monitor flavor and seasoning.

BLENDER, IMMERSION BLENDER, OR FOOD PROCESSOR. Some sauces, including pesto and tomato sauce, are puréed in order to give the sauce a finer texture.

STRAINER. Many sauces benefit from straining. Produce a smoother sauce by using cheesecloth or a fine-mesh sieve to remove any lumps.

LADLE. A ladle allows you to easily place the proper portion of a finished sauce onto the plate.

Basic Preparations

LIAISON. A mixture of egg yolks and cream that is used to enrich and slightly thicken a sauce is called a liaison. When properly simmered, the combination of eggs and cream in a liaison adds smoothness, body, color, and flavor to a sauce. To make a liaison, blend the cream and egg yolks together. (The common ratio is 3 parts cream to 1 part egg yolk.)

USING A LIAISON. Add about one-third of the hot liquid to the liaison, a ladleful at a time, whisking constantly. This process, known as tempering, reduces temperature extremes so that the finished sauce remains smooth. Combine the tempered liaison with the rest of the sauce in the pot. Heat the sauce over low heat, stirring frequently, until it thickens slightly.

WHITE SAUCES: VELOUTÉ AND BÉCHAMEL

Velouté and béchamel are both classical white sauces. They have the same preparation technique and only vary in that velouté is made with stock (chicken, fish, or vegetable) and béchamel is made with milk. Both are thickened with a roux. Blond roux is traditionally used, and the amount of roux will determine the sauce's consistency. In French, the word *velouté* literally means "velvety soft and smooth to the palate," and, in keeping, the final texture of this sauce should be silky smooth. Vegetables or aromatics are sometimes added to strengthen the flavor, but they are normally strained out after cooking to preserve the characteristic smooth texture.

Chef's Lesson
WHITE SAUCES

1. In a saucepan over medium heat, soften the aromatics, if using, in a small amount of butter or oil. Add the flour, stirring frequently, to form the roux (or use a prepared blond roux; see page 16). If not using armoatics, heat the fat over medium and add the flour, stirring to combine. Cook until the roux is golden with a slightly nutty aroma.

2. Add the liquid, stirring or whisking well to combine. Bring to a simmer and cook until the sauce develops good flavor and consistency. Add the sachet d'épices or other seasoning, if using, and simmer over low to medium heat for 30 minutes, stirring frequently. (Simmering for 30 minutes is long enough to cook away any raw flour flavor from the roux.) Use a wooden spoon to stir the sauce while it simmers, making sure that the spoon scrapes the bottom and corners of the pot, to prevent scorching.

3. The finished white sauce should be translucent, smooth, and thick enough to coat the back of a spoon. Strain the sauce through a fine-mesh sieve or moistened cheesecloth. As the sauce simmers, it will almost inevitably develop a thick skin on its surface as well as a heavy, gluey layer on the bottom and sides of the pot. Straining the sauce removes any lumps and develops a very smooth texture. The sauce is now ready to use.

TOMATO SAUCE

Good tomato sauce (page 73) can be made from fresh or canned tomatoes. When fresh tomatoes are at their peak, it is a good idea to use them, but at other times of the year, good-quality canned tomatoes are a better choice. Plum tomatoes, sometimes referred to as Romas (a variety of plum tomato), are generally preferred for tomato sauces because they have a high ratio of flesh to skin and seeds. Fresh tomatoes may be skinned and seeded for sauce, or they may be simply rinsed, cored, and quartered or chopped. Canned tomatoes come peeled and whole, diced, crushed, or puréed. Tomato paste is sometimes added to the sauce as well. A good tomato sauce has a concentrated flavor of tomatoes and no trace of bitterness or excess acidity or sweetness. The ingredients selected to flavor the sauce should provide only subtle underpinnings. All tomato sauces should pour easily, but for a smoother texture, you may choose to purée the sauce using a blender, immersion blender, or food processor.

Choose a heavy-gauge pot made of nonreactive materials such as stainless steel or anodized aluminum, because tomatoes have a high acid content. Because of the high sugar content of some tomatoes, they have a tendency to scorch, so it is important to avoid hot spots in the pan.

EXPERT tip

WHEN MAKING A TOMATO SAUCE, add any of the following ingredients to develop different flavors:

Fresh and/or dried herbs

Smoked meats

Smoked ham bone or pork bone

Vegetables, such as onions and carrots

The tomato sauce on the left has been puréed, while the tomato sauce on the right has been left with a coarser texture.

Chef's Lesson
TOMATO SAUCE

1. In a sauce pot over medium heat, cook the onions and garlic until tender. For a more complex roasted flavor, continue cooking the vegetables until lightly browned.

2. Add the tomatoes and, if using, any additional ingredients. Simmer, stirring frequently and skimming as needed, until the flavor is fully developed. Cooking time varies depending on the ingredients you include, but in general, the less cooking time, the better for any sauce based on fruits or vegetables. Extended cooking time can diminish the fresh flavors. Most tomato sauces should be cooked just long enough for the flavors to meld together.

3. Add the herbs and season the sauce, adjusting the flavor and consistency as desired. If desired, purée the sauce using a blender or food processor. Adding a small amount of oil during puréeing will help emulsify the sauce, creating a lighter yet thicker consistency. Be aware that puréeing the sauce will intensify the flavors and lighten the color.

HOLLANDAISE

Hollandaise sauce is prepared by combining melted butter and water with partially cooked egg yolks. Since the largest part of a hollandaise is butter, much of the success or failure of the sauce depends on the quality of the butter itself. High-quality butter will give the sauce its characteristic rich, creamy flavor. For the hollandaise to emulsify, the butter must be quite warm but not too hot. An acidic ingredient is included in hollandaise both for flavor and liquid, but it also helps to prevent the egg proteins from curdling as well as provides the water necessary to form an emulsion. Using a reduction as the acidic ingredient will give the sauce a more complex flavor, particularly if lemon juice is also used as a seasoning.

Chef's Lesson
HOLLANDAISE SAUCE

1. An acidic ingredient is included in the hollandaise both for flavor and for the effect it has on the protein in the egg yolk. It also provides the water necessary to form an emulsion. To make the standard reduction for hollandaise, cook the wine and/or vinegar, shallots, and peppercorns in a pan over medium heat until the liquid has almost completely reduced. Add a small amount of water to cool and moisten the reduction. Strain through a fine-mesh sieve into a bowl.

2. Place the bowl of the reduction over a pot of simmering water. (Be sure the water is barely simmering with no visible signs of boiling, just plenty of steam rising from its surface.) Whisk the egg yolks into the reduction until it is thickened and warm. As the yolks warm up, they will increase in volume. When the yolks have tripled in volume and fall in ribbons into the bowl and the whisk leaves trails in them, remove the bowl from the simmering water. Do not overcook the yolks, or it will be impossible to successfully bring the hollandaise sauce together. If the yolks seem to be getting too hot and coagulating slightly around the sides and bottom of the bowl as you whisk them, remove the bowl from the heat immediately. Set the bowl on a cool surface and whisk until the mixture has cooled slightly. Return the bowl to the pot of barely simmering water and continue cooking. If the hollandaise becomes too hot and begins to curdle, remove the sauce from the heat and add a small amount of cool water. Whisk the sauce until it is smooth, and, if necessary, strain it to remove any bits of overcooked yolk.

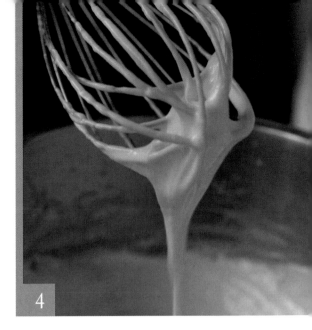

3. Remove the bowl from the heat. To keep the bowl from slipping on the countertop, stabilize it by setting it on a kitchen towel. Slowly add the melted butter to the egg yolks in a thin stream, whisking constantly until it is fully incorporated. The sauce will begin to thicken as more butter is blended in. If the sauce becomes too thick, add a bit of water or lemon juice. This makes it possible to finish adding the correct amount of butter without breaking the sauce.

4. The sauce should be a lemon yellow color with a satiny smooth texture. It should have a luster and not appear oily, and the consistency should be light and pourable. When the sauce is nearly finished, season with salt, pepper, cayenne, and lemon juice as desired. If the sauce is too thick at this point, add a little warm water to reach the desired light texture. It is best to serve hollandaise immediately. Holding the sauce for later use presents an unusual challenge, because it must be kept warm in a bowl over a pot of warm water or in an insulated bottle. Since the sauce contains eggs, it should never be held for more than 2 hours.

EXPERT tips

HOLLANDAISE IS A FRAGILE SAUCE that, unlike many other sauces, is prepared in a single operation, so a key to success is having all of the ingredients measured out and ready to go before you begin.

ADD ANY OF THE FOLLOWING INGREDIENTS to hollandaise to develop different flavor profiles:

Cayenne

Tarragon

Mint

Finely diced tomato, tomato purée, or tomato juice

Citrus fruit

THE ACIDIC INGREDIENT CAN BE VARIED when making the sauce, depending on the desired flavor. A reduction will give the sauce a more complex flavor, particularly if lemon juice is also used as a seasoning. Lemon juice will lighten the sauce's flavor and texture, but do not add so much that it becomes dominant. Butter is the predominant flavor and aroma of a good hollandaise sauce, so add just enough lemon juice to give the flavor a lift.

IF A HOLLANDAISE STARTS TO BREAK as you incorporate the butter, try adding a small amount of water and whisking until the sauce is smooth before adding more butter. If that doesn't work, cook another egg yolk in 1 teaspoon of water over simmering water until thickened, then gradually whisk the broken hollandaise into the new egg yolk.

BEURRE BLANC

EXPERT
tips

A STANDARD REDUCTION FOR BEURRE BLANC is made from dry white wine and shallots. Other ingredients that can be used to give the reduction additional flavor are:

- Vinegar
- Citrus juice
- Red wine
- Chopped herbs
- Cracked peppercorns
- Garlic
- Ginger
- Lemongrass
- Saffron

STRAINING IS COMPLETELY OPTIONAL for this sauce. You can choose to strain either the reduction before adding the butter or the finished sauce. If you decide to strain, be sure to use a fine-mesh sieve.

The flavor of beurre blanc is that of whole butter with piquant accents from the reduction. A good beurre blanc is cream in color, although garnishes may change the color. The sauce should have a distinct sheen. The body should be light. If the sauce is too thin, it probably does not contain enough butter. As with hollandaise, high-quality butter is critical to the success of a beurre blanc sauce. It's best to use unsalted butter so that you can more strictly control the salt level of the sauce. Before making beurre blanc, be sure to cube the butter and keep it cool.

A small amount of heavy cream is sometimes added to beurre blanc to stabilize the mixture. To use the cream, first simmer it in a pot over medium-high heat until it has reduced by half and has a rich, ivory yellow color. The more reduced the cream, the more stable the final sauce will be, but be aware that the flavor of the reduced cream will overpower the fresh taste of butter.

Chef's Lesson
BEURRE BLANC

1. To make the standard reduction for beurre blanc, combine the wine, vinegar, shallots, and peppercorns in a saucepan over medium-high heat, and cook until the mixture reduces to a syrupy consistency.

2. Over low heat, gradually incorporate the butter with a whisk. Do not let the sauce get too hot. If the sauce begins to look oily rather than creamy or appears to be separating, it has gotten too hot. Immediately pull the pan off of the stovetop and set it on a cool surface. Continue to add the butter a little at a time, whisking until the mixture regains the proper appearance. Then return it to the stovetop and continue to incorporate the remainder of the butter over low heat.

3. The reduction ingredients can be left in the sauce for texture and garnish, or you can choose to strain the sauce through a fine-mesh sieve. If you do strain the sauce, work quickly in order to keep the sauce warm. Serve immediately. The finished beurre blanc should be frothy and should in no way be greasy or oily. Adjust the seasoning and add any desired flavoring ingredients.

VEGETABLE STOCK

2 tbsp olive oil

1 large yellow onion, thinly sliced

1 celery stalk, thinly sliced

1 leek, thinly sliced

1 carrot, thinly sliced

1 parsnip, thinly sliced

1 cup thinly sliced broccoli stems

1 cup thinly sliced fennel

1 sachet d'épices (see page 2)

3 qt water, plus more as needed

Salt, as needed

1. Heat the olive oil in a stockpot over medium heat. Add the onion, celery, leek, carrot, parsnip, broccoli, and fennel and sauté until the vegetables begin to release juices, 3 to 5 minutes.

2. Add the sachet and 3 quarts of water, or more if necessary, to cover the vegetables by about 2 inches. Bring to a boil over medium heat, then reduce the heat to establish a slow simmer. Cover the pot, and simmer, stirring occasionally and skimming as necessary, until the stock is flavorful, about 1 hour.

3. Strain the stock and discard the solids and sachet. Season with salt. The stock is ready to use, or it may be cooled and stored in the refrigerator for up to 5 days, or in the freezer for up to 3 months.

CHICKEN STOCK

4 lbs chicken bones, cut into 3-inch-long pieces

3 qt cold water, plus more as needed

1 cup medium-dice yellow onion

½ cup medium-dice carrot

½ cup medium-dice celery

1 sachet d'épices (see page 2)

Salt, as needed

1. Rinse the bones under cool running water and place them in a stockpot.

2. Add 3 quarts of cold water, or more if necessary, to cover the bones by about 2 inches. Slowly bring the water to a simmer, and cook at a gentle simmer, skimming the surface as necessary, 3 to 4 hours.

3. Add the onion, carrot, celery, and sachet d'épices and continue to simmer for 1 hour more, skimming as necessary.

4. Strain the stock and discard the solids and sachet. Season with salt. The stock is ready to use, or it may be cooled and stored in the refrigerator for up to 5 days, or in the freezer for up to 3 months.

BEEF STOCK *Replace the chicken bones with an equal amount of beef bones and simmer for 8 to 10 hours.*

FISH OR SHELLFISH STOCK

MAKES 2½ QUARTS STOCK

2 tbsp olive oil

1 large yellow onion, cut into medium dice

1 leek, coarsely chopped

1 celery stalk, cut into medium dice

5 lb bones from mild, lean white fish; or shrimp, crab, and/or lobster shells

1 sachet d'épices (see page 2)

3 qt water, plus more as needed

Salt, as needed

1. Heat the oil in a stockpot over medium heat. Add the onion, leek, and celery and sauté until the onion is translucent, about 5 minutes. Add the bones or shells and cook over low heat until the flesh on the bones is opaque or the shells turn bright red, 5 to 6 minutes.

2. Add the sachet and 3 quarts of water, or more if necessary, to cover the bones or shells by about 2 inches. Bring to a boil over medium heat, then reduce the heat to establish a slow simmer. Cover the pot, and simmer, skimming as necessary, until the stock is flavorful, 30 to 45 minutes.

3. Strain the stock and discard the solids. Season with salt. The stock is ready to use, or it may be cooled and stored in the refrigerator for up to 5 days, or in the freezer for up to 3 months.

CHICKEN BROTH

4 lb stewing hen parts, including backs and necks

3 qt cold water, plus more as needed

1 large yellow onion, cut into medium dice

1 celery stalk, cut into medium dice

1 carrot, cut into medium dice

1 sachet d'épices (see page 2)

1½ tsp salt, plus more as needed

1. Put the chicken in a stockpot and cover with 3 quarts of water, or more if necessary, to cover the chicken by at least 2 inches. Bring to a boil over medium heat, and skim off any foam that rises to the surface.

2. Reduce the heat to establish a slow simmer. Cover partially and simmer for 2 hours, skimming the foam from the surface as necessary.

3. Add the onion, celery, carrot, sachet d'epices, and salt. Continue to simmer, skimming as necessary, until the broth is flavorful, about 1 hour more. Season with additional salt.

4. Remove the meaty parts of the chicken and save for another use. Strain the broth and discard the solids. Skim the fat from the surface, or cool down the broth in an ice bath, chill, and then lift away the hardened fat. The broth is ready to use, or it may be cooled and stored in the refrigerator for up to 5 days, or in the freezer for up to 3 months.

BEEF BROTH *Replace the chicken with 4 lb bony beef cuts such as short ribs or shank. Brown the bones and vegetables, along with ½ cup tomato purée, in a 350°F oven for 45 minutes. Proceed as directed, increasing the simmering time to a total of 4 to 4½ hours and adding 1 leek, chopped, and ¼ cup celery leaves along with the vegetables.*

CLEAR VEGETABLE SOUP

3 tbsp olive oil

⅔ cup small-dice carrot

1¼ cups small-dice yellow onion

½ cup small-dice celery

⅓ cup small-dice turnips

¾ cup small-dice leeks

½ cup small-dice cabbage

2 qt Vegetable Stock (page 38)

1 sachet d'épices (see page 2)

½ cup peeled, seeded, and diced plum tomatoes

½ cup small-dice peeled yellow or white potatoes

½ cup fresh or frozen lima beans

½ cup fresh or frozen corn kernels

¼ cup chopped flat-leaf parsley

Salt, as needed

1. Heat the oil in a soup pot over medium heat. Add the carrot, onion, celery, turnips, leeks, and cabbage and cook until softened, 10 to 15 minutes.

2. Add the stock and sachet d'epices, bring to a simmer, and cook for 10 minutes.

3. Add the tomatoes, potatoes, lima beans, corn, and parsley. Continue to simmer until the potatoes are tender, 10 to 15 minutes.

4. Remove and discard the sachet. Season with salt and serve immediately.

ONION SOUP GRATINÉE

¼ cup olive oil or vegetable oil

4 yellow onions, thinly sliced

2 garlic cloves, minced

½ cup brandy

6 cups Beef or Chicken Broth (page 40), warm

1 sachet d'épices (see page 2), including 1 sprig fresh or ½ tsp dried tarragon

Salt, as needed

Freshly ground black pepper, as needed

8 slices French bread (about ¼ inch thick)

1 cup shredded Gruyère, plus more as needed

1. Heat the oil in a soup pot over medium-low heat. Add the onions and cook, without stirring, until they begin to brown on the bottom. Increase the heat to medium, stir, and continue to cook, stirring occasionally, until the onions are deeply caramelized to a dark golden brown and very soft, 30 to 45 minutes. If the onions begin to scorch, add a few tablespoons of water.

2. Add the garlic and continue to cook for 1 minute more. Add the brandy and stir to deglaze the pan, scraping up any browned bits from the bottom of the pan. Simmer until the liquid has nearly evaporated, 2 to 3 minutes.

3. Add the broth and the sachet and bring to a simmer. Cook, partially covered, for 45 to 60 minutes, skimming any foam that rises to the surface. Remove and discard the sachet. Season with salt and pepper.

4. Serve immediately, or cool and refrigerate to allow the flavors to develop.

5. To serve, preheat the oven to 350°F. Ladle the soup into 8 individual ovenproof onion soup crocks. Top each crock with a slice of bread and sprinkle with grated cheese, covering the bread completely and coming to the edges of the crocks. Set the soup crocks in a large baking dish and add enough boiling water to the baking dish to reach two-thirds of the way up the sides of the crocks, making a water bath. Bake until the soup is thoroughly heated, if needed, and the cheese is lightly browned, 10 to 15 minutes.

POTATO AND LEEK SOUP

MAKES 8 SERVINGS

1 tbsp butter

2 medium leeks, white and light green parts, thinly sliced

2 large russet potatoes, thinly sliced

2 quarts Vegetable Stock (page 38) or Chicken Stock (page 38)

¼ cup heavy cream

¼ cup whole milk

1 to 2 tsp chopped rosemary

Salt, as needed

Freshly ground black pepper, as needed

1. In a large soup pot, melt the butter over medium heat. Add the leeks and sauté until tender, 3 to 4 minutes.

2. Add the potatoes and stock and bring to a simmer. Cook until the potatoes are tender and the soup is flavorful, 15 to 20 minutes.

3. Stir in the cream and milk.

4. Working in batches if necessary, purée the soup in a blender or food processor until smooth. Alternatively, purée the soup in the pot using an immersion blender.

5. Transfer the mixture back to the pot, if necessary. Stir in the rosemary and season with salt and pepper. Bring the soup back to a simmer. Serve immediately in warm bowls.

Minestrone

2 tbsp olive oil

1 oz pancetta (5 to 6 thin slices), chopped

1½ cups chopped green cabbage

1 cup chopped yellow onion

1 cup sliced carrot

⅓ cup chopped celery

2 garlic cloves, minced

2 qt Chicken Broth (page 40)

½ cup peeled, medium-dice potatoes

1 piece Parmesan rind (about 3 inches square)

¾ cup vermicelli or capellini (broken into 2-inch-long pieces), cooked and drained

½ cup peeled, seeded, and chopped plum tomatoes

¼ cup canned chickpeas, drained and rinsed

⅓ cup canned kidney beans, drained and rinsed

⅓ cup Pesto (page 79)

½ tsp salt

¼ tsp freshly ground black pepper

Freshly grated Parmesan, as needed

1. Heat the oil in a soup pot over medium heat. Add the pancetta and cook until the fat melts, 3 to 5 minutes; do not allow the pancetta to brown.

2. Add the cabbage, onion, carrot, celery, and garlic and cook until the onions are translucent, 6 to 8 minutes.

3. Add the broth, potatoes, and cheese rind and bring to a simmer. Cook until the vegetables are tender, about 30 minutes; do not overcook.

4. When the vegetables are tender, add the pasta, tomatoes, chickpeas, and kidney beans. Cook until heated through.

5. Remove and discard the cheese rind, and stir in the pesto, salt, and pepper.

6. Serve immediately, topped with grated cheese.

WHITE BEAN AND ESCAROLE SOUP

MAKES 10 SERVINGS

2 oz tubettini pasta, cooked and drained

3½ tbsp olive oil

5 oz pancetta, cut into small dice

1 cup small-dice yellow onion

1½ tbsp minced shallot

1½ tbsp chopped garlic plus ½ cup garlic cloves, sliced

½ lb navy beans, soaked overnight in cold water

3 cups canned tomatoes, seeded and chopped

2 qt Chicken Broth (page 40)

1 sachet d'épices (see page 2)

1 cup small-dice carrot

Salt, as needed

Freshly ground black pepper, as needed

¾ lb escarole, blanched

Freshly grated Parmesan, as needed

1. In a large bowl, toss the pasta lightly with 1 tablespoon of the oil, and reserve.

2. In a large soup pot over medium-high heat, heat 1½ tablespoons of the oil. Add the pancetta. Cook until lightly browned, stirring frequently. Using a slotted spoon, remove the pancetta from the pan, transfer to a plate lined with a paper towel, and reserve.

3. Reduce the heat to low. Add the onion, shallot, and chopped garlic and cook until tender, 3 to 4 minutes.

4. Add the beans, tomatoes, broth, sachet d'epices, and reserved pancetta. Bring the mixture to a simmer over medium heat, and continue simmering until the beans are almost tender, 1 to 1½ hours.

5. Add the carrot and cook until both the beans and carrots are tender, about 5 minutes. Remove and discard the sachet. Season with salt and pepper.

6. Meanwhile, in a sauté pan, heat the remaining 1 tablespoon oil over medium heat. Add the sliced garlic and cook until golden brown, 3 to 5 minutes.

7. Add the garlic to the soup, and bring to a simmer over medium to medium-high heat. Stir in the escarole and reserved cooked pasta.

8. Serve immediately, topped with grated cheese.

TORTILLA SOUP

4 corn tortillas

2 tsp vegetable oil

¾ cup finely grated or puréed onion

1 garlic clove, finely minced

¾ cup tomato purée

1 tbsp chopped cilantro leaves

1½ tsp mild chili powder

1 tsp ground cumin

6 cups Chicken Broth (page 40)

1 bay leaf

½ cup shredded cooked chicken breast

Grated cheddar, as needed

Diced avocado, as needed

1. Preheat the oven to 350°F.

2. Cut the tortillas into strips. Place the strips in an even layer on a baking sheet and toast them in the oven for about 15 minutes or until lightly browned. Reserve about ½ cup of the strips for garnish. Crush the remaining strips into small pieces using a food processor or blender.

3. Heat the oil in a soup pot over medium heat. Add the onion and garlic and cook, stirring frequently, until they have a sweet aroma, 5 to 6 minutes.

4. Add the tomato purée and continue to cook for 3 minutes more. Add the cilantro, chili powder, and cumin and cook for 2 minutes more.

5. Add the broth, crushed tortillas, and bay leaf and stir well to combine. Bring the soup to a simmer and cook for 25 to 30 minutes. Remove and discard the bay leaf.

6. Serve immediately, garnished with the shredded chicken, grated cheese, reserved tortilla strips, and diced avocado.

BEEF NOODLE SOUP
PHO BO

MAKES 8 SERVINGS

8 lb beef marrow bones

1½ lb beef shoulder clod

2½ gallons water, plus more as needed

8 oz ginger, cut in half lengthwise and dry roasted (see Note)

8 shallots, peeled and dry roasted (see Note)

¾ cup fish sauce

¾ cup sugar

6 cinnamon sticks

10 star anise pods, lightly toasted

5 cloves, lightly toasted

Salt, as needed

Freshly ground black pepper, as needed

¾ lb rice noodles, about ⅛ inch wide

1½ cup bean sprouts

1 onion, thinly sliced

6 oz beef strip loin, slightly frozen, sliced paper thin

3 green onions, thinly sliced

24 Thai basil leaves

24 cilantro leaves

24 mint leaves

24 rau ram leaves (Vietnamese coriander leaves)

4 Thai chiles, sliced paper thin

8 lime wedges

¼ cup Vietnamese chili sauce

1. Place the marrow bones and beef shoulder in a large pot. Add the water, plus more if needed, to cover. Add the roasted ginger, shallots, fish sauce, and sugar and bring to a boil over medium-high heat.

2. Reduce the heat to establish a simmer. Simmer until the shoulder is tender, about 1½ hours, skimming as necessary.

3. Remove the shoulder from the liquid and submerge it in a bowl of cool water for 15 minutes.

4. Add the cinnamon sticks, star anise, and cloves to the broth and continue to simmer until their flavor has infused the broth, about 30 minutes. Strain the broth, return it to the pot, and season with salt and pepper. Reserve on the stovetop at a low boil over low to medium heat.

5. Remove the beef shoulder from the water, slice it into thin pieces, and reserve.

6. Bring a large pot of salted water to a boil. Add the noodles and cook until just tender, and drain.

7. To serve, divide the noodles equally among 8 soup bowls. Place some bean sprouts and onion slices over the noodles, followed by a few slices of the beef shoulder. Lay 2 to 3 slices of the raw beef over the beef shoulder slices and ladle the boiling broth into the bowl. The broth should cover the meat by at least 1 inch. Garnish each bowl with the green onions, 3 leaves each of the Thai basil, cilantro, mint, and rau ram, and the chiles. Serve immediately with the lime wedges and chili sauce on the side.

NOTE *To roast the ginger and shallots, brush the halved ginger and peeled shallots with vegetable oil and place them on a lightly oiled baking sheet. Roast in a 400°F oven for about 10 minutes.*

Thai Hot and Sour Soup

MAKES 8 SERVINGS

¼ lb small medium shrimp (41/50), peeled, deveined, and butterflied

2 oz thin rice noodles (rice vermicelli)

2 qt Chicken Broth (page 40) or Fish Stock (page 39)

1 lemongrass stalk, cut into 2-inch pieces, smashed

¼ cup nam pla (Thai fish sauce)

2 tbsp chile oil

1 tbsp fresh lemon juice

2 tsp lime zest plus 1 tbsp fresh lime juice

½ pickled Thai chile

⅓ cup rinsed and drained canned straw mushrooms

Salt, as needed

Freshly ground black pepper, as needed

¼ cup chopped cilantro

1. Bring a pot of water to a boil. Add the shrimp and boil until cooked through, about 3 minutes. Using a slotted spoon, transfer the shrimp to a colander, and reserve the boiling water. Rinse the shrimp under cold running water to stop the cooking, drain, and reserve.

2. In the same pot of boiling water, cook the noodles until tender, 2 to 3 minutes. Drain, rinse under cold running water, drain, and reserve.

3. In a soup pot, combine the chicken broth or fish stock with the lemongrass, fish sauce, chile oil, lemon juice, lime zest, lime juice, pickled chile, and mushrooms. Bring the broth to a simmer over medium to medium-high heat and simmer for 10 minutes. Using tongs, remove the lemongrass. Season with salt and pepper.

4. To serve, place a few shrimp and some of the noodles in each bowl. Ladle the soup over the noodles and garnish with the cilantro.

WONTON SOUP

WONTONS

3 oz ground pork

½ cup finely chopped Napa cabbage

2 tbsp Chicken Broth (page 40)

1 tbsp finely chopped green onions, green parts only

½ tsp peeled, minced ginger

¾ tsp soy sauce

¾ tsp dark (Asian) sesame oil

¼ tsp salt

¼ tsp freshly ground black pepper

32 wonton wrappers, plus more as needed

1 egg, beaten

SOUP

2 tsp vegetable oil

1 tsp minced green onions, green parts only

½ tsp peeled, minced ginger

5 cups Chicken Broth (page 40)

1½ tsp Chinese black soy sauce

Salt, as needed

Freshly ground black pepper, as needed

1 egg, lightly beaten

1 oz ham, cut into thin strips

1. To make the wontons, in a large bowl, combine the pork, cabbage, broth, green onions, ginger, soy sauce, sesame oil, salt, and pepper. Place ½ teaspoon of the mixture in the center of a wonton wrapper. With a pastry brush dipped in the beaten egg, brush the edges of the wrapper. Fold it in half to form a triangle. Twist and press together the two triangle points along the long edge to form a wonton. Repeat with the remaining filling and wrappers to make about 32 wontons.

2. Bring a large pot of salted water to a boil. Add the wontons to the boiling water and cook until they float, about 2 minutes. Drain and rinse under cool water. Transfer the wontons to a bowl, cover, and reserve.

3. To make the soup, in a large wok or soup pot, heat 1 teaspoon of the oil over medium-high heat. Add the green onions and ginger and stir-fry for 30 seconds. Add the broth and bring to a simmer. Add the soy sauce and season with salt and pepper.

4. In a nonstick omelet pan or small skillet over medium-low heat, heat the remaining 1 teaspoon oil. Add the beaten egg and cook until set on the bottom, about 1 minute. Flip the egg and cook until completely set, 1 to 2 minutes. Transfer the omelet to a cutting board and slice it into thin strips.

5. To serve, divide the wontons equally among 8 bowls (using at least 4 per bowl), ladle the soup over the wontons, and garnish with the egg strips and ham.

Sopa de Albóndigas

MEATBALLS

¼ lb ground beef

¼ lb ground pork

¼ cup grated yellow onion

⅓ cup dried bread crumbs

1 egg yolk

1½ tbsp chopped flat-leaf parsley

½ garlic clove, finely minced

¼ tsp ground cinnamon (optional)

¼ tsp ground cumin (optional)

½ tsp salt

¼ tsp freshly ground black pepper

SOUP

2 tbsp extra-virgin olive oil

½ cup small-dice yellow onion

¼ tsp saffron, crushed

3 cups Chicken Broth (page 40)

½ lb dried chickpeas, soaked overnight and drained

½ cup peeled, medium-dice potatoes

Salt, as needed

Freshly ground black pepper, as needed

2 tbsp chopped flat-leaf parsley

2 Hard-Cooked Eggs (page 330), peeled and chopped

1. To make the meatballs, in a bowl, combine the beef, pork, onion, bread crumbs, egg yolk, parsley, garlic, cinnamon and cumin, if using, salt, and pepper. Knead by hand until all of the ingredients are fully incorporated. If possible, cover and refrigerate the mixture for 1 hour to make forming the meatballs easier.

2. Using your hands, shape the mixture into tiny meatballs, and reserve on a plate or baking sheet.

3. To make the soup, heat the oil in a pot over medium heat. Add the onion, and sauté until translucent, 3 to 5 minutes. Add the saffron and broth and increase the heat to bring the broth to a boil.

4. Add the chickpeas and reduce the heat to establish a simmer. Simmer until tender, about 90 minutes. Add the potatoes and continue cooking until the potatoes are tender, about 15 minutes.

5. Carefully add the meatballs to the broth and simmer gently until cooked through, about 20 minutes. Season with salt and pepper.

6. To serve, using a slotted spoon, divide the meatballs equally among 8 bowls. Ladle the broth and vegetables over the meatballs and garnish with the parsley and chopped eggs.

Cream of Tomato Soup with Gastrique and Savory Churros (page 54)

CREAM OF TOMATO SOUP

2 tbsp olive oil

1½ cups chopped yellow onion

1 tbsp chopped garlic

1 qt Vegetable Stock (page 38)

¼ cup chopped basil

One 28-oz can plum tomatoes

1 cup heavy cream, warm

Salt, as needed

Ground white pepper, as needed

Basil chiffonade, as needed (optional)

Gastrique, as needed (recipe follows)

1. Heat the oil in a soup pot over medium heat. Add the onion and garlic and cook until the onions are translucent, 5 to 7 minutes.

2. Add the stock, chopped basil, and tomatoes, reserving a little bit of the juice from the tomatoes. Simmer until the onions and tomatoes are completely tender, about 20 minutes.

3. Purée the soup using an immersion blender, or in batches using a blender or food processor.

4. Return the puréed soup to the pot, if necessary, bring to a gentle simmer over medium-low heat, and stir in the heavy cream. If necessary, thin the soup with the reserved tomato juice. Season with salt and white pepper. Serve immediately, garnished with the basil, if using, and a drizzle of gastrique. Serve extra gastrique on the side, if desired.

NOTE *The consistency of the soup may be adjusted to suit your taste. Leave some chunks of tomato, if desired, or continue to purée until the soup is completely smooth.*

GASTRIQUE

2 cups packed light brown sugar

2 cups apple cider vinegar

Combine the sugar and vinegar in a nonreactive saucepan and bring to a boil. Continue to boil until the syrup registers 220°F on a candy thermometer. Serve immediately, or refrigerate in a nonreactive airtight storage container until ready to serve, up to 2 weeks.

Savory Churros

½ cup whole milk

½ cup water

Pinch salt

Pinch sugar

3 tbsp butter

½ cup all-purpose flour

½ cup bread flour

2 eggs, beaten

2 oz ham, cut into small dice

2 oz Pepper Jack, shredded

Vegetable oil, as needed

Salt, as needed

Cayenne pepper, as needed

1. In a saucepan, bring the milk, water, salt, sugar, and butter to a boil. Rremove from heat.

2. Sift together the flours. Add the flours to the saucepan, stir briefly, and allow the flours to hydrate for a few seconds.

3. Return the pan to the stovetop over medium heat, and stir vigorously until the dough is dry and forms a ball.

4. Transfer the dough to a mixer fitted with the paddle attachment. Mix on low to cool slightly, then slowly add the eggs. Mix until fully incorporated.

5. Allow the dough to cool almost to room temperature, then add the ham and cheese. Mix to combine.

6. Chill the dough in the refrigerator for 5 minutes, or until needed. Transfer the chilled dough to a piping bag fitted with a medium star tip.

7. Cut twenty-four 3 x 2-inch strips of parchment paper and lightly oil the paper on one side. Place the strips on a baking sheet, oiled side up. Pipe the churro dough onto the strips and chill until ready to fry.

8. Heat about 3 inches of vegetable oil in a 5-quart pot or a deep fryer until it registers 310°F on a deep-fry thermometer. To cook the churros, lower each strip of paper into the hot oil and gently pull the paper away; the dough will release from the paper. The churros will eventually float and turn themselves as they cook; they will take 3 to 4 minutes to fully cook.

9. Using a slotted spoon, transfer the churros to a wire rack set over a baking sheet and sprinkle with salt and cayenne. Repeat with remaining dough until all the churros are fried.

SPICY CHICKPEA SOUP

SOUP

1 lb dried chickpeas, soaked and drained (see page 257)

¼ cup extra-virgin olive oil

2 cups small-dice onion

4 cloves garlic, minced

Harissa paste, as needed

1 tbsp plus 1½ tsp ground cumin

1 tbsp coriander

2 tsp ground turmeric

2 tsp ground black pepper

Salt, as needed

CONDIMENTS

8 oz canned tuna, drained and flaked

2 lemons, quartered

8 Hard-Cooked Eggs (page 330), coarsely chopped

1 tbsp ground cumin

Harissa paste, as needed

2 bunches scallions, sliced

Extra-virgin olive oil, as needed

8 oz country-style bread, ripped into irregular pieces

Salt, as needed

Freshly ground black pepper, as needed

1. To make the soup, place the chickpeas in a large pot of unsalted water over low to medium heat. Simmer until very tender, 45 to 90 minutes. Reserve in the cooking liquid.

2. In a separate large soup pot, heat the oil over medium heat. Add the onion and cook until very tender, 3 to 5 minutes. Add the garlic, harissa paste, cumin, coriander, turmeric, and pepper, and sweat until aromatic, 10 to 20 seconds.

3. Add the cooked chickpeas to the onion mixture along with enough of the chickpea cooking liquid to just cover them. Bring the mixture to a simmer, and simmer until the mixture is the consistency of a stew, about 15 minutes. Season with salt.

4. Arrange the condiments in serving bowls or in sectioned relish dishes and serve with salt and pepper alongside the soup.

CREAM OF BROCCOLI SOUP

2 lb broccoli, separated into stems and florets, stems peeled

¼ cup olive oil

1 yellow onion, chopped

1 leek, white and light green parts, chopped

1 celery stalk, chopped

¼ cup all-purpose flour

6 cups Vegetable Stock (page 38) or Chicken Broth (page 40)

½ cup heavy cream, warm

1 tsp fresh lemon juice

Salt, as needed

Freshly ground black pepper, as needed

1. Reserve 1 cup of the nicest-looking small broccoli florets for garnish.

2. Coarsely chop the remaining broccoli florets and stems.

3. Heat the oil in a soup pot over medium heat. Add the onion, leek, celery, and chopped broccoli and cook, stirring frequently, until the onion is translucent, 6 to 8 minutes.

4. Add the flour and cook, stirring frequently with a wooden spoon, to make a blond roux, about 5 minutes. Gradually add the stock or broth to the pot, whisking well to work out any lumps. Bring the soup to a simmer and cook until flavorful and thickened, about 45 minutes, stirring frequently and skimming as necessary.

5. Meanwhile, bring a large pot of water to a boil. Prepare a large bowl of ice water. Add the reserved broccoli florets to the boiling water and cook just until tender, 3 to 4 minutes. Using a slotted spoon, remove the florets from the pot and plunge them into the bowl of ice water. When cool, drain and reserve.

6. Strain the soup and reserve both the solids and the stock or broth. Purée the solids in a blender or food processor, adding broth as needed to facilitate puréeing. Combine the purée with enough of the reserved broth to achieve the consistency of heavy cream. Strain the soup through a fine-mesh sieve, if desired.

7. Return the soup to the pot and bring to a simmer over medium heat. Remove the soup from the heat and stir in the cream and lemon juice. Season with salt and pepper.

8. Serve immediately, garnished with the reserved florets.

COLD CANTALOUPE CREAM SOUP

MAKES 8 SERVINGS

4½ cups peeled, seeded, and cubed cantaloupe

2 cups apricot nectar

Juice of ½ lemon

2 tbsp honey, plus more as needed

1 sachet d'épices (see page 2), including ½ tsp ground ginger, 3 whole allspice berries, 1 whole clove, and one 2-inch cinnamon stick

1 cup yogurt, chilled

8 mint leaves

1. Combine the melon, nectar, lemon juice, honey, and sachet d'épices in a soup pot and bring to a simmer over low heat. Simmer, stirring frequently, until the melon is tender, 10 to 15 minutes. Remove and discard the sachet.

2. Purée the soup in batches in a food processor or blender until smooth. Transfer the soup to a bowl or storage container, cover, and refrigerate until thoroughly chilled.

3. Just before serving, whisk ½ cup of the yogurt into the soup.

4. Serve immediately, each serving garnished with a dollop of the remaining yogurt and a mint leaf.

MANHATTAN CLAM CHOWDER

MAKES 8 SERVINGS

2 strips bacon, minced

2 leeks, white and light green parts, diced

1 medium onion, cut into medium dice

1 medium carrot, cut into medium dice

1 large celery stalk, cut into medium dice

1 medium red bell pepper, seeded and ribs removed, cut into medium dice

2 garlic cloves, minced

2 canned plum tomatoes, seeded and chopped

2 yellow or white potatoes, peeled and cut into medium dice

3 cups bottled clam juice

1 cup tomato juice

1 bay leaf

Pinch dried thyme

3 dozen chowder clams, shucked, juices reserved

Salt, as needed

Freshly ground black pepper, as needed

Tabasco sauce, as needed

1. In a soup pot over medium heat, cook the bacon until crisp and browned, about 10 minutes.

2. Add the leeks, onion, carrot, celery, bell pepper, and garlic. Cover and cook over medium-low heat, stirring occasionally, until the vegetables are soft and translucent, about 10 minutes.

3. Add the tomatoes, potatoes, clam juice, tomato juice, bay leaf, and thyme. Bring to a simmer and cook until the potatoes are tender, 15 to 20 minutes. Add the clams with their juices and simmer until the clams are cooked, 5 to 10 minutes more.

4. Using a shallow, flat spoon, remove and discard any surface fat. Remove and discard the bay leaf. Season with salt, black pepper, and Tabasco and serve immediately.

New England Seafood Chowder

1¼ lb mussels, scrubbed and debearded

8 chowder clams (quahogs), scrubbed

5 black peppercorns, crushed

2 sprigs thyme, plus 1 tbsp leaves

2 sprigs parsley

½ bay leaf

5 cups water

2 strips bacon, minced

1½ yellow onions, cut into medium dice

2 celery stalks, cut into medium dice

½ cup all-purpose flour

2 large yellow or white waxy potatoes, peeled and cut into medium dice

¼ lb cod fillet

¼ lb sea scallops, diced

1 cup whole milk

1 cup heavy cream

Salt, as needed

Freshly ground black pepper, as needed

1. In a large stockpot, combine the mussels, clams, peppercorns, thyme sprigs, parsley, and bay leaf with the water. Bring to a simmer over medium heat, cover, and steam until the shells open, 12 to 15 minutes. Discard any mussels and clams that do not open.

2. Remove the mussels and clams and set aside. Strain the broth through a fine-mesh sieve, then through a coffee filter; reserve the cooking liquid.

3. Remove the mussels and clams from their shells and dice the meat. Refrigerate.

4. Heat a soup pot over medium heat and add the bacon. Cook, stirring frequently, until the fat renders and the bits of meat become crisp, 6 to 8 minutes.

5. Add the onions and celery and cook, stirring occasionally, until tender, about 5 minutes.

6. Reduce the heat to medium-low, add the flour, and cook, stirring frequently with a wooden spoon, to make a blond roux, about 5 minutes. Stir in the thyme leaves, then gradually add the reserved cooking liquid, whisking well to work out any lumps. Simmer, stirring occasionally, for 30 minutes.

7. Add the potatoes and simmer until tender, about 20 minutes more.

8. Add the cod fillet and simmer until opaque throughout, 4 to 6 minutes more.

9. Remove the cod, use two forks to flake it apart, and return it to the chowder.

10. Add the reserved mussels and clams, the scallops, milk, and cream. Cook the chowder gently, but do not allow it to simmer, until the scallops are opaque throughout, about 3 minutes.

11. Season with salt and pepper and serve immediately.

PACIFIC SEAFOOD CHOWDER

¾ cup dry white wine

1 sachet d'épices (see page 2), including 1 crushed garlic clove, one 1-inch piece peeled ginger, 2 lemongrass stalks, cut into 1-inch pieces, and 6 kaffir lime leaves

1 qt bottled clam juice

3 cups unsweetened coconut milk

½ cup heavy cream, warm

2 tbsp red curry paste

Cornstarch slurry: 1 tsp cornstarch combined with 1 tsp cold water, or as needed (see page 210)

½ lb snapper fillet, skinned, and cut into medium dice

½ lb shrimp (16/20), peeled, deveined, and cut into medium dice

Juice of ½ lemon

Salt, as needed

¼ cup basil chiffonade

1. In a soup pot over high heat, combine the wine and the sachet and bring to a boil. Reduce the heat and simmer for 10 minutes. Add the clam juice, coconut milk, and cream and bring the mixture back to a boil. Stir in the curry paste.

2. Stir the cornstarch slurry into the soup. Simmer until the soup thickens, about 5 minutes. Remove and discard the sachet.

3. Add the snapper and shrimp and continue simmering until the seafood is cooked through, 5 to 7 minutes.

4. Season with the lemon juice and salt and serve immediately, garnished with the basil.

SHRIMP AND ANDOUILLE GUMBO

¼ cup olive oil or vegetable oil

¼ cup all-purpose flour

2 qt Chicken Broth (page 40)

½ lb medium or large shrimp (16/20 count), peeled, deveined, and diced

½ lb fresh okra, stem ends trimmed, sliced ¼ inch thick

¼ lb andouille sausage, diced

2 bay leaves

½ tsp ground cayenne pepper

Tabasco sauce, as needed

Salt, as needed

Freshly ground black pepper, as needed

2 tsp filé powder (optional)

4 cups steamed white rice

1. Heat the oil in a soup pot over high heat. Reduce the heat to medium-low. Add the flour and cook, stirring frequently with a wooden spoon, to make a dark roux with an intensely nutty aroma, 10 to 15 minutes.

2. Gradually add the broth, whisking well to work out any lumps. Simmer for 15 to 20 minutes, stirring frequently.

3. Add the shrimp, okra, sausage, and bay leaves. Cook until the okra is tender, about 15 minutes.

4. Remove and discard the bay leaves. Season with the cayenne, Tabasco, salt, and black pepper.

5. Remove the gumbo from the heat and gradually stir in the filé powder, if using.

6. Divide the steamed rice and gumbo evenly among 8 bowls and serve immediately.

CIOPPINO

GARLIC CROSTINI

2 tbsp olive oil

1 garlic clove, minced

Salt, as needed

Freshly ground black pepper, as needed

10 slices crusty French or Italian bread (about ½ inch thick)

STEW

2 tbsp olive oil

1 yellow onion, cut into medium dice

10 green onions, white and green parts, diced

1 green bell pepper, seeded and cut into medium dice

1 fennel bulb, cored and thinly sliced

8 garlic cloves, minced

1 cup dry white wine

One 32-oz can diced tomatoes

2 cups bottled clam juice

2 cups Chicken Broth (page 40)

½ cup tomato purée

3 bay leaves

12 littleneck clams, scrubbed

3 blue crabs, disjointed

1½ lb swordfish fillet, coarsely chopped

1 lb large shrimp (31/30), peeled and deveined

½ lb scallops

¼ cup basil, chopped

¼ tsp salt, plus more as needed

Pinch freshly ground black pepper, plus more as needed

1. To make the crostini, preheat the broiler. In a small bowl, whisk together the oil and garlic, and season with salt and pepper. Brush the mixture evenly over the bread slices. Place the crostini on a baking sheet and broil on both sides until browned, about 2 minutes per side, watching carefully to prevent the garlic from burning. Reserve.

2. To make the stew, heat the oil in a soup pot over medium-high heat. Add the yellow onion, green onions, bell pepper, fennel, and garlic. Sauté until the onions are translucent, 6 to 8 minutes. Add the white wine and cook until reduced by half, about 5 minutes.

3. Add the tomatoes, clam juice, broth, tomato purée, and bay leaves and cover the pot. Reduce the heat to establish a slow simmer and cook until very flavorful, about 45 minutes. If necessary, add a small amount of water to adjust the consistency; cioppino should be more of a broth than a stew.

4. Remove and discard the bay leaves. Add the clams and crabs. Simmer until the crab shells are bright red and the clams have just started to open, about 10 minutes. Add the swordfish, shrimp, and scallops and continue simmering just until the fish is cooked through, 8 to 10 minutes more. The clams should be completely open. Discard any that are not. Add the basil, salt, and pepper. Taste, and season with additional salt and pepper if needed. Serve immediately, garnished with the crostini.

UDON NOODLE POT

24 oz fresh or dry udon noodles

1 tbsp peanut oil or canola oil

6 cups prepared instant dashi

24 littleneck clams, thoroughly scrubbed

12 oz boneless, skinless chicken thighs, cut into bite-size pieces

12 oz small shrimp (31/36 count), peeled and deveined

1½ cups sliced shiitake mushroom caps

1½ cups finely shredded Napa cabbage

1½ cups finely shredded spinach

1 cup thinly sliced carrot

1 cup snow peas, trimmed

⅓ cup soy sauce

1 tbsp mirin

2 green onions, thinly sliced on the diagonal

1. Bring a large pot of salted water to a boil over medium heat. Add the noodles and cook until just tender, 2 to 3 minutes. Drain the noodles and rinse them under cold water. Drain the noodles again, toss with the oil, and reserve.

2. In another pot, bring the dashi to a simmer over medium heat. Add the clams, chicken, shrimp, and mushrooms. Cover and cook until the clams open and the chicken is cooked through, 10 to 12 minutes. Discard any clams that do not open. Transfer the clams, chicken, shrimp, and mushrooms to a bowl and keep warm.

3. Add the cabbage, spinach, carrot, and snow peas to the pot and simmer until all of the vegetables are cooked through and very hot, about 10 minutes. Return the noodles to the pot and simmer until they are very hot, 3 to 4 minutes. Add the soy sauce and mirin and continue to simmer until the soup is flavorful, 2 to 3 minutes.

4. To serve, divide the noodles, vegetables, clams, chicken, shrimp, and mushrooms equally among 8 bowls. Ladle the broth over the top, and garnish each bowl with green onions.

N Chowder

3 tbsp butter

½ cup medium-dice yellow onion

¾ cup medium-dice celery

⅓ cup medium-dice green bell peppers

⅓ cup medium-dice red bell peppers

⅓ cup all-purpose flour

2 cups Vegetable Stock (page 38)

2¾ cups corn kernels

2½ cups medium-dice peeled potatoes

1 bay leaf

½ cup heavy cream, warmed

½ cup whole milk, warmed

Salt, as needed

Ground white pepper, as needed

Tabasco sauce, as needed

1. Melt the butter in a large soup pot over medium heat. Add the onion, celery, and bell peppers and cook until the vegetables are tender and the onions are translucent, 4 to 5 minutes.

2. Add the flour, stirring to combine, and cook until light brown to form a white roux, about 3 minutes.

3. Add half of the stock and stir the mixture until it is well combined. Add the remaining stock, stirring to ensure there are no lumps. Bring the soup to a simmer and cook until thickened, 30 to 40 minutes.

4. In a food processor or blender, purée half of the corn and add it to the soup with the potatoes. Add the remaining corn kernels and the bay leaf and simmer until the potatoes are tender, about 15 minutes.

5. Stir the cream and milk into the soup and bring to a simmer. Remove and discard the bay leaf. Season with salt, white pepper, and Tabasco and serve immediately.

CHEDDAR AND BEER SOUP

MAKES 8 SERVINGS

¼ cup canola oil

1 cup all-purpose flour

3 cups Vegetable Stock (page 38)

2 tbsp butter

1 cup minced yellow onion

1 cup small-dice white mushrooms

½ cup small-dice celery

½ cup small-dice carrot

1 garlic clove, minced

One 12-oz bottle beer

2 tbsp dry mustard powder

6 cups grated sharp cheddar (about 1½ lbs)

¾ cup heavy cream, warm

Tabasco sauce, as needed

Salt, as needed

Freshly ground black pepper, as needed

1. In a soup pot over medium heat, combine the oil and flour. Cook, stirring constantly, to make a pale golden roux, about 12 minutes.

2. Gradually add the stock and whisk constantly to work out any lumps. Bring to a simmer and cook until the soup has deepened in flavor and has a velvety texture, about 45 minutes.

3. Meanwhile, melt the butter in a pan over medium heat. Add the onion, mushrooms, celery, carrot, and garlic. Sauté until the vegetables are tender, 6 to 8 minutes. Keep warm.

4. While the vegetables are sautéing, in a small bowl, whisk together the beer and mustard powder. Pour the beer mixture into the simmering soup, whisking constantly. The beer will foam up a little bit—don't worry.

5. Add the cheese to the soup and stir constantly until the cheese is melted and well incorporated. Stir in the cream. Season with Tabasco, salt, and pepper, stir in the vegetables, and serve immediately.

PURÉE OF SPLIT PEA SOUP

2 tbsp vegetable oil

1 cup small-dice yellow onion

½ cup small-dice parsnips

½ cup small-dice celery

1 tsp minced garlic

3 qt Chicken Stock (page 38)

8 oz potatoes, peeled and cut into large dice

1 lb green split peas

1 ham hock

1 bay leaf

Salt, as needed

Freshly ground black pepper, as needed

1 oz bacon (about 1 thick slice), minced and cooked

Croutons (page 294), as needed

1. Heat the oil in a large soup pot over medium heat. Add the onion, parsnips, and celery and sauté until the onions are translucent, 5 to 7 minutes. Add the garlic and sauté for 1 minute more. Do not brown the onion.

2. Add the stock, potatoes, split peas, ham hock, and bay leaf and bring to a simmer. Allow the soup to simmer until the peas are tender, about 45 minutes. Remove the bay leaf and the ham hock. Discard the bay leaf. If desired, dice the lean meat of the ham hock and reserve for a garnish.

3. Using a blender or food processor, purée the soup in batches until it is smooth. Season with salt and pepper.

4. Serve immediately, garnished with the bacon bits, croutons, and reserved diced ham, if using.

PURÉE OF YELLOW SPLIT PEA SOUP *Replace the green split peas with an equal amount of yellow split peas.*

PURÉED LENTIL SOUP

2 tbsp olive oil

1 yellow onion, finely diced

1 garlic clove, minced

1 leek, white and light green parts, finely diced

2 carrots, finely diced

1 celery stalk, finely diced

1 tbsp tomato paste

7 cups Vegetable Stock (page 38)

1¾ cups French green lentils

¼ cup Riesling wine

2 tbsp sherry vinegar

½ lemon, seeded

1 sachet d'épices (see page 2)

Salt, as needed

Freshly ground black pepper, as needed

1. Heat the oil in a soup pot over medium heat. Add the onion and garlic and cook, stirring occasionally, until the onion is translucent, 4 to 6 minutes.

2. Add the leek, carrots, and celery and cook, stirring occasionally, until the vegetables have softened, 5 to 7 minutes.

3. Add the tomato paste, stir well, and cook until it darkens, about 5 minutes.

4. Add the stock, lentils, wine, vinegar, lemon, and sachet d'épices and bring the soup to a simmer over medium-high heat. Cook, uncovered, until the lentils are tender, about 40 minutes. Remove and discard the sachet and lemon half.

5. Transfer half of the soup to a blender or food processor and purée until smooth. Return the purée to the pot with the remaining soup and stir to combine well. Season with salt and pepper and serve immediately.

Gazpacho Verde

2 tbsp minced jalapeños

3 cups cored and cubed tomatoes

½ cup small-dice green bell peppers

1 cup small-dice green onions

1 cup small-dice seeded cucumbers

1½ cups small-dice celery

½ cup chopped basil

1 tsp chopped tarragon

2 qt Vegetable Stock (page 38)

2 tbsp olive oil

3 tbsp balsamic vinegar

Tabasco sauce, as needed

Salt, as needed

Ground white pepper, as needed

Croutons (page 294), as needed

1. In a large bowl, combine the jalapeños, tomatoes, bell peppers, green onions, cucumbers, celery, basil, tarragon, stock, oil, and vinegar. Season with Tabasco. Refrigerate until well chilled, at least 30 minutes.

2. Purée the soup in a blender or food processor until it is coarse, but even in texture. Season with salt and pepper, garnish with the croutons and serve immediately.

SHRIMP BISQUE

MAKES 6 SERVINGS

4 lb shrimp (26/30), peeled and deveined, shells reserved

10 tbsp (1¼ sticks) butter

1½ cups minced onion

1 tbsp minced garlic

1½ tsp paprika, plus more as needed

2 tbsp tomato paste

¼ cup brandy

½ cup flour

2 qt clam juice

⅓ cup long-grain rice

Salt, as needed

Freshly ground black pepper, as needed

2 cups heavy cream, hot

1 tsp Old Bay Seasoning

1 tsp Tabasco sauce, plus more as needed

1 tsp Worcestershire sauce, plus more as needed

½ cup dry sherry

1. Rinse the shrimp shells thoroughly and drain them. In a medium stockpot over medium-high heat, melt 8 tablespoons of the butter. Add the shrimp shells and sauté until the shells turn bright pink, 1 to 2 minutes.

2. Reduce the heat to medium. Add the onion, and sauté until translucent, about 2 minutes.

3. Add the garlic, paprika, and tomato paste and cook until there is a sweet, cooked tomato aroma and the shells soften slightly, about 2 minutes.

4. Add the brandy to the pot and deglaze the onion mixture. Reduce over medium heat until nearly dry, 2 to 3 minutes. Add the flour and cook for another 1 to 2 minutes.

5. Add the clam juice and bring the mixture to a simmer. Add the rice and simmer for 45 minutes over medium-low heat until the bisque is intensely rust-colored and has thickened slightly. Season with salt and pepper. Purée the bisque (including the shells) in a food mill (preferably), blender, or food processor. Strain the bisque through a fine-mesh strainer into another pot.

6. Return the bisque to a simmer and add the cream.

7. Cut the shrimp into small dice. In a medium sauté pan over medium-high heat, melt the remaining 2 tablespoon of butter. Add the shrimp and sauté, stirring with a spoon, until cooked thoroughly and pink, 3 to 6 minutes. Add the shrimp to the bisque and simmer for 5 minutes.

8. Add the Old Bay, Tabasco, and Worcestershire. Taste, and adjust the seasoning with additional salt and pepper.

9. Add the sherry, bring the bisque to a simmer, and serve immediately. Or the soup may be rapidly cooled in an ice bath, refrigerated, and brought to a simmer before serving.

LOBSTER BISQUE

¼ cup vegetable oil

½ to 1 lb lobster shells, coarsely chopped

1 yellow onion, thinly sliced

1 leek, white part only, thinly sliced

1 celery stalk, thinly sliced

1 tbsp minced shallot

½ cup tomato purée

1 tbsp sweet paprika

¼ cup brandy

2 qt Fish Stock (page 39) or Vegetable Stock (page 38)

½ cup dry white wine

1 sachet d'épices (see page 2)

1 cup long-grain white rice

½ cup heavy cream, warm

Salt, as needed

Cayenne pepper, as needed

1 cup sliced cooked lobster tail meat

1. Heat the oil in a soup pot over high heat. Add the lobster shells, reduce the heat to medium, and cook, stirring occasionally, until the shells turn bright red, about 10 minutes.

2. Add the onion, leek, celery, and shallot and continue to cook until the vegetables have softened, 4 to 6 minutes. Add the tomato purée and paprika and cook until the purée darkens, about 3 minutes. Add the brandy and let the liquid reduce until nearly dry.

3. Add the stock, wine, and sachet d'épices and bring to a simmer. Cook until well flavored, about 30 minutes. Add the rice and continue to simmer until the rice is very soft, about 30 minutes more.

4. Remove and discard the sachet. Purée the bisque (including the shells) in a food mill (preferably), blender, or food processor. Strain through a fine-mesh sieve.

5. Return the bisque to a simmer, then remove from the heat, add the warm cream, and stir well. Season with salt and cayenne.

6. In a medium saucepan, reheat the lobster in a small amount of bisque over low heat. Divide the lobster slices equally among 8 bowls, ladle the bisque over the lobster, and serve.

VELOUTÉ

MAKES 1 QUART SAUCE

3 tbsp butter

½ cup all-purpose flour

1 tbsp vegetable oil

¼ cup small-dice yellow onion

2 tbsp small-dice parsnip

2 tbsp small-dice celery

5 cups Chicken Stock (page 38), warm

1 sachet d'épices (see page 2)

Salt, as needed

Ground white pepper, as needed

1. Melt the butter in a small saucepan over medium heat. Add the flour, stirring to combine, and cook until light brown to form a white roux, about 2 minutes. Remove from the heat and set aside.

2. In a large saucepan over medium heat, heat the oil. Add the onion, parsnips, and celery and cook, stirring occasionally, until the onions are soft and have begun to release their juices, about 15 minutes. The onions may start to take on a light color, but should not be allowed to brown.

3. Add the roux to the pan and cook, stirring occasionally, until the roux is very hot, about 2 minutes.

4. Gradually add the stock to the pan, stirring or whisking to work out any lumps. Bring the mixture to a full boil, then reduce the heat to establish a simmer. Add the sachet d'épices and continue to simmer, skimming as necessary, until the sauce has thickened and the starchy feel and taste of the flour have cooked away, 45 minutes to 1 hour.

5. Remove from the heat and strain the sauce through a fine-mesh sieve into a bowl.

6. Return the sauce to the pot and bring to a simmer over medium heat. Season with salt and pepper. Use immediately, or refrigerate for later use.

FISH VELOUTÉ *Replace the chicken stock with an equal amount of Fish Stock (page 39).*

SHRIMP VELOUTÉ *Replace the chicken stock with an equal amount of Shellfish Stock (page 39).*

VEGETABLE VELOUTÉ *Replace the chicken stock with an equal amount of Vegetable Stock (page 38).*

Béchamel Sauce

3 tbsp butter

½ cup all-purpose flour

2 tsp vegetable oil

¼ cup minced yellow onion

5 cups milk, warm

Salt, as needed

Ground white pepper, as needed

Freshly grated nutmeg, as needed (optional)

1. Melt the butter in a small saucepan over medium heat. Add the flour, stirring to combine, and cook until light brown to form a white roux, about 2 minutes. Remove from the heat and reserve.

2. In a saucepan over medium heat, heat the oil. Add the onion and cook, stirring frequently, until the onions are soft and translucent, about 6 minutes.

3. Add the roux and cook until the roux is very hot, about 2 minutes.

4. Gradually add the milk to the pan, stirring or whisking to work out any lumps. Bring the mixture to a full boil, then reduce the heat to low to establish a simmer. Simmer until the sauce has thickened and the starchy feel and taste of the flour have cooked away, about 30 minutes. Be sure to stir frequently and skim as necessary.

5. Season the sauce with salt, white pepper, and nutmeg, if using, and strain through a fine-mesh sieve.

6. Return the sauce to the pan and bring to a simmer over low heat. Adjust the seasoning with salt and pepper if necessary. Use immediately, or refrigerate for later use.

CHEDDAR CHEESE SAUCE *After straining, return to the pan and stir in 4 oz grated sharp cheddar as the sauce simmers over low heat.*

CREAM SAUCE *Add ½ cup heated heavy cream to the finished sauce and simmer over low heat for an additional 4 to 5 minutes.*

MORNAY SAUCE *After straining, return to the pan and add 2 oz each grated Gruyère and Parmesan. Finish with up to 4 tbsp butter if desired.*

Tomato Sauce

MAKES 1 QUART SAUCE

1 tbsp olive oil

¾ cup small-dice yellow onion

2 tsp minced garlic

5 cups cored and chopped plum tomatoes with their juice (fresh or canned)

½ cup basil chiffonade

Salt, as needed

Freshly ground black pepper, as needed

1. Heat the oil in a shallow pan over medium-low heat. Add the onion and cook, stirring occasionally, until light golden brown, about 8 minutes.

2. Add the garlic and continue to cook, stirring frequently, until the garlic is soft and fragrant, about 1 minute more.

3. Add the tomatoes and their juice and bring the sauce to a simmer over low heat. Simmer, stirring occasionally, until the mixture develops a saucelike consistency, about 45 minutes. (The exact cooking time will vary depending on the quality and moisture content of the tomatoes.)

4. Add the basil and simmer for 2 to 3 minutes more. Season with salt and pepper.

5. The sauce may be left chunky, broken up with a whisk to make a rough purée, or puréed using a food mill, blender, or food processor. Serve immediately, or refrigerate for later use.

HOLLANDAISE SAUCE

MAKES 1 QUART SAUCE

6 tbsp white wine vinegar or apple cider vinegar

1 tsp cracked black peppercorns

6 tbsp water, plus more as needed

6 egg yolks, lightly beaten

2¼ cups (4½ sticks) butter, melted and kept warm

1 tbsp fresh lemon juice, plus more as needed

Salt, as needed

Ground white pepper, as needed

Pinch cayenne pepper (optional)

1. In a small saucepan, heat the vinegar and peppercorns over medium heat. Simmer until nearly dry, 3 to 4 minutes. Add the water to a medium bowl. Strain the vinegar-peppercorn mixture into the bowl; discard the peppercorns.

2. Whisk the egg yolks into the mixture and set the bowl over a pot of barely simmering water. Cook, whisking constantly, until the yolks have tripled in volume and fall in ribbons from the whisk when it is lifted, about 4 minutes.

3. Remove the bowl from the heat and set it on a damp towel to keep the bowl from slipping on the work surface. Gradually ladle in the warm, melted butter in a thin stream, whisking constantly. As the butter is blended into the yolks, the sauce will thicken and emulsify. If it becomes too thick, add a little water or lemon juice to loosen the yolks enough to absorb the remaining butter.

4. Add the lemon juice, salt, pepper, and cayenne, if using. Taste, and adjust the seasoning as needed.

5. Serve the sauce within 2 hours. If not using immediately, keep the sauce warm over a pot of barely simmering water or in an insulated container.

BEURRE BLANC

MAKES 1 QUART SAUCE

1 cup heavy cream

3 tbsp minced shallots

7 black peppercorns

1 cup dry white wine

¼ cup fresh lemon juice

⅓ cup apple cider vinegar or white wine vinegar

3 cups (6 sticks) butter, cubed, chilled

Salt, as needed

Ground white pepper, as needed

1 tbsp grated lemon zest (optional)

1. In a small saucepan, bring the cream to a simmer over medium heat and continue simmering until the cream has reduced to half its volume. Reserve.

2. In a medium saucepan over medium-high heat, combine the shallots, peppercorns, wine, lemon juice, and vinegar. Cook until the liquid has reduced and the pan is nearly dry, 4 to 6 minutes.

3. Add the reduced heavy cream and simmer over low heat for 2 to 3 minutes to reduce the sauce slightly.

4. With the pan over low heat, add the butter, a few cubes at a time, whisking constantly to blend the butter into the reduced cream. Continue adding the butter until the full amount has been incorporated. Season the sauce with salt and white pepper, and stir in the lemon zest, if using.

5. If desired, the sauce can be strained through a fine-mesh sieve for a smoother texture. Serve immediately, or refrigerate for later use.

Jus de Veau Lié

MAKES 1 QUART SAUCE

1 tbsp vegetable oil

½ lb lean veal trim

½ cup chopped yellow onion

¼ cup chopped carrot

¼ cup chopped celery

1 tbsp tomato purée

5 cups Beef Stock (page 38)

1 sachet d'épices (see page 2)

Cornstarch slurry: ¼ cup cornstarch mixed with enough cold water or beef stock to make a slurry (optional) (See page 210)

Salt, as needed

Freshly ground black pepper, as needed

1. Heat the oil in a wide saucepan over medium heat. Add the veal, onion, carrot, and celery and cook, stirring occasionally, until the veal and vegetables have turned a deep brown color, about 20 minutes.

2. Add the tomato purée and continue to cook over medium heat until the veal and tomato mixture turns a rusty brown and has a sweet aroma, 3 to 5 minutes.

3. Add the stock and bring the mixture to a simmer. Continue to simmer, skimming the surface as necessary, for about 1 hour. Add the sachet d'éspices and continue simmering until the sauce develops a good flavor, about 1 hour more.

4. If the sauce needs thickening, prepare the cornstarch slurry: Combine the cornstarch with cold water or stock until it has the consistency of heavy cream. With the sauce at a simmer, gradually stir in the slurry. Continue simmering, stirring often, until the sauce has thickened enough to coat the back of a wooden spoon. Season with salt and pepper.

5. Strain the sauce through a fine-mesh sieve. Serve immediately, or refrigerate for later use.

SHERRY VINEGAR SAUCE

MAKES 1 QUART SAUCE

½ cup sherry vinegar

⅓ cup packed dark brown sugar

3¼ cups Jus de Veau Lié (opposite)

Salt, as needed

Freshly ground black pepper, as needed

½ cup (8 tbsp/1 stick) butter, cubed

1. In a medium saucepan, combine the vinegar and sugar and cook over medium-high heat until the mixture comes to a boil and the sugar has completely dissolved, 4 to 6 minutes.

2. Remove the saucepan from the heat, add the jus de veau lié to the vinegar mixture, and stir to combine. Return the pan to the stovetop and bring to a simmer over medium heat. Simmer until the sauce has reduced to a consistency thick enough to coat the back of a spoon, about 15 minutes. Season with salt and pepper.

3. Strain the sauce through a fine-mesh sieve and return it to the pan. Over medium heat, gradually add the butter cubes, stirring constantly. Once the butter is fully incorporated into the sauce, remove the pot from the heat. Serve immediately, or refrigerate for later use.

MUSHROOM SAUCE

MAKES 1 QUART SAUCE

4 tbsp butter, plus 4 tbsp, cubed

3 tbsp minced shallots

2 lb 4 oz sliced white mushrooms

1 cup dry white wine

1 qt Jus de Veau Lié (opposite)

Salt, as needed

Freshly ground black pepper, as needed

1. In a medium pan over medium heat, melt 4 tablespoons of the butter. Add the shallots and cook until they are translucent, 2 to 3 minutes.

2. Increase the heat to high, add the mushrooms, and cook, stirring often, until the mushrooms' juices have cooked away.

3. Add the wine and deglaze the pan. Continue to cook until the wine has reduced by two-thirds.

4. Add the jus de veau lié and simmer until the sauce has a good consistency and flavor, about 5 minutes.

5. Reduce the heat to medium. Gradually add the cubed butter, stirring constantly. Once the butter is fully incorporated into the sauce, remove the pan from the heat. Season with salt and pepper. Serve immediately, or refrigerate for later use.

BOLOGNESE MEAT SAUCE

MAKES 1 QUART SAUCE

2 oz finely diced pancetta

1 tbsp extra-virgin olive oil

1 tbsp butter

1¼ cups small-dice onion

½ cup small-dice carrot

¼ cup small-dice celery

8 oz lean ground beef

8 oz lean ground pork

2 tbsp plus 1 tsp tomato paste

1 cup white wine

Salt, as needed

Freshly ground black pepper, as needed

Freshly grated nutmeg, as needed

2 cups Chicken Stock (page 38)

1 cup heavy cream, warmed

1. In a large pot over medium heat, combine the pancetta, oil, and butter and cook, stirring frequently, until the pancetta is golden brown and the fat has rendered, about 15 minutes.

2. Increase the heat to medium-high and add the onion, carrot, and celery. Cook, stirring frequently, until the vegetables are soft and the onions are translucent, 5 to 7 minutes.

3. Add the beef and pork to the pan and cook, stirring constantly and breaking up the meat, until the meat is browned, 3 to 4 minutes. If necessary, drain off excess fat.

4. Stir in the tomato paste and cook until it turns brown, 2 to 3 minutes. Stir in the wine and continue cooking until the wine has almost completely reduced and the pan is nearly dry.

5. Season with salt, pepper, and nutmeg and add the stock. Bring the sauce to a boil over high heat, then reduce the heat to low to establish a simmer. Simmer, uncovered, until the sauce has reduced to a good consistency and the flavors have concentrated.

6. Just before serving, stir in the cream and bring the sauce to a simmer; do not allow the sauce to boil. If necessary, adjust the seasoning with additional salt and pepper. Serve immediately, or refrigerate for later use.

PESTO

MAKES 2 CUPS PESTO

6 garlic cloves

Salt, as needed

⅓ cup pine nuts

4 cups tightly packed basil leaves, no stems

½ cup extra-virgin olive oil, plus more as needed

1 cup grated Parmigiano-Reggiano

1. On a cutting board, using the side of a chef's knife, mash the garlic and salt together into a smooth paste.

2. In a food processor, blend the garlic paste and pine nuts until smooth. Add the basil and oil and blend slowly until the sauce reaches a smooth, fluid consistency.

3. Add the cheese and more oil, if needed, and blend until smooth. Adjust the seasoning with salt if needed. Use immediately, or refrigerate for later use. If storing, pour a thin layer of oil over the surface to prevent browning.

SALSA VERDE

MAKES 2 CUPS SALSA

12 tomatillos, hulled, rinsed well, and halved

1 serrano

1 cup diced onion

2 garlic cloves

2 tbsp vegetable oil

Salt, as needed

Freshly ground black pepper, as needed

Water, as needed

½ cup Vegetable Stock (page 38)

3 tbsp chopped cilantro

1. Preheat the oven to 450°F.

2. In a large bowl, toss the tomatillos, chile, onion, and garlic with 1 tablespoon of the oil to coat. Season with salt and pepper. Pour the mixture onto a baking sheet in an even layer.

3. Roast the tomatillo mixture for 20 minutes, making sure the vegetables do not become too dark. Let cool completely to room temperature.

4. In a food processor or blender, purée the tomatillo mixture, adding water as needed, until the mixture is smooth.

5. In a medium pot, heat the remaining 1 tablespoon oil over medium heat. Add the puréed tomatillo mixture and cook, stirring constantly, until the mixture is heated through, 2 to 3 minutes.

6. Add the stock and bring the mixture to a boil. Reduce the heat to low and simmer until the salsa is thick enough to coat the back of a spoon, about 10 minutes. Let cool. Garnish with the cilantro and serve chilled.

MINT SAUCE

3 mint sprigs, chopped, plus 3 tbsp chopped mint

1 tsp cracked black peppercorns

⅓ cup apple cider vinegar

3 tbsp dry white wine

⅓ cup water

1 cup egg yolks (about 8)

3 cups (48 tbsp/6 sticks) butter, melted and kept warm

Salt, as needed

1. In a small saucepan over medium heat, combine the chopped mint sprigs, peppercorns, and vinegar and cook, stirring occasionally, until the liquid has reduced and the pan is nearly dry.

2. Stir the wine and water into the reduction, remove the pan from the heat, and strain the reduction through a fine-mesh sieve into a medium bowl.

3. Whisk the egg yolks into the reduction, then place the bowl over a pot of gently simmering water. Cook, whisking constantly, until the yolks have thickened and form ribbons when they fall from the whisk.

4. Gradually add the butter in a thin stream, whisking constantly, until all of the butter has been incorporated and the sauce has thickened.

5. Stir in the chopped mint leaves and season with salt. If not serving immediately, the sauce may be held in a warm place for up to 2 hours.

BARBECUE SAUCE

MAKES 3 CUPS SAUCE

2 tbsp corn oil

½ cup minced onion

2 cups ketchup

¼ cup packed brown sugar

¼ cup molasses

2 tbsp prepared yellow mustard

¼ cup apple cider vinegar

½ tsp garlic powder

Pinch cayenne pepper

½ tsp salt

½ tsp freshly ground black pepper

½ cup water, or as needed

1. Heat the oil in a medium saucepan over medium heat. Add the onion, reduce the heat to low, and cover the pot with a lid. Cook until the onion is translucent but not browned, about 4 minutes.

2. Add the ketchup, brown sugar, molasses, mustard, vinegar, garlic powder, cayenne, salt, and black pepper. Increase the heat to establish a simmer, and simmer for 10 minutes. Adjust the consistency by adding the water, if needed. (If you plan to brush this sauce onto a meat while it's cooking, then make a thinner sauce by adding more water.)

3. Strain the sauce through a fine-mesh sieve into a bowl. Use immediately, or refrigerate for later use.

RED PEPPER COULIS

2 lb red bell peppers, seeded and diced

2 tbsp minced shallot

¼ cup olive oil

¾ cup dry white whine

¾ cup Vegetable Stock (page 38)
or Chicken Broth (page 40)

Salt, as needed

1. In a sauté pan, sauté the bell peppers and shallots in the olive oil over medium heat until tender, about 8 minutes.

2. Stir in the wine and continue to cook until the pan is dry.

3. Add the stock or broth and cook over medium heat until the liquid has reduced by approximately half.

4. Transfer the mixture to the bowl of a food processor and purée until smooth. Season with salt. Serve immediately, or refrigerate for later use.

Yellow Mole

2 tbsp olive oil

3 cups sliced onion

1 tsp sliced garlic

4¾ cups chopped yellow bell peppers

1¼ cups trimmed, cored, and chopped fennel

1 cinnamon stick (about 2 inches long)

¼ tsp ground allspice

1½ tsp dried epazote

1 tbsp plus 1 tsp sugar

1 cup water

3 tomatillos, hulled, rinsed well, and quartered

2 tbsp fresh lime juice, plus more as needed

Salt, as needed

1. Heat the oil in a medium saucepan over medium-high heat. Add the onion and garlic and cook until translucent, about 8 minutes.

2. Add the bell peppers, fennel, cinnamon stick, allspice, epazote, sugar, and water. Cover the pot and simmer over low heat until the peppers are soft, about 25 minutes.

3. Transfer the mixture to a blender, add the tomatillos, and purée until very smooth. Strain through a large-holed sieve into a bowl.

4. Season the mole with the lime juice and salt. The mole is now ready to serve, or it may be refrigerated for later use.

Salsa Fresca

1 cup seeded and diced tomatoes

¼ cup minced onion

2 tbsp small-dice green bell peppers

1 tbsp minced jalapeños

1 tbsp extra-virgin olive oil

1 garlic clove, minced

2 tsp chopped cilantro

½ tsp chopped oregano

1 tbsp fresh lime juice, plus more as needed

½ tsp salt, plus more as needed

Freshly ground black pepper, as needed

1. In a medium bowl, combine the tomatoes, onion, bell peppers, jalapeños, oil, garlic, cilantro, and oregano. Add the lime juice, salt, and black pepper as needed. Taste, and adjust seasoning.

2. Cover the bowl and chill the salsa in the refrigerator for at least 30 minutes before serving.

Pico de Gallo

6 plum tomatoes, seeded and diced
(about 3 cups)

1 cup minced onion

2 serranos, seeded and minced

Juice of 1 lime

¼ cup chopped cilantro

Salt, as needed

Freshly ground black pepper, as needed

1. In a medium bowl, toss together the tomatoes, onion, chiles, lime juice, and cilantro to combine. Season with salt and pepper.

2. Cover the bowl and chill the salsa in the refrigerator for at least 15 minutes before serving.

Tapenade

1 cup pitted green olives, rinsed

1 cup pitted black Niçoise olives, rinsed

½ cup brined capers, drained and rinsed

2 garlic cloves, minced

1½ tbsp fresh lemon juice

¼ cup extra-virgin olive oil

Freshly ground black pepper, as needed

1 tbsp chopped oregano

1 tbsp chopped basil

1. In a food processor, pulse to combine the green and black olives, capers, and garlic. Slowly incorporate the lemon juice and oil until the mixture is chunky and easy to spread. It is very important not to overmix. The tapenade should not be a purée.

2. Season with pepper and stir in the oregano and basil. The tapenade is now ready to serve, or it may be refrigerated for later use.

GUACAMOLE

2 avocados, peeled, pitted, and diced

2 tomatoes, seeded and chopped

½ red onion, diced

1 jalapeño, seeded and minced

Juice of 2 limes

1 garlic clove, minced

2 tbsp chopped cilantro

Salt, as needed

Freshly ground black pepper, as needed

1. In a large bowl, combine the avocados, tomatoes, onion, jalapeño, lime juice, garlic, and cilantro. Season with salt and pepper. Mash lightly with a fork to obtain a chunky consistency.

2. Serve immediately, or cover the surface of the guacamole directly with plastic wrap to prevent browning and refrigerate until needed.

HUMMUS

1 cup cooked chickpeas

3 tbsp fresh lemon juice

2 cloves garlic

⅓ cup tahini

¾ cup extra-virgin olive oil, plus more as needed

¼ cup water, or as needed

Salt, as needed

Paprika, as needed

Chopped flat leaf parsley, as needed

1. In a food processor or blender, pulse the chickpeas, lemon juice, and garlic to form a smooth paste.

2. Add the tahini and oil and blend until smooth, adding water as needed to adjust the consistency. Season with salt.

3. Serve garnished with a drizzle of olive oil and sprinkled with paprika and parsley.

Facing page, from top: Tapenade (page 83), Guacamole, and Hummus

PINEAPPLE-JÍCAMA SALSA

¼ cup olive oil

Juice of 4 limes

Salt, as needed

Freshly ground black pepper, as needed

¼ cup chopped cilantro

2 jícama, peeled and cut into fine julienne

1 pineapple, peeled, cored, and cut into small dice

2 cups minced red onion

2 red bell peppers, seeded and cut into small dice

3 serranos, minced

1. In a medium bowl, whisk together the oil, lime juice, salt, black pepper, and cilantro to combine.

2. Gently fold in the jícama, pineapple, onion, bell peppers, and chiles.

3. Cover and refrigerate until ready to serve.

GRAPEFRUIT SALSA

2 tbsp olive oil

2 tbsp roughly chopped cilantro

½ cup small-dice red onion, rinsed

1 tsp seeded and minced Scotch Bonnet chile

2 tsp chopped flat-leaf parsley

4 ruby red grapefruits, segmented

2 seedless oranges, segmented

½ tsp salt, plus more as needed

1. In a medium bowl, combine the oil, cilantro, onion, chile, and parsley.

2. Just before serving, add the grapefruit and orange segments and season with salt. The salsa is now ready to serve, or it may be refrigerated for later use.

MINT AND YOGURT CHUTNEY

MAKES 1 QUART CHUTNEY

1¾ cups cilantro stems and leaves

1⅓ cups mint leaves

2 tsp cumin seeds

16 Thai bird chiles

¾ cup fresh lemon juice

1 tbsp plus 1 tsp sugar

Salt, as needed

2½ cups yogurt, drained

1. In a blender, combine the cilantro, mint, cumin, and chiles and purée until the mixture is smooth. If necessary, add 2 tablespoons of the lemon juice to facilitate the blending. The mixture should not be watery; if it is, drain it through a colander lined with cheesecloth.

2. Combine the herb mixture with the remaining lemon juice, the sugar, salt, and yogurt. Adjust the seasoning, if necessary. The chutney is now ready to serve, or it may be refrigerated for later use.

TAHINI SAUCE

MAKES 2 CUPS SAUCE

¼ cup plus 2 tbsp tahini

¼ cup plus 2 tbsp Greek-style yogurt

¼ cup plus 2 tbsp fresh lemon juice

¾ cup water

3 tbsp honey

2 tsp salt

½ tsp freshly ground black pepper

1. In a medium bowl, whisk together the tahini, yogurt, lemon juice, water, honey, salt, and pepper until completely combined. The sauce should be smooth, but slightly runny.

2. The sauce is now ready to serve, or it may be refrigerated for later use.

HARISSA

9 dried New Mexico or Ancho chiles
1 garlic clove
¼ tsp salt
½ tsp ground caraway
¼ tsp ground coriander
¼ tsp ground cumin
1 tbsp extra-virgin olive oil

1. Stem, seed, and break up the dried chiles and soak in a bowl of cold water for 15 minutes. Drain well, wrap in cheesecloth or place in a strainer, and press out any excess moisture.

2. Chop the garlic, sprinkle with the salt, and mash to a paste using the flat side of a chef's knife.

3. Grind the chiles, garlic paste, caraway, coriander, and cumin with a mortar and pestle or in a spice grinder.

4. Place the mixture in a small jar or other airtight container and drizzle the oil over the harissa sauce in a thin layer. Cover tightly and store in the refrigerator until needed.

CRANBERRY-ORANGE COMPOTE

MAKES 2 CUPS COMPOTE

5 cups whole cranberries, fresh or frozen
¾ cup fresh orange juice
½ cup sugar, plus more as needed
⅓ cup orange zest, blanched
Salt, as needed
Freshly ground black pepper, as needed

1. In a sauce pot, combine the cranberries, orange juice, and enough water to barely cover the berries. Add the sugar, bring to a simmer over medium heat, and simmer until the berries have softened and the liquid has thickened, 15 to 20 minutes.

2. Stir in the orange zest. Season with salt and pepper and add additional sugar, if necessary. Serve hot.

FIG COMPOTE

2⅔ cups dried figs

2 cups raisins

1 vanilla bean, split lengthwise, seeds scraped

1½ tsp fresh lemon juice

Zest of 1 orange

⅔ cup honey

1 tsp ground cinnamon

¾ cup almonds, lightly toasted and finely chopped

¼ cup plus 2 tbsp tawny Port

1. Coarsely chop the figs and raisins by hand or in a food processor. Transfer the fruit to a medium bowl.

2. Add the vanilla seeds, lemon juice, orange zest, honey, cinnamon, almonds, and port to the fig mixture.

3. Serve immediately, or cover and refrigerate until ready to serve.

NORTH CAROLINA PIEDMONT SAUCE

2 cups apple cider vinegar

2 cups white vinegar

3 tbsp Tabasco

¼ cup sugar

1 tbsp plus ½ tsp red pepper flakes

1 tbsp plus 1 tsp cracked black peppercorns

Combine the vinegars, Tabasco, sugar, red pepper flakes, and peppercorns in a large bowl and mix well. The sauce is ready to use now, or it may be refrigerated for later use.

Barbecue Sauce
NORTH CAROLINA WESTERN SAUCE

`MAKES 4 CUPS SAUCE`

3 cups ketchup

¾ cup white vinegar

¼ cup water

2 tbsp Worcestershire sauce

3 tbsp brown sugar

1 tbsp plus 1½ tsp chili powder

1 tbsp plus 1½ tsp dry mustard

1 tbsp plus 1½ tsp paprika

¾ tsp cayenne pepper, plus more as needed

1 tsp salt, plus more as needed

1. Combine all of the ingredients and mix well. Adjust the seasoning with additional salt and cayenne, if necessary.

2. The sauce is ready to use now, or it may be refrigerated for later use.

Mustard Barbecue Sauce
NORTH CAROLINA EASTERN LOW COUNTRY SAUCE

`MAKES 4 CUPS SAUCE`

2 tbsp vegetable oil

3 cups chopped onion

¼ cup minced garlic

2 cups white vinegar

1¼ cups spicy brown mustard

¼ cup sugar

2 tsp celery seeds

Salt, as needed

Freshly ground black pepper, as needed

1. Heat the oil in a saucepan over medium heat. Add the onion and sauté until translucent, about 4 minutes. Add the garlic and cook until aromatic, about 1 minute.

2. Add the vinegar, mustard, sugar, and celery seeds, bring the mixture to a simmer, and cook until the sugar has melted. Remove the pan from the heat and allow the flavors to blend, about 30 minutes. Adjust the seasoning with salt and pepper as needed. The sauce is now ready to use, or it may be refrigerated for later use.

GREMOLATA

1½ cups fresh bread crumbs

2 tbsp blanched, minced orange zest

2 tbsp plus 1½ tsp blanched, minced lemon zest

4 garlic cloves, minced

½ cup chopped flat-leaf parsley

Salt, as needed

Freshly ground black pepper, as needed

1. Preheat the oven to 400°F.

2. Pulse the bread crumbs in a food processor. Spread out into a thin, even layer on a dry baking sheet. Toast the bread crumbs in the oven until lightly browned, about 7 minutes. Transfer to a bowl.

3. Add the orange and lemon zests, garlic, parsley, salt, and pepper to the bread crumbs and toss to combine. The gremolata is now ready to use, or it may be refrigerated for later use.

NOTE *For a more traditional gremolata, combine 4 large minced garlic cloves, the zest of 1 lemon, 1½ cups chopped flat-leaf parsley, and, if desired, 2 anchovy fillets smashed to a paste.*

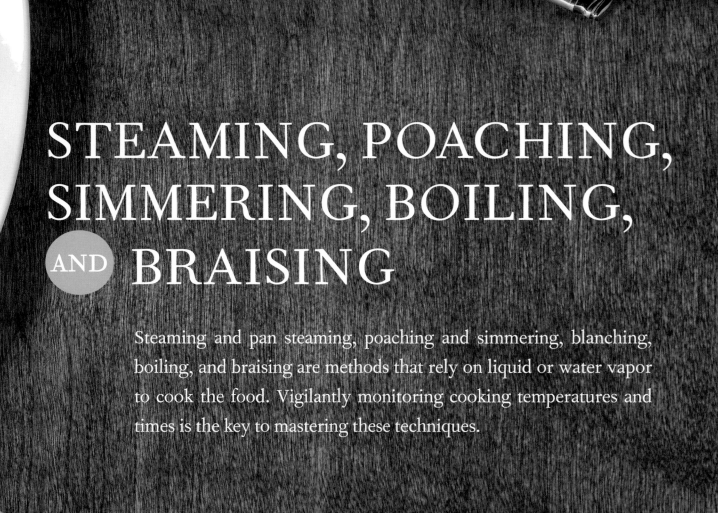

STEAMING, POACHING, SIMMERING, BOILING, AND BRAISING

Steaming and pan steaming, poaching and simmering, blanching, boiling, and braising are methods that rely on liquid or water vapor to cook the food. Vigilantly monitoring cooking temperatures and times is the key to mastering these techniques.

STEAMING

THE BEST FOODS FOR STEAMING are naturally tender and of a size and shape that allow them to cook in a short amount of time. Cut food into the appropriate size, if necessary, making sure all pieces are the same size. Fish are generally cooked as fillets, though there are some classic presentations of whole fish. Boneless, skinless poultry breasts also steam well. Shellfish should be left in the shell unless otherwise indicated; for example, scallops are customarily removed from the shell. Shrimp may also be peeled before steaming.

Steamed foods often retain more of their natural flavor than foods prepared using other cooking methods because steaming generally does not impart much flavor of its own. Water is a common liquid used for steaming, but a flavorful broth or stock, wine, or beer can also be used, especially if the steaming liquid is going to be served along with the food. Adding aromatic ingredients such as herbs and spices, citrus zest, lemongrass, ginger, garlic, and mushrooms to the liquid boosts its flavor as well as that of the food being steamed. Sometimes food is steamed on a bed of vegetables in a closed vessel, such as a bamboo steamer, and the vegetables' natural moisture becomes part of the steam bath cooking the food. Fillings, marinades, and wrappers can all be used in preparing steamed foods. Fish in particular is sometimes wrapped to keep it exceptionally moist.

Basic Equipment for Steaming

STEAMER. A steamer consists of two stacked pots. The bottom pot holds the cooking liquid, and the lidded top pot has a perforated bottom to allow the steam to reach the food inside.

TIERED STEAMER. Often made out of bamboo, tiered steamers consist of several baskets that stack together with a tight-fitting lid. The stacked baskets fit over a wok or pot. The cooking liquid is simmered in the pot below, and the steam rises, cooking the food situated inside the baskets. The baskets are usually lined with a bed of vegetables, such as cabbage, before the food is placed inside.

WOK. A wok is a round-bottomed pan, usually made of rolled steel and traditionally used in Asian cooking. Its shape is perfect for holding a tiered steamer.

PARCHMENT PAPER. This paper is used primarily for baking to line pans to prevent sticking, but it is also used for cooking en papillote. It may also have a silicone coating, which further prevents sticking during baking or cooking.

EXPERT tips

FOR ADDITIONAL FLAVOR, replace some or all of the water for steaming with:

Broth

Stock

Fruit juice, such as orange, apple, or cranberry

DEPENDING ON THE FLAVOR PROFILE that you want to achieve, the cooking liquid could also be flavored with:

Carrots

Celery

Onion

Chopped garlic

Grated ginger

Bay leaf

Parsley

Thyme

Coriander seeds

Cracked peppercorns

Cumin seeds

COOKING EN PAPILLOTE

In the *en papillote* method of steaming, which literally translates from French as "in paper," the main item and accompanying ingredients are wrapped in a parchment-paper package and cooked in the steam produced by their own juices (see photos below). En papillote indicates a specific preparation, but there are similar dishes, known by regional names, throughout the world. Like other methods of steaming, cooking en papillote is best suited to naturally tender foods like chicken, fish, and shellfish. Trim and portion the food as required by the recipe. It may be marinated or seared as an initial step, if appropriate.

The classic wrapper for a dish en papillote is parchment paper, but the effect is similar when aluminum foil, lettuce, plantain, grape or banana leaves, corn husks, or similar wrappers are used to enclose foods as they cook—the wrapper traps the steam driven from the food as it heats up. The dish is often presented to the guest still in its wrapper, and when the packet is opened, it releases a cloud of aromatic steam.

BELOW, LEFT:
To cook en papillote, cut the parchment paper to the appropriate size and butter or oil it. Place a bed of aromatics, vegetables, or sauce on one half of the paper, then top the bed with the main item.

BELOW, CENTER:
Fold the parchment paper in half, and crimp the edges to seal the pouch. Place the paper packet on a hot baking sheet or shallow pan.

BELOW, RIGHT:
Bake the packet in the oven until it is puffed and browned. Serve immediately.

1

2

3

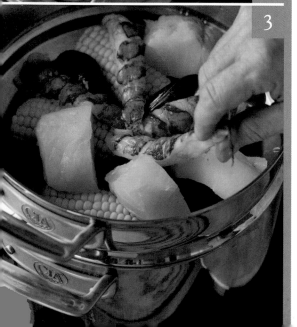

1

2

3

Chef's Lesson
STEAMING

1. Sweat the aromatics in the pot to build a flavor base for the steamed foods. Add enough liquid to last throughout cooking. (Adding more liquid to the pot during cooking will lower the temperature and lengthen the cooking time needed, so if you must add more liquid, preheat it.) Bring the liquid to a full boil, then adjust the heat to maintain a simmer. For the best results, maintain even, moderate heat. Liquids do not need to be at a rolling boil in order to produce steam. In fact, rapid boiling may cause the liquid to cook away too fast.

2. Arrange the main item in a single layer inside the steamer. If cooking more than one layer of food at a time, depending on the recipe, use a tiered steamer. You can place each food on a bed of vegetables, such as cabbage leaves, or on plates or in shallow dishes inside the steamer baskets. Alternatively, stack the foods in the steamer as pictured, layering them evenly to ensure proper cooking.

3. Continue layering. Replace the lid and steam until the food is done. Always remember to tilt the lid away from you as you open it so that the steam will safely vent away from your face and hands. Since steaming is done in a closed cooking vessel, it can be more difficult than other methods to gauge how long food needs to cook. Recipes may tell approximately how long to steam foods for the correct doneness. Start checking for doneness at the earliest point at which the food might be done, since steamed foods can easily become rubbery and dry when overcooked. Any juices from the food should be nearly colorless. When done, the flesh of fish and shellfish loses its translucency, taking on a nearly opaque appearance. The shells of mollusks (mussels, clams, and oysters) open, the flesh turns opaque, and the edges curl. Crustaceans (shrimp, crab, and lobster) have a bright pink or red color when done. Poultry turns opaque, and the flesh offers little resistance when pressed with a fingertip.

Steaming Vegetables

STEAMED VEGETABLES PRODUCE DISHES THAT HAVE PURE, UNDILUTED FLAVORS. Since steaming cooks through direct contact with steam rather than liquid, a steamed vegetable may be less soggy than the same vegetable boiled. Steamed vegetables are generally considered to have greater nutritional value as well. Properly steamed vegetables will be bright in color and tender.

Although the most commonly used steaming liquid is water, flavorful stocks, broths, or other aromatic liquids are sometimes used to replace some or all of the water. The amount of liquid required depends on how long the vegetable will take to cook: the shorter the cooking time, the less liquid needed.

Salt, pepper, and other seasonings may be combined with the vegetables as they steam or as they are finished. Aromatic vegetables, spices, herbs, or citrus zest can be added to the steaming liquid to produce specific flavors. Steamed vegetables are often reheated or finished with flavorful oils, butter, cream, or a sauce.

Small quantities of vegetables can be cooked using a steaming insert. Larger quantities, or a combination of vegetables that require different cooking times, are best prepared in a tiered steamer. It is important to allow enough room for steam to circulate completely around foods as they cook to encourage even cooking.

Pan Steaming Vegetables

SPEED IS THE MAJOR ADVANTAGE TO PAN STEAMING. Green vegetables that sometimes discolor when cooked, such as green beans, are done quickly enough with pan steaming to retain a bright color. Another advantage is that the cooking liquid can be reduced to easily make a pan sauce or glaze.

Vegetables of virtually all sorts can be prepared by pan steaming. Inspect the vegetables for quality and freshness. Rinse, trim, peel, and cut the vegetables as close to the cooking time as possible for the best flavor and nutrition.

Water is often used to prepare pan-steamed vegetables, but stocks or broths can be used for added flavor, if desired. Check the seasoning of any cooking liquid and add salt or other flavorings, including wine, fruit juice, herbs, and spices.

If the cooking liquid will be used to prepare a pan sauce, add additional seasonings and garnishing ingredients as indicated by the recipe. If preparing a glaze, add a sweetener, such as white or brown sugar, maple syrup, honey, or molasses.

To pan steam, place the prepared vegetables in a shallow pan and add just enough cooking liquid to nearly cover the vegetables. Cover the pan with a tight-fitting lid, and cook over medium heat. Covering the pan with a tight-fitting lid captures the steam that is released by the cooking liquid, and the steam condenses on the lid and falls back onto the vegetables. Check under the lid periodically during cooking to maintain the level of the cooking liquid and test the vegetables for doneness. Pan-steamed vegetables may be cooked to a range of doneness, according to their intended use. To make a pan sauce for pan-steamed vegetables, remove the cover and continue cooking until the cooking liquid has reduced to the desired consistency. If the vegetables are delicate or if they might overcook before the sauce is finished, remove them from the pan before making the sauce. For glazes, leave the vegetables in the pan while the cooking liquid reduces to form the glaze.

SHALLOW POACHING

SHALLOW-POACHED FOODS ARE COOKED WITH a combination of steam and simmering liquid. The food is partially submerged in liquid, which often contains an acid, such as wine or lemon juice, and the pan is covered to capture the steam released by the liquid during cooking. The aim of shallow poaching is to produce tender and moist food. The liquid, or *cuisson*, in the shallow poach is most often used to prepare a sauce that will accompany the finished dish.

A significant amount of flavor is transferred from the food to the cooking liquid during shallow poaching, so the cooking liquid is usually reduced and used as the base for a sauce to be served with the main item. The sauce may be a Beurre Blanc (page 75) or simply the reduced cooking liquids. Refer to specific recipes for additional suggestions or guidance.

As for steaming, naturally tender foods of a size and shape that allow for quick cooking are the best choices for shallow poaching. Fish, shellfish, and chicken breasts are among the most common options. Trim them as appropriate.

Aromatics, such as shallots and herbs, are often added to the cooking liquid for more flavor. Finely chop or mince aromatics; other ingredients that will be served as a garnish for the sauce should be diced or cut into strips, julienne, or chiffonade (see page 19 for more information on knife cuts). These ingredients are sometimes sautéed or parcooked first to develop the best possible flavor.

TO DEVELOP ADDITIONAL FLAVOR, choose well-seasoned poaching liquids such as:

  Stock

  Broth

  Wine

  Prepared sauce

DEPENDING ON THE DESIRED RESULT, the cooking liquid can be used to create a sauce to serve alongside the poached item, or the cooking liquid can be left as a broth-like liquid in which the poached item is served.

Basic Equipment for Shallow Poaching

PAN. Use an appropriately sized shallow pan or dish for shallow poaching. If too much or too little space is left around the food, it may over or undercook, or there may be too much or too little liquid for the sauce. Use a lid to loosely cover the pan, or use a piece of buttered or oiled parchment paper.

SLOTTED SPATULA. A slotted spatula is a handy tool for removing shallow-poached foods from the pan.

FINE-MESH STRAINER. Use a fine-mesh strainer to strain the sauce for shallow poached foods.

1

2

3

SHALLOW POACHING

1. Lightly butter a shallow pan and add the desired aromatics. If the aromatics can cook completely in the time required to cook the main item, they can be added raw; otherwise, cook them separately beforehand.

Place the main item on top of the aromatics, then pour the cooking liquid around the food. The poaching liquid contributes flavor to the food as well as to the sauce prepared from it. Choose rich broths or stocks and add wine, vinegar, or citrus juice as appropriate. Make sure that the level of the liquid goes no higher than halfway up the food; generally, less is required. If too much liquid is used, either a great deal of time will be needed to reduce it properly or only part of it will be usable in the sauce. It is not necessary in most cases to preheat the cooking liquid, though for very large quantities, it may be helpful to do so.

2. On the stovetop over medium heat, bring the cooking liquid up to 160° to 180°F, just under a simmer. Temperature is very important when shallow poaching, so take the time to use a thermometer. When the liquid reaches the proper temperature, loosely cover the pan with a piece of buttered parchment paper, known as a cartouche. The parchment traps enough steam to cook the unexposed part of the food, but not so much that the food cooks too quickly. Place the pan in a 300°F oven. It is best to finish poaching foods in the oven because oven heat is more even and gentle than the heat on a stovetop. Do not allow the liquid to boil at any time. A rapid boil will cook the food too quickly and may cause all of the liquid to evaporate from the pan, which could scorch the food.

3. Cook shallow-poached foods until just done. Fish and shellfish should appear opaque and feel slightly firm; the flesh of oysters, clams, and mussels should curl around the edges. Chicken should appear opaque and offer slight resistance when pressed with a fingertip. All shallow-poached foods should be very tender and exceptionally moist. Since this technique is most often used with delicate foods, they have an almost fragile texture; if the food is falling apart or dry, however, it has been overcooked.

If preparing a sauce from the cooking liquid, transfer the food to a heatproof dish, moisten with a small amount of the cooking liquid, and cover tightly with plastic wrap to keep it from drying out while you make the sauce. Add any additional flavoring ingredients to the cooking liquid as directed in the recipe, and simmer over medium heat on the stovetop to concentrate the flavor and thicken the sauce to the desired consistency.

Deep Poaching and Simmering

Deep poaching and simmering call for the food to be cooked at a constant, moderate temperature while completely submerged in a liquid. The aim of deep poaching and simmering is the same—to produce foods that are moist and extremely tender. The distinguishing factor between the two methods is that deep poaching is done at a lower temperature and is better suited to naturally tender cuts of meat, poultry, or fish. Simmering occurs at a slightly higher temperature, so that the tougher cuts can become tender and moist during cooking. Though portion-size cuts are often used—chicken quarters, for example—poached and simmered items also include dressed fish, whole birds, and large pieces of meat.

To keep it from breaking apart during cooking, dressed fish is usually wrapped in cheesecloth. Stuff the poultry, if desired, and truss it to help retain its shape. Stuff meats, if desired, and tie them to maintain their shape.

The liquid used in deep poaching and simmering should be flavorful. For meat and poultry, use beef or chicken stock; for fish and shellfish, use white wine or fish stock. Herbs and spices, vegetables, vegetable juices, wine, or citrus zest may be added to the cooking liquid to enhance the flavor.

Deep-poached and simmered foods are often served with a sauce that is prepared separately. See specific recipes for sauce suggestions.

Basic Equipment for Deep Poaching or Simmering

POT. The pot used for deep poaching or simmering should hold the food, liquid, and aromatics comfortably, with enough room to allow the liquid to expand as it heats. There should also be enough space so that the surface can be skimmed if necessary throughout cooking. A tight-fitting lid may be helpful for bringing the liquid up to temperature.

LADLE OR SKIMMER. Use a ladle or skimmer to skim off any fat or impurities that rise to the surface during deep poaching or simmering.

INSTANT-READ THERMOMETER. An instant-read thermometer is helpful to monitor the temperature of the cooking liquid. It can be difficult to see the difference between a liquid at a perfect temperature and one that is a degree or two too hot, and the difference to the final product can be significant.

EXPERT tips

CHOOSE WELL-SEASONED POACHING LIQUIDS such as:

Stock

Broth

Wine

Vegetables

Fresh herbs

Lemon or lime juice

Bay leaf

Cracked peppercorns

ADDING FLAVORING INGREDIENTS directly to the poaching liquid will infuse flavor throughout the cooking process. Try using:

THE COOKING LIQUID from deep poaching or simmering may be used to poach or simmer other items. You may want to strain it first, depending on the desired usage.

DEEP POACHING AND SIMMERING

1. For deep poaching, in a pot over medium heat, bring the liquid just under a simmer to 160° to 185°F. The surface of the liquid may show some motion, sometimes called shivering, but no air bubbles should break the surface.

For simmering, bring the liquid to a gentle simmer, 185° to 200°F. Small bubbles should be gently breaking the surface of the liquid. Use an instant-read thermometer to monitor the temperature of the cooking liquid since it is vital to the quality of the finished product. The remainder of this method applies to both deep poaching and simmering. Lower the food completely into the cooking liquid. If a part of the food is above the level of the liquid, the cooking will be uneven and the finished food may look raw where the liquid did not cover it completely. Also be sure that the pan is not overcrowded or the food will cook unevenly.

If the recipe calls for the pot to be covered, monitor the cooking temperature regularly. Covering a pot creates pressure, which raises the temperature of the liquid. Setting the lid slightly ajar is a good precaution to ensure that the liquid does not accidentally come to a boil.

2. Maintain the liquid's temperature throughout the poaching or simmering process, skimming as and adjusting the seasoning as necessary, until the food is properly done.

Tests for doneness vary from one food type to another. Properly deep-poached or simmered poultry and meat should feel tender when pierced with a fork, and any juices from poultry should be nearly colorless. Poultry flesh should look opaque and offer little resistance when pressed with a fingertip. When whole birds are fully cooked, the legs should move around easily in the sockets.

When properly cooked, the flesh of fish and shellfish should feel slightly firm and take on a nearly opaque appearance. Shellfish shells should open and the edges of the flesh should curl. Shrimp, crab, and lobster should have a bright pink or red color.

Deep poached and simmered foods are often served with a sauce that is prepared separately. Remove the main item, moisten it with a small amount of the cooking liquid, and keep it warm while preparing the sauce.

BLANCHING VEGETABLES

Remove vegetables from the boiling water either by draining off the water through a colander or sieve or by lifting the vegetables from the pot, then submerge them in an ice bath to stop the cooking.

THE TERM BLANCHING refers to the process of briefly submerging a vegetable in boiling water. Depending on the type and ripeness of a vegetable, it may be in the water from 30 seconds to 1 minute. Blanching is typically used as the first step in another cooking method or for vegetables that will be served cold. Blanching also makes the skin easy to remove, reduces or eliminates strong odors or flavors, and sets the vegetable color. Many vegetables are also blanched for preserving. Green beans, for example, are typically blanched as the first step for freezing, pickling, or jarring.

The water is typically brought to a rolling boil before the vegetables are added; however dense, starchy vegetables are an exception to this rule.

Parboiled and tender-crisp vegetables follow the procedure for blanching, however their doneness indicators are different. Parboiled vegetables are cooked beyond the blanched stage but are not cooked to full doneness. The vegetable should still be resistant when bitten or pierced. Tender-crisp vegetables are boiled long enough that they can be bitten easily but still offer a slight resistance and sense of texture.

Chef's Lesson
BLANCHING VEGETABLES

1. Trim the vegetable as necessary. Meanwhile, bring a pot of water to a boil over high heat.

2. Submerge the vegetable in the boiling water for 30 seconds to 1 minute, depending on the size, type, and ripeness of the vegetable. Immediately remove the vegetable from the water and submerge it in a bowl of ice water to stop the cooking process (photo, left). Drain the vegetable from the ice water, and serve or use as instructed in the specific recipe.

BOILING VEGETABLES

BOILING IS A FUNDAMENTAL VEGETABLE COOKING TECHNIQUE that can result in a wide range of textures and flavors, depending on how the technique is applied. Vegetables that are submerged in boiling water long enough to cook to partial doneness are said to be parboiled. Vegetables are often parboiled so that they can be finished with another cooking method, such as grilling, sautéing, pan frying, deep frying, or stewing. Fully boiled vegetables are said to be tender-crisp. Tender-crisp vegetables are submerged in boiling water until they can be bitten into easily but still offer a slight resistance and a sense of texture.

Prepare vegetables for boiling by properly rinsing or scrubbing them to remove all traces of dirt. They may be trimmed and cut before cooking, or they may be cooked whole. If a vegetable has a tendency to turn brown once it is cut and exposed to the air (as artichokes do), try to cut it immediately before cooking, or hold the cut vegetables in a bowl of water mixed with a bit of lemon juice. Vegetables boiled whole or cut should be of a similar size, shape, and diameter to ensure even cooking.

Water is the most common liquid for boiling vegetables, though other liquids can be used if desired. Salt or other seasonings added to the liquid can enhance the flavor of a vegetable. Additional flavor and interest can also be provided with a garnish.

Delicate green vegetables must be cooked in heavily salted water that should never stop boiling, and they must always be shocked in ice water immediately after cooking. If cooking a large volume of green vegetables, cook them in batches so that the water in the pot remains at a constant boil.

To preserve the vibrant color, green vegetables such as broccoli, asparagus, and green beans should always be boiled uncovered. For the best color in red cabbage, beets, and white vegetables, cover the pot after placing them in the boiling water. This helps retain acids that set the color in these vegetables. If desired, you can also cover the pot when boiling orange and yellow vegetables, such as carrots and squash.

DETERMINING DONENESS IS CRUCIAL to all vegetable preparations. Cook vegetables until they are tender-crisp—that is, they can be bitten into easily but still offer a slight resistance.

EXPERT
tip

Basic Equipment for Boiling Vegetables

POT. The pot should be large enough to hold the vegetables, liquid, and aromatics comfortably, with enough room for the liquid to expand as it heats. Leave enough headspace for the surface to be skimmed if necessary. A tight-fitting lid is helpful for bringing the liquid up to temperature, but it isn't essential.

COLANDER OR STRAINER. Use a colander or strainer to drain the water from the boiled vegetables.

LADLE OR SKIMMER. Use a ladle or skimmer to skim off any impurities that rise to the surface of the liquid during the boiling process. As an alternative to draining the vegetables in a colander or strainer, a skimmer may be used to lift the boiled vegetables out of the water.

ICE BATH. Be sure to have a container of ice water ready whenever boiling delicate green vegetables. After boiling, drain the cooking liquid and immediately submerge the vegetables in the ice bath. This will stop any additional cooking and help keep the vegetables' vibrant color.

Mashed and Puréed Potatoes

MASHED AND PURÉED POTATOES are classic dishes that can be made as rustic or as elegant as you like. Low- to moderate-moisture potatoes, such as mealy yellow potatoes and russets, are the best for mashing and puréeing.

These preparations begin with fork-tender, boiled, steamed, or baked potatoes that have been drained and dried but are still hot. For the best result, dry boiled or steamed potatoes on a baking sheet in a medium oven. Mashed potatoes are then smashed with a fork or potato masher to yield a coarser texture, while puréed potatoes are processed through a food mill or potato ricer until smooth. Food processors and blenders should be avoided to prevent the potatoes from taking on a gluey or watery texture.

Basic mashed and puréed potatoes contain milk or heavy cream, butter, salt, and pepper, but they may be blended with many other ingredients including chicken or beef broth, puréed vegetables, mustard, garlic, horseradish, shallots, green onions, or grated cheese. If using milk or heavy cream, it must be at room temperature or warmed to the same temperature as the potatoes.

1. Before adding most vegetables, bring the water to a rolling boil over high heat. Dense, starchy vegetables such as potatoes are the exception: Put them in the pot, then cover with cold water and bring to a boil.

2. Add the vegetables to the pot, and leave the heat on high to bring the water back to a rolling boil. Continue cooking until the vegetables reach the appropriate doneness. Remove the vegetables from the water either by draining off the water using a colander or strainer or by lifting the vegetables from the water with a skimmer.

3. Some vegetables must be shocked after boiling. To do this, immediately submerge the drained vegetables in ice water to thoroughly chill them. As soon as they are cool, drain them again. The vegetables should not be allowed to sit in water for extended periods of time.

BRAISING AND STEWING

BRAISES AND STEWS frequently call for less tender (and less expensive) main ingredients than other cooking techniques. They have a robust, hearty flavor, so they are often considered cool-weather comfort foods. However, by replacing the traditional ingredients with poultry, fish, or shellfish, braises and stews can be lighter in flavor and color and faster to prepare.

BRAISING

One of the benefits of braising is that tough cuts of meat become tender as the moist heat gently penetrates the meat and causes the connective tissues to soften. Another benefit is that flavor is released into the cooking liquid, lending the accompanying sauce exceptional body. The less tender cuts of meat to be braised come from more mature and more exercised animals. Braised foods are often left in a single large piece that can be sliced or carved. It's a good idea to truss or tie the meat in order to maintain the proper shape. Tender foods, even delicate fish and shellfish, can also be braised. To properly braise these kinds of foods, use less cooking liquid and cook the food at a lower temperature for a shorter period of time. Consult specific recipes for cooking temperatures and times.

The cooking liquid for a braised dish is usually a stock or a combination of a stock and a sauce, such as velouté, that is suited to the main item's natural flavor. Broths or vegetable juices may also be used. Wine is often used to deglaze the pan before the braising liquid is added. Aromatic vegetables or herbs are sometimes added for more flavor. Prepare a sachet d'épices (see page 2) or bouquet garni (see page 2) including spices, herbs, and other aromatic ingredients as desired or indicated in the recipe. Tomato concassé (see page 24), tomato purée, or tomato paste may also be added for color and flavor. A whole garlic head can be roasted with a little oil and added to give a deeper, sweeter flavor to the dish.

Basic Equipment for Braising

POT. Choose a heavy-gauge pot of a size and shape that best fits the meat or poultry that you're braising. Be sure the pot has a tight-fitting lid.

FORK. Pierce braised meats with a fork to test for doneness. Properly braised, fork-tender meats should slide easily from the tines of the fork.

STRAINER. Use a strainer or fine-mesh sieve to strain the sauce, if desired.

SERVING SPOON. Use a serving spoon to remove the braised food and sauce from the pan.

CARVING KNIFE. Use a sharp carving knife to slice or carve foods that were braised in large pieces.

Chef's Lesson
BRAISING

1. Season the meat or other main item with salt and freshly ground pepper, spice blends, or marinades before searing. Long simmering times reduce the volume of liquid and make relatively small amounts of seasoning more intense; taste and adjust the seasoning throughout the entire cooking process.

Heat the pot and oil over high heat, and sear the main item on high heat, turning it as often as necessary, just until each side is deep brown. After searing, remove the food from the pot.

2. Lower the heat to medium, add any aromatic vegetables, and cook to the desired color. Onions are typically added to the pan first and cooked until tender and translucent for a light-colored braise, or deep golden for a brown braise. Add other vegetables, herbs, and spices to the pot in order of cooking time. These ingredients can later be removed, puréed, or used as a garnish in the final product.

3. Acidic ingredients such as tomatoes or wine are often added to a braise. They are used to deglaze the pot, add flavor and color, as well as help soften the tough tissue of some braised foods. If using a tomato product, add it to the pot and continue cooking over medium heat until it turns a deep rust color and smells sweet.

4. Add enough cooking liquid to the pot to cover the main item by one-third to one-half. Bring the liquid to a simmer. Add the main item to the simmering liquid, along with any additional flavoring ingredients. Cover the pot and place it in the oven.

Braise in the oven until the main item is fully cooked and tender. Stir, skim, and adjust the seasoning and amount of liquid as needed throughout the cooking time. Baste or turn the foods from time to time to keep all surfaces evenly moistened with the cooking liquid. This helps to ensure that the food cooks evenly.

During the final part of the cooking time, remove the lid from the pot. This will allow the cooking liquid to reduce adequately so that the sauce will have the right consistency and flavor. Cook until the main item reaches the proper doneness. Fork-tender braised foods should slide easily from a kitchen fork or be easily cut with the side of a fork.

5. Well-made braises have an intense flavor—as a result of the long, gentle cooking—and a soft, almost melting texture. The main item's natural juices, along with the cooking liquid, become concentrated, providing both a deep flavor and a full-bodied sauce.

Transfer the braised food to a pan and keep it warm while finishing the sauce. (Even though carryover cooking is not as big a factor for these dishes as it is for roasts, grills, and sautés, it is still easier to carve foods after they are allowed to rest for several minutes.) As the braised food rests, the sauce can be finished in a number of ways. Remove and discard the sachet d'épices or bouquet garni if used. Bring the braising liquid to a simmer on the stovetop over medium heat, skimming away any fat that has risen to the surface. Once the sauce reaches the desired consistency, adjust the seasoning as needed. Straining the sauce is optional. Add any final garnishing ingredients just before serving the braise.

STEWING

STEWS DIFFER FROM BRAISES in that the food is cut into bite-size pieces and cooked in more liquid. Stews are often thought of as one-dish meals, producing a tender and highly flavored dish including not only meat, poultry, or seafood, but also a variety of vegetables in an aromatic sauce. It is also possible to finish a stew with heavy cream, herbs, or a liaison of eggs and heavy cream. (For more information on using a liaison, see page 30.)

Stews usually contain the same cuts of meat, poultry, or fish as a braise. These cuts require slow, moist-heat cooking in order to become tender. The size into which you cut the main item will vary according to the style of stew, but typically meat is cut into 1-inch cubes. If the pieces are cut too small, too much of the surface area will be exposed and the meat will dry out.

Season the food with salt, pepper, marinades, or dry rubs before stewing to give the finished dish a complex and dynamic flavor. Select the cooking liquid according to the food being stewed or the specific recipe's instructions. Flavorful stocks or combinations of stocks and sauces, vegetable or fruit juices, or water may be used.

Choose a heavy-gauge pot with a lid for slow, even cooking. Have a ladle or skimmer available to skim the stew as it cooks. To test for doneness, use a table fork to cut a piece, or bite into a small portion.

Some stews call for the main meat or poultry to be dusted with flour and then cooked in hot oil just until it starts to stiffen, with no browning. Other stews call for the main item to be cooked to a deep brown. Once the meat, poultry, or fish is properly colored, remove it from the pot and keep it warm while sweating, smothering, or browning the aromatic vegetables, if required.

White stews do not call for the main item to be seared before the cooking liquid is added. Instead, a seasoned cooking liquid is added directly to the uncooked meat. Otherwise, the stewing liquid is added to the pot with the aromatics and the main item is returned to the stew.

A well-made stew has a rich flavor and a soft, almost melting texture. Stews often taste better a day or two after preparation.

Basic Equipment for Stewing

POT. Choose a heavy-gauge pot with a lid, such as a Dutch oven or other similar pot (as may be indicated in a recipe), for the slow, even cooking that is required when stewing.

LADLE OR SKIMMER. Have a ladle or skimmer available to skim off any fat or impurities that rise to the surface of the stew as it cooks.

FORK. Use a fork to test for doneness in stewed foods. When properly cooked, stewed foods should be easy to cut with the side of a table fork.

1
2
3

Chef's Lesson
STEWING

1. Prepare the main item by seasoning it and cutting it into pieces as desired, generally 1-inch cubes. Searing the main item assists in developing color and flavor.

Heat the pot and oil over high heat. In order to develop the best color, the pieces of food should not touch each other; add the main item in batches if necessary, and cook on all sides until golden brown.

2. Turn the main item during cooking to make sure it is well seared on all sides. Repeat with remaining batches, if necessary.

3. Add the cooking liquid to the main item in the pot. The amount of cooking liquid required varies from one cut of meat or poultry to another. Delicate or tender foods, such as fish or shellfish, may require very little added moisture to stew successfully. Bring the cooking liquid to a simmer over low heat. You can choose to finish the stew by covering the pot and placing it in a moderate oven or by leaving the pot uncovered and cooking it over low heat on the stovetop. Stir, skim, and adjust the seasoning and amount of liquid throughout the cooking time as needed. Add any additional aromatics and vegetable garnish in the proper sequence throughout the cooking time for a rich, complex flavor and perfect texture.

4. Before removing the meat or main item to finish the sauce, check a few pieces to be sure that they are fully cooked and tender. Properly cooked stewed foods should be easy to cut with the side of a table fork. Discard the sachet d'épices or bouquet garni if used.

Remove the main item and other solid ingredients with a slotted spoon or skimmer. Moisten them with a little of the cooking liquid, cover, and keep warm. Finish the stewing liquid into a sauce: Strain if desired, and thicken the sauce by reducing it over medium heat on the stovetop. Add any additional thickeners, such as a prepared roux (see page 15) or a pure starch slurry (see page 210), and continue to cook, skimming as necessary, until the sauce has the desired flavor and consistency. Return the solid ingredients to the sauce, and bring the stew just back to a simmer over medium heat.

Make the final adjustments to the stew's flavor. Season with salt, pepper, lemon juice, or other ingredients. If desired, add heavy cream or temper a liaison (see page 30) into the stew to enrich it. If necessary, adjust the consistency with additional simmering. Add garnishes to the stew either in batches or by individual servings.

EXPERT tips

SEARING THE MAIN ITEM assists in developing color and flavor before stewing. For searing, the main item should not be added to the pot in quantities so large that the pieces are touching one another. If they are touching, the pot's temperature will be lowered significantly, hindering proper coloring. Instead, sear the item in batches, and remove each batch when it has developed the appropriate color.

STEWS OFTEN TASTE BETTER a day or two after preparation. Reheating can take place on low direct heat or in the oven or microwave.

FOR A HEALTHIER OPTION, use puréed vegetables (especially those high in starch) to thicken the stew in place of a roux or slurry.

VEGETABLE BRAISES AND STEWS INCLUDE A WIDE SPECTRUM OF DISHES, from delicate to sturdy and robust. Stewed or braised vegetables literally cook in their own juices. The vegetables in a stew are customarily cut into small pieces, while those in a braise are cut into large pieces or left whole. Occasionally, a pure starch slurry is added to the juices to give the dish more substance and to improve its appearance. The thickened sauce lightly coats the vegetable, providing an attractive sheen. Vegetable stews and braises have deep, concentrated flavors. Stews and braises should be fork-tender or, in some cases, meltingly soft.

Vegetable stews and braises may be composed of one main ingredient or a combination of vegetables. Braised fennel, for example, contains a single main ingredient; ratatouille is a stew that melds several different vegetables. Braises and stews generally include some aromatic ingredients such as shallots.

Prepare the vegetables according to their type and the desired result. Rinse, peel, trim, and cut the vegetables, as necessary. Blanch them to remove bitterness or to aid in removing peels (see page 104 for more information on blanching).

The fat chosen should have a good flavor that is appropriate to the dish. Vegetables that do not release a significant amount of liquid as they cook may need additional liquid such as stock, wine, juice, or water.

Prepare and use seasonings and aromatics such as salt and pepper, shallots, garlic, minced herbs, or spices. Some braised and stewed vegetable dishes include a pork product (salt pork, bacon, or ham) or an acid (vinegar, citrus zest or juice, or wine) to develop a complex flavor. Various finishing ingredients, such as reduced heavy cream, a cream sauce, butter, or a liaison, may be added to give a vegetable stew a rich flavor, some sheen, and a smooth texture. A vegetable stew or braise may also be garnished with bread crumbs and cheese to create a gratin.

Sea Bass and Scallops en Papillote

2 tbsp butter, melted

1½ cups Vegetable Stock (page 38)

½ cup vermouth

5 cups julienned celeriac

1½ cups thinly sliced Red Bliss potatoes

1 cup julienned carrot

1 cup julienned cucumber

½ lb sea bass fillets, cut into five 1½-oz portions

½ lb sea scallops, muscle tabs removed

½ cup Gremolata (page 91)

½ tsp crushed black peppercorns

1. Preheat the oven to 425°F. Place two baking sheets in the oven to preheat.

2. Cut 5 heart shapes out of parchment paper, large enough to enclose the fillets, scallops, and vegetables. Lightly butter both sides of the paper with a pastry brush.

3. Combine the stock and vermouth in a large saucepan and bring to a simmer (185°F). In separate batches, blanch the celeriac, potatoes, and carrot in the stock mixture until tender. Drain the vegetables and toss with the cucumber in a large bowl.

4. Arrange a bed of about ¾ cup of the vegetables on one half of each paper heart. Top each mound of vegetables with 1 portion of the bass and ¼ cup of the scallops. Top each portion with about 1 tablespoon of the gremolata and sprinkle with the crushed peppercorns.

5. Fold the top of each heart over the fish and vegetables. Crimp the edges of the paper to seal tightly. Refrigerate until needed.

6. Place the parchment packages on the preheated baking sheets and bake for about 7 minutes, rotating the pans halfway through, until each is puffy and brown. Serve immediately. For a dramatic presentation, let each diner cut their package open at the table and enjoy the wonderful aroma.

New England Shore Dinner

MAKES 4 SERVINGS

1 tbsp butter

1 garlic clove, minced

1 small onion, minced

1½ cups Fish, Chicken, or Vegetable
Stock or Broth (see pages 38 to 40)

1 bay leaf

1 sprig thyme

3 to 4 black peppercorns

2 ears of corn, shucked and halved
lengthwise

4 small Red Bliss potatoes, cooked

2 boiling onions, peeled and steamed

2 lobster tails, split lengthwise

4 pieces scrod fillet (about 2 oz each)

8 mussels, scrubbed and debearded

1. Heat the butter in a large pot over medium heat. Add the garlic and minced onion and sauté until the onion is limp.

2. Add the stock or broth, bay leaf, thyme, and peppercorns to the pot and bring to a simmer.

3. Arrange the remaining ingredients in a steamer insert. Place the corn, potatoes, boiling onions, and lobster tails as the first layer, and top with the fillets and mussels. If a tiered bamboo or aluminum steamer basket is being used, place the ingredients in separate tiers.

4. Place the steamer insert over the simmering stock, cover the pan tightly, and reduce heat to low. Steam for about 20 minutes.

5. To serve, arrange the vegetables, seafood, and fish on a platter, or serve them directly from the pot. If desired, strain the broth and serve it separately.

NOTE *If you do not have a steamer insert for a pot, or a tiered steamer, it is possible to make this dish by fitting a heatproof colander inside a pot large enough to accommodate it. A lid can be created by covering the pot with aluminum foil.*

CREAMED CORN

1½ cups small-dice leeks

2 cups heavy cream

Salt, as needed

Freshly ground black pepper, as needed

Freshly grated nutmeg, as needed

1½ lb fresh or frozen corn kernels

1 tbsp chopped chervil

1. Combine the leeks and the cream in a nonreactive medium saucepan. Season with salt, pepper, and nutmeg. Simmer over medium heat, stirring occasionally, until the cream has reduced by half.

2. Steam the corn in a steamer insert over boiling water until fully cooked, 4 to 5 minutes. Add the corn to the leek mixture and simmer 2 to 3 minutes more.

3. Adjust the seasoning with additional salt and pepper, if needed. Serve immediately, garnished with the chervil.

STEAMED BROCCOLI

2 lb broccoli (about 4 bunches)

Salt, as needed

Freshly ground black pepper, as needed

1. Trim the broccoli, peel the stems, and cut them into spears. Arrange the broccoli on a steamer rack or perforated insert, and season with salt and pepper.

2. In the bottom of a tightly covered steamer, bring water to a full boil. Add the rack or insert, replace the cover, and steam the broccoli until tender, 5 to 7 minutes.

3. Remove the broccoli from the steamer. If serving immediately, season with additional salt and pepper. Otherwise, cool to room temperature, refrigerate, and adjust the seasoning before serving.

BROCCOLI AND TOASTED GARLIC *Sauté about 4 thinly sliced garlic cloves in about 1 tablespoon butter in a medium sauté pan until lightly browned. Add the steamed broccoli and toss or roll it in the butter or oil until very hot. Adjust the seasoning with salt and pepper, as necessary. Serve immediately.*

PAN-STEAMED CARROTS

MAKES 10 SERVINGS

2½ lb carrots, cut into ¼-inch pieces

6 tbsp butter

1 tsp chopped flat-leaf parsley

Salt, as needed

Freshly ground black pepper, as needed

1. Add about 1 inch of salted water to a large pan and bring to a boil. Add the carrots to the water, adding more water if necessary to barely cover the carrots. Return the water to a boil. Cover the pan tightly and reduce the heat slightly.

2. Pan steam the carrots until they are fully cooked and tender to the bite, 5 to 6 minutes. When done, drain excess water from the pan. Return the carrots to the heat and allow any excess moisture to evaporate. Add the butter and parsley, and season with salt and pepper. Stir or toss until the carrots are evenly coated and very hot. Serve immediately.

PAN-STEAMED HARICOTS VERTS *Substitute 2½ lb trimmed haricots verts for the carrots. Pan steam the haricots verts according to the above method. To finish the haricots verts, omit the parsely and instead sauté 1 tbsp shallots in 2 tbsp olive oil until translucent. Add the cooked haricots verts and toss to coat. Season with salt and pepper and serve immediately.*

Pescada à la Veracruzana

10 red snapper fillets (about 6 oz each)

1 tsp salt

½ tsp freshly ground black pepper

¾ cup fresh lime juice

SAUCE

¼ cup plus 2 tbsp olive oil

4 cups minced onion

3 garlic cloves, minced

2 cups peeled, seeded, medium-dice tomatoes

15 green olives, pitted and chopped

1 tbsp plus 2 tsp brined capers, drained and rinsed

5 pickled jalapeños, julienned

3 bay leaves

1½ tsp chopped marjoram or oregano

1½ tsp chopped thyme

4 cups Fish Stock (page 39), plus more as needed

Salt, as needed

Freshly ground black pepper, as needed

GARNISH

¼ cup chopped flat-leaf parsley

¼ cup brined capers, drained and rinsed

30 to 40 green olives, drained and rinsed

1. Cut a shallow crisscross into the skin of all the fillets with a boning knife. Season the fish with the salt and pepper and marinate it in the lime juice, in a covered container in the refrigerator, for at least 1 hour.

2. Meanwhile, prepare the sauce: Heat ¼ cup of the oil in a saucepan over medium-high heat. Add the onion and garlic and sauté until they start to turn golden. Add the tomatoes, chopped olives, capers, jalapeños, bay leaves, marjoram or oregano, thyme, and stock. Bring the sauce to a simmer and cook until the tomatoes are soft and the flavors have blended. Adjust the seasoning with salt and pepper, if necessary.

3. Preheat the oven to 350°F.

4. Lightly grease a large shallow ovenproof sauté pan with the remaining 2 tablespoons oil. Place the fillets in the pan. Pour the sauce over and around the fish.

5. Bring the liquid to just under a simmer over medium heat. Place a piece of buttered parchment paper, trimmed to fit inside the pan, over the fish to cover. Transfer the entire pan to the oven.

6. Poach the fish until cooked through (140°F), 6 to 8 minutes.

7. Serve immediately with the sauce, garnished with the parsley, capers, and olives.

Poached Sea Bass with Clams, Bacon, and Peppers

MAKES 5 SERVINGS

4 tbsp butter, cold

5 sea bass fillets

25 littleneck clams, thoroughly scrubbed

½ cup dry white wine

⅓ cup Fish Stock (page 39)

⅓ cup bottled clam juice

Salt, as needed

Freshly ground black pepper, as needed

¼ cup julienned green bell pepper, blanched

5 oz (about 7 slices) bacon, minced, cooked until crisp

1 tbsp chopped chives

1. Preheat the oven to 350°F.

2. Lightly butter a large shallow ovenproof pan with 2 tablespoons of the butter. Add the fillets, clams, wine, stock, and clam juice.

3. Bring the liquid to just under a simmer over medium heat. Place a piece of buttered parchment paper, trimmed to fit in the pan, over the fillets to cover. Transfer the entire pan to the oven.

4. Poach the fish and clams until the fish is slightly underdone and the clams are barely open, 10 to 12 minutes. Remove from the oven. Remove the fish and clams and keep warm in a heatproof container.

5. Place the pan with the parchment paper back over medium heat, bring the liquid back to a simmer, and cook until the liquid has reduced by two-thirds. Stir in the remaining 2 tablespoons butter to slightly thicken the sauce. Season with salt and black pepper.

6. Strain the sauce through a fine-mesh sieve into a clean saucepan, if desired. Add the bell peppers and bacon.

7. Divide the fish and clams among 5 plates, ladle the sauce over each portion, and garnish with the chives.

POACHED SOLE WITH VEGETABLE JULIENNE AND VIN BLANC SAUCE

MAKES 5 SERVINGS

5 sole fillets (5 to 6 oz each)

1 tsp salt, plus more as needed

¼ tsp ground white pepper, plus more as needed

1 cup julienned red bell peppers, blanched

1 cup julienned carrot, blanched

1 cup julienned yellow squash, blanched

1 cup julienned zucchini, blanched

1 tbsp butter

2 shallots, minced

5 sprigs parsley, plus 2 tbsp finely chopped parsley

5 sprigs chive, plus 2 tbsp minced chives

¼ tsp coarsely cracked white peppercorns

¾ cup dry white wine

½ cup Fish Stock (page 39)

¾ lb shrimp (21/25 count), peeled and deveined

¾ cup Fish Velouté (page 71)

¾ cup heavy cream

1 tbsp fresh lemon juice, plus more as needed (optional)

1. Preheat the oven to 300°F.

2. Arrange the fillets, best-looking side up, on a clean work surface. Season with the salt and white pepper. Combine the bell peppers, carrot, squash, and zucchini. Place a generous portion of the vegetables across each fillet, leaving the vegetables extending over the edge of the fillets on both sides. Roll (or fold) the fillets tail to head. Place them on a baking sheet, seam side down, until ready to poach.

3. Lightly butter a large ovenproof sauté pan and sprinkle it evenly with the shallots. Add the parsley sprigs, chive sprigs, and peppercorns. Place the rolled fillets, seam side down, on top. Add the wine and stock.

4. Cook over medium heat until the liquid in the pan just begins to simmer. Remove the pan from the heat. Place a buttered piece of parchment paper, trimmed to fit inside the pan, over the fillets to cover. Transfer the pan to the oven.

5. After 6 minutes, add the shrimp to the pan. Poach until the flesh of the sole and shrimp is opaque and gives under slight pressure, 4 to 6 minutes more. Transfer the sole and shrimp to a baking dish, add a small amount of the stock from the pan, cover with plastic wrap, and keep warm.

6. Place the pan with the remaining stock on the stovetop, return to a simmer, and reduce by two-thirds. Add the velouté and simmer for 1 to 2 minutes. Stir in the cream. Reduce the sauce until it is thick enough to coat the back of a spoon. Add the lemon juice, if desired, and adjust the seasoning with salt and white pepper.

7. Strain the sauce through a fine-mesh sieve into a clean saucepan. Add the chopped parsley and minced chives and stir to combine.

8. Blot the sole rolls and shrimp dry with paper towels. Serve immediately with the sauce.

SEAFOOD POACHED IN SAFFRON BROTH WITH FENNEL

MAKES 10 SERVINGS

4 cups Fish Stock (page 39)

1 tsp saffron, crushed

1 sachet d'épices (see page 2)

½ cup Pernod

½ cup dry white wine

4 cups julienned fennel

Salt, as needed

Freshly ground black pepper, as needed

3 lb assorted seafood (see Note)

2¾ cups tomato concassé (see page 24)

1 tbsp chopped flat-leaf parsley or fennel fronds

1. Combine the stock, saffron, sachet d'épices, Pernod, wine, and fennel in a large sauté pan. Simmer until the fennel is barely tender and the broth is well flavored, about 12 minutes. Season with salt and pepper.

2. Add the seafood and poach, keeping the liquid just under a smimmer, until it is just cooked through, 6 to 8 minutes. Add the tomatoes and continue to cook until heated through. Serve immediately with the broth, and garnish with the parsley or fennel fronds.

NOTE *A variety of seafood may be used, including shrimp, monkfish, squid, shark, scallops, and lobster.*

POULE AU POT

1 broiler chicken (about 3 lb)

2 qt Chicken Broth (page 40), **plus more as needed**

1 sachet d'épices (see page 2)

1½ tsp salt, plus more as needed

¾ cup coarsely diced carrot

¾ cup coarsely diced parsnips

¾ cup coarsely diced peeled celeriac

1½ cups coarsely diced Yukon gold potatoes

¾ cup coarsely diced leeks, white part only

Freshly ground black pepper, as needed

3 tbsp minced chives

1. Cut the chicken into quarters, reserving the backbone, wing tips, neck, heart, and gizzards. Save the liver for another use.

2. Bring the broth to a simmer in a soup pot over medium heat. Add the chicken quarters and other parts, the sachet d'épices, and the salt. Simmer over low heat until the broth is flavorful, about 45 minutes.

3. Using tongs, remove and discard the backbone, wing tips, gizzard, heart, neck, and sachet. Skim the broth to remove any excess fat from the surface. Add more broth if needed to cover the chicken by 2 inches.

4. Add the vegetables to the pot in stages so that they all finish cooking at the same time: Add the carrot and parsnips and simmer for 5 minutes; add the celeriac and simmer for 5 minutes; add the potatoes and simmer for 7 minutes; and then add the leeks and simmer for 2 to 3 minutes more.

5. Continue to simmer, skimming as needed, until the chicken is fork-tender and all of the vegetables are tender. Taste and adjust the seasoning with salt and pepper.

6. Remove the chicken from the pot. Cut the drumsticks from the thighs and cut the breast pieces in half on the diagonal.

7. Arrange the chicken in soup bowls, placing in each a breast portion and either a drumstick or thigh. Ladle in some vegetables and broth, and garnish with the chives.

THAI RED CURRY CHICKEN

MAKES 4 SERVINGS

3 tbsp vegetable oil

1 cup diced Spanish onion

3 garlic cloves, minced

1 tbsp prepared red curry paste

1 tsp salt, plus more as needed

½ tsp freshly ground white pepper, plus more as needed

3 boneless, skinless chicken breast halves (7 to 8 oz each), cut into large cubes

6 small red potatoes, scrubbed, each cut into 6 pieces

1½ cups Chicken Broth (page 40)

¼ cup unsweetened shredded dried coconut

½ cup unsweetened coconut milk

2 tbsp packed brown sugar

1 tsp grated lemon zest

Cornstarch slurry as needed: 1 tbsp cornstarch combined with 4 tsp cold water or chicken broth (see page 210)

1 tbsp coarsely chopped basil

1 tbsp coarsely chopped mint

1 qt cooked white rice

4 green onions, white and green parts, sliced on the diagonal

1. Preheat the oven to 350°F.

2. Heat the oil in a large sauté pan over medium heat. Add the onion and sauté until translucent, 5 to 7 minutes. Add the garlic and cook until aromatic, about 2 minutes.

3. Add the red curry paste, salt, and white pepper. Stir to coat the onions and garlic evenly with the curry paste. Add the chicken and potatoes and stir to coat.

4. Add the broth and bring to a simmer. Simmer until the potatoes are tender, 15 to 20 minutes.

5. Meanwhile, spread the shredded coconut on a baking sheet and bake until golden, about 5 minutes. Transfer to a bowl and set aside.

6. Using a slotted spoon, transfer the chicken and potatoes to a platter and cover to keep warm while completing the sauce. Add the coconut milk, brown sugar, and lemon zest to the pan and bring to a simmer, stirring constantly. Taste and adjust the seasoning with salt and white pepper. If needed, add just enough of the cornstarch slurry, while stirring constantly, to thicken the sauce slightly.

7. Add the basil and mint. Return the chicken and the potatoes to the pan and stir to coat them thoroughly with the sauce.

8. Serve immediately over rice, garnished with the green onions and toasted coconut.

CORNED BEEF WITH WINTER VEGETABLES

MAKES 6 SERVINGS

5 lb corned beef brisket, trimmed

1½ qt Beef Stock (page 38), Beef Broth (page 40), or cold water

7 new potatoes, halved

1 small head green cabbage, cut into wedges

7 baby turnips, peeled

15 baby carrots, peeled

½ lb pearl onions, blanched and peeled

Salt, as needed

Freshly ground black pepper, as needed

1. Split the brisket along the natural seam into two pieces.

2. Put the meat in a deep pot and add enough stock, broth, or water to cover the meat. Bring to a simmer, skimming as necessary. Reduce the heat to establish a slow simmer, cover, and continue simmering until the meat is nearly fork-tender, about 2½ hours.

3. Add the potatoes, cabbage, turnips, carrots, and onions to the corned beef and continue to simmer until the vegetables are tender and flavorful and the corned beef is fork-tender, 35 to 45 minutes. Season with salt and pepper as needed throughout the cooking time.

4. Remove the corned beef from the cooking liquid and carve into slices. Serve immediately with the vegetables.

Potatoes au Gratin
GRATIN DAUPHINOISE

1¾ lb russet potatoes

5 garlic cloves

2 cups whole milk

Freshly grated nutmeg, as needed

Salt, as needed

Freshly ground black pepper, as needed

¾ cup heavy cream

4 tbsp butter, cut into small pieces

1. Preheat the oven to 350°F. Butter a 9 x 13-inch baking pan.

2. Scrub, peel, and thinly slice the potatoes using a mandoline, electric slicer, or chef's knife.

3. Combine the garlic with the milk in a medium saucepan and bring to a boil. Season the milk with nutmeg, salt, and pepper and add the sliced potatoes.

4. Bring the milk mixture to a simmer and cook the potatoes for 10 to 12 minutes, taking care that the milk does not boil over. Remove the saucepan from the heat and discard the garlic cloves.

5. Transfer the potatoes and milk to the prepared baking pan, pour the cream over the top, and dot with the butter.

6. Bake until golden brown and the milk has been absorbed, about 45 minutes.

7. Allow the potatoes to rest for 10 to 15 minutes before serving.

TRADITIONAL SCALLOPED POTATOES *The sliced potatoes may be "shingled," or arranged in overlapping rows, in the baking dish. Before baking, layer with 4 to 5 oz grated cheddar and then top with an additional 5 oz grated cheddar. Cover the pan with aluminum foil and bake for 35 minutes. Uncover and continue to bake to allow the cheese to brown lightly.*

NOTE *To make individual servings, assemble the potatoes in five small, shallow, oven-safe ramekins. Bake for about 25 minutes.*

Lamb and Chicken Stew with Couscous

MAKES 10 SERVINGS

2 lb boneless lamb shoulder or leg, cut into 1-inch cubes

3 lb skinless, bone-in chicken legs, thighs and drumsticks separated

1 tbsp salt, plus more as needed

1½ tsp freshly ground black pepper, plus more as needed

½ cup olive oil

2 cups diced onion

3 tbsp minced garlic

1 tbsp peeled, grated ginger

2 tbsp plus 1 tsp ground cumin, plus more as needed

2 tbsp ground turmeric, plus more as needed

1 tsp ground coriander, plus more as needed

½ tsp freshly grated nutmeg, plus more as needed

2 bay leaves

Pinch saffron threads

Dash ground cloves

2½ qt Beef Stock (page 38)

2 cups large-dice carrots

1 cup large-dice turnips

1 lb couscous

2¼ cups small-dice zucchini

1½ cups small-dice green bell peppers

½ cup cooked chickpeas

½ cup cooked lima beans

1 lb tomatoes, peeled and cut into wedges

1½ cups artichoke bottoms, quartered

4 oz Arabic white truffles, sliced (optional)

2 tbsp Harissa (page 88)

5 tbsp chopped flat-leaf parsley

1. Season the lamb and chicken with the salt and black pepper.

2. Heat ¼ cup of the oil over medium-high heat in a medium pan until it starts to shimmer. Place the lamb carefully in the oil and sear until deep brown on as many sides as possible.

3. Add the onion, garlic, ginger, cumin, turmeric, coriander, nutmeg, bay leaves, saffron, and cloves. Add enough stock to cover the lamb. Bring the stock to a simmer, cover, and cook for 45 minutes.

4. Add the carrot, turnips, and chicken to the stew and return to a simmer over low heat, skimming as necessary.

5. Meanwhile, fill the bottom of a steamer or couscousciere with water and bring to a boil. Line the insert with cheesecloth and add the couscous. Cover and steam over the boiling water for another 30 minutes, or until the couscous is light and fluffy and all the moisture has evaporated. Season with salt and add the reaining ¼ cup of oil, stirring to break up any clumps. Cover the pot and place in a warm oven (about 250°F) to keep hot while finishing the stew.

6. Add the zucchini and bell peppers to the stew and cook for 4 minutes.

7. Add the chickpeas, lima beans, tomatoes, artichoke bottoms, and truffles, if using, and simmer the stew until all of the ingredients are tender and very hot. Adjust the seasoning with additional salt, pepper, and spices, if necessary.

8. Transfer the couscous to a serving dish and ladle the stew on top. Garnish with droplets of harissa and the parsley. Serve immediately.

Lamb Khorma

MAKES 5 SERVINGS

MARINADE

¾ cup yogurt

1 tsp ground white pepper

1 tsp ground cardamom

2 tsp garlic paste

2 tsp ginger paste

LAMB

2½ lb lamb, cut into 1½-inch cubes

¾ cups ghee or vegetable oil

3¼ cups small-dice onion

1 tbsp ground coriander

1 tbsp ground cumin

½ tsp ground cardamom

2 tsp ground fennel

1½ tsp ground white pepper, plus more as needed

1 tbsp peeled, chopped ginger

7 Thai chiles, minced

¼ cup chopped cilantro stems, plus 6 tbsp chopped cilantro leaves

1⅓ cups cashews, soaked in hot water, then ground to a paste

Water, as needed

½ cup heavy cream

Salt, as needed

1. To make the marinade, combine the yogurt, white pepper, cardamom, garlic paste, and ginger paste in a large bowl and mix to combine. Add the lamb, cover, and marinate in the refrigerator for 30 minutes.

2. Heat the ghee or oil in a Dutch oven over medium-high heat. Add the onion and sweat until translucent.

3. In 1- to 2-minute intervals and still over medium-high heat, stir in the coriander, cumin, cardamom, fennel, white pepper, and ginger. When the spices are aromatic, add the chiles and cilantro stems. Cook the mixture for 1 to 2 minutes. Add the cashew paste, stirring to make sure nothing sticks to the bottom of the pan. Add water if the mixture becomes too dry.

4. Drain the lamb from the marinade and add it to the pot. Increase the heat and stir until the lamb is evenly covered with the spices. Bring to a simmer, cover the pot, and reduce the heat to medium-low. Cook for 45 minutes, stirring occasionally to prevent the meat from sticking. Add water if the mixture becomes too dry.

5. Add the cream and adjust the seasoning with additional salt and white pepper. Mix well and continue to cook until the meat is tender. Serve the curry garnished with the chopped cilantro leaves.

PORK VINDALOO

SPICE PASTE

1 cup tamarind pulp, strained

14 oz dried red chiles

20 garlic cloves, thinly sliced

½ cup salt

½ cup sugar

¼ cup peeled and sliced ginger

⅓ cup plus 2 tsp coriander seeds

3 tbsp cumin seeds

2 tbsp ground turmeric

1 tbsp plus 1½ tsp methi seeds

1 tbsp ground cinnamon

1 tsp cardamom pods

1 tsp cloves

2¼ cups palm vinegar

MARINADE

⅓ cup sugar

2 tbsp chili powder

1 tbsp ground turmeric

½ cup palm vinegar

10 lb pork butt, cut into 1-inch cubes

¼ cup vegetable oil

2 onions, cut into large dice

4 oz tomato paste

½ cup water

Salt, as needed

Freshly ground black pepper, as needed

1. To make the spice paste, combine the tamarind, chiles, garlic, salt, sugar, ginger, coriander, cumin, turmeric, methi, cinnamon, cardamom, cloves, and vinegar in a medium bowl. Cover the mixture and refrigerate for 1 day. Purée the mixture in a blender to make a coarse paste.

2. To make the marinade, combine the sugar, chili powder, turmeric, and vinegar in a large bowl. Add the pork, toss well, cover, and refrigerate overnight.

3. Heat the oil in a medium pan over medium-high heat. Add the onions and sauté until golden brown. Add the spice paste and cook until aromatic. Combine the tomato paste and water and add it to pot. Cook until most of the water has evaporated and the mixture is almost dry.

4. Drain the pork from the marinade and add it to the pot. Stir to cover the pork cubes with the spice mixture.

5. Bring to a gentle simmer over medium-low heat, cover the pot, and stew the pork until tender, stirring occasionally to make sure that the meat does not scorch or burn, and skimming as necessary.

6. Season with salt and pepper and serve immediately.

NEW MEXICAN GREEN CHILE STEW

1 cup white beans, soaked overnight (see page 257)

1¾ lb pork shoulder, cut into large dice

1 qt Chicken Stock (page 38)

12 oz Anaheim peppers

2 tbsp vegetable oil

1½ cups small-dice onion

2 tbsp minced garlic

3 cups medium-dice russet potatoes

1 tbsp seeded and chopped jalapeños

1 cup chopped cilantro, plus ¼ cup cilantro leaves

2 tsp salt

1. Drain the soaked beans, transfer to a small pot, and cover with water. Simmer over medium-low heat for about 1 hour, or until completely tender. Add more water throughout the cooking process, if necessary. Reserve the beans in their cooking liquid.

2. Bring a large pot of water to a boil while the beans are simmering. Blanch the pork for 6 minutes to remove any impurities. Skim any scum that forms on the surface. Drain and rinse the pork.

3. Place the blanched pork in a large pot and add the stock. Simmer over low heat until the pork is tender, about 2 hours.

4. Flame-roast the Anaheim peppers for 6 to 8 minutes or until the skins blacken and the flesh is tender. Place the peppers in a bowl and cover with plastic wrap to steam. Peel the peppers and remove the seeds. Reserve.

5. Heat the oil in a medium sauté pan over medium-high heat. Add the onion and garlic and sweat until the onions are translucent, about 5 minutes. Add the onions and garlic to the pork.

6. Add the potatoes and beans to the pork and simmer until the potatoes are tender, about 10 minutes.

7. Place the roasted Anaheim peppers, the jalapeños, and chopped cilantro in a blender and purée until completely smooth. Add some of the cooking liquid from the stew to facilitate puréeing, if needed. Strain the mixture through a large-holed strainer, if desired.

8. Just before serving, add the purée to the stew, simmer for 1 to 2 minutes, and add the salt. Serve immediately, garnished with the cilantro leaves.

Beef Stew

7 lb 8 oz boneless beef shank or chuck, cut into 2-inch cubes

1 tbsp salt, plus more as needed

1½ tsp freshly ground black pepper, plus more as needed

¼ cup vegetable oil

1⅓ cups minced onion

5 garlic cloves, minced

¼ cup tomato paste

3¾ cups red wine

5 cups Beef Stock (page 38), plus more as needed

10 cups Jus de Veau Lié (page 76)

1 sachet d'epices (see page 2)

1 bouquet garni (see page 2)

4 tbsp butter

1 cup Chicken Stock (page 38)

5¼ cups large-dice or bâtonnet carrots, blanched

4½ cups large-dice or bâtonnet white turnips, blanched

4½ cups large-dice or bâtonnet yellow turnips, blanched

5¼ cups green beans, cut into 1-inch pieces, blanched

5 tbsp chopped parsley

1. Season the beef with the salt and pepper.

2. Heat the oil over medium-high heat in a large pot until it starts to shimmer. Working in batches, if necessary, place the beef carefully in the oil and sear until deep brown on as many sides as possible. Transfer the beef to a baking dish and reserve.

3. Degrease the pan, if necessary. Add the onion to the pan and cook, stirring occasionally, until caramelized, about 10 minutes. Add the garlic and tomato paste and cook until the tomato paste turns a deeper color and gives off a sweet aroma, about 1 minute.

4. Add the wine, stirring to release any browned bits from the bottom of the pot. Cook until the wine has reduced by three-quarters. Return the beef to the pan along with any juices it may have released.

5. Add the beef stock, jus lié, sachet d'épices, and bouquet garni. Reduce the heat to medium-low to establish a gentle simmer. Cover the pot and stew the beef, skimming as necessary, until tender, about 2 hours. Add more stock during cooking, if necessary. Remove and discard the sachet and bouquet garni.

6. Heat the butter and chicken stock in a large sauté pan over medium-high heat. Add the carrot, turnips, and green beans and toss to coat. Cook until the stock has reduced and the vegetables are hot, about 15 minutes. Adjust the seasoning with additional salt and pepper.

7. To serve, garnish the stew with the parsley and serve immediately with the vegetables.

Saag Paneer

4 lb spinach, washed

½ cup vegetable oil

1½ cups chopped onion

2 tbsp ground cumin

2 tsp turmeric powder

1 tsp garam masala

1 tsp Korean chili powder

1 tbsp ground coriander

5 garlic cloves, chopped

2 tbsp chopped ginger

1 Thai bird chili, chopped

1 lb chopped tomatoes

Kosher salt, as needed

1 lb cubed paneer cheese

1 cup Greek yogurt

Sugar, as needed

Freshly ground black pepper, as needed

1. Prepare an ice-water bath. Bring a large pot of salted water to a boil. Blanch the spinach until just wilted and then shock in the ice water.

2. Drain the spinach and squeeze out the excess moisture. Coarsely chop the spinach and reserve.

3. Heat the oil in a large sauté pan over medium-high heat and add the onion. Cook until slightly brown and then stir in the cumin, turmeric, garam masala, chili powder, and coriander.

4. Reduce the heat to low. Cook for 2 minutes more, then add the garlic, ginger, and chopped chile. Cook until the garlic is fragrant, about 1 minute more.

5. Add the tomatoes and cook for 5 minutes. When the tomatoes are cooked, add the spinach. Season with salt.

6. Cook, stirring, until the flavors of the spices have blended, about 5 minutes. Cover and cook for 3 minutes more.

7. Add the cheese and cook for 4 minutes more. Stir in the yogurt. Adjust the seasoning with sugar, pepper, and additional salt, if necessary, and serve.

RATATOUILLE

¼ cup olive oil, plus more as needed

1½ cup medium-dice onion

3 tbsp minced garlic

2 tbsp tomato paste

½ cup medium-dice red bell peppers

4 cups medium-dice eggplant

4 cups medium-dice zucchini

1½ cups peeled, seeded, medium-dice tomatoes

½ cup Chicken Stock (page 38) or Vegetable Stock (page 38), plus more as needed

Salt, as needed

Freshly ground black pepper, as needed

2 tbsp chopped herbs such as thyme, parsley, and oregano

1. Heat the oil in a large pot over medium heat. Add the onion and sauté until translucent, 4 to 5 minutes. Add the garlic and sauté until soft, about 1 minute.

2. Reduce the heat to medium-low. Add the tomato paste and cook until it completely coats the onions and develops a deeper color, 1 to 2 minutes.

3. Add the vegetables in the following sequence, cooking each vegetable until it softens, 2 to 3 minutes each, before adding the next: bell peppers, eggplant, zucchini, and tomatoes.

4. Add the stock, reduce the heat to low, and simmer until the vegetables are tender and flavorful. (They should be moist, but not soupy.) Season with the salt, pepper, and the herbs. Serve immediately.

French-Style Peas

MAKES 10 SERVINGS

⅓ cup small pearl onions

½ cup (8 tbsp/1 stick) butter

1 lb 4 oz shelled green peas

10 cups Boston lettuce chiffonade

½ cup Chicken Stock (page 38)

Salt, as needed

Freshly ground black pepper, as needed

3 tbsp all-purpose flour

1. Bring a large pot of water to a rolling boil. Add the pearl onions and blanch for 1 minute. Remove the onions, rinse under cool running water until cool enough to handle, and then remove the skins.

2. Melt 4 tablespoons of the butter in a large sauté pan over low heat and add the pearl onions. Cook, covered, until they are tender and translucent, 8 to 10 minutes.

3. Add the peas, lettuce, and stock. Season with salt and pepper. Bring the stock to a gentle simmer over low heat and cover the pan. Simmer until the peas are fully cooked and tender, 3 to 4 minutes.

4. Blend the remaining 4 tablespoons butter with the flour and gradually add it to the peas in small pieces until the cooking liquid is slightly thickened. Adjust the seasoning with additional salt and pepper, if needed, and serve immediately.

Glazed Beets

MAKES 10 SERVINGS

2½ lb red or golden beets, tops trimmed, skin on

¼ cup sugar

1 tbsp red or white wine vinegar

¼ cup fresh orange juice

1 cup Chicken Stock (page 38)

3 tbsp butter

Salt, as needed

Freshly ground black pepper, as needed

1. Place the beets in a large pot and add enough water to cover. Bring the water to a boil, reduce to a simmer, and cook the beets until they are soft when pierced with a fork or skewer, about 40 minutes, depending on size.

2. Drain the beets and let cool slightly. Peel and slice the beets into ¼-inch-thick rounds, or in wedges.

3. In a small sauté pan over medium heat, combine the sugar, vinegar, juice, stock, and butter and bring to a simmer. Cook gently until the glaze has the consistency of light syrup, about 15 minutes.

4. In a large bowl, toss the cut beets in the glaze. Season with salt and pepper and serve immediately.

Braised Bok Choy

BRAISED GREENS

MAKES 10 SERVINGS

4 lb collard greens or kale

¼ cup minced bacon

1½ cups minced onion

3 garlic cloves, minced

1¼ cups Chicken Stock (page 38)

1 tbsp sugar

1 ham hock

Salt, as needed

Freshly ground black pepper, as needed

2 tbsp apple cider vinegar

1. Preheat the oven to 350°F. Bring a large pot of water to a boil.

2. Strip the leaves from the collards or kale; discard the tough stems. Cut the leaves into bite-size pieces and blanch (see page 104).

3. In a large ovenproof skillet over medium heat, cook the bacon until it is light golden and the fat has rendered. Add the onion and garlic and sweat until aromatic. Add the blanched greens. Deglaze the pan with some stock and cook until reduced by half. Stir in the sugar.

4. Add the ham hock and the remaining stock and season with salt and pepper. Transfer the skillet to the oven and braise until tender, 30 to 45 minutes.

5. Remove the greens and ham hock from the pan. Add the vinegar to the braising liquid and cook over medium heat until the liquid is reduced by half. Add the greens back to the liquid and adjust the seasoning with salt and pepper. Remove the meat from the ham hock, dice it, and add it to the finished greens, if desired. Serve immediately.

BRAISED BOK CHOY

MAKES 5 SERVINGS

1 lb baby bok choy

2 tbsp vegetable oil

8 garlic cloves, thinly sliced

Salt, as needed

1. Cut the bok choy in half lengthwise. Score the cores to promote even cooking.

2. Prepare a bowl of ice water. Bring a pot of salted water to a boil. Blanch the bok choy, then shock it in the ice water bath and drain well.

3. Heat the oil in a wok over high heat, add the garlic, and stir-fry until aromatic and light brown.

4. Add the bok choy and stir-fry until the bok choy is just cooked through. Add a small amount of water to the wok to keep the garlic from burning, if necessary. Season with salt and serve immediately.

BRAISED SHORT RIBS

5 beef short ribs (about 1 lb)

1½ tsp salt, plus more as needed

1 tsp freshly ground black pepper, plus more as needed

2 tbsp vegetable oil

½ cup medium-dice onion

½ cup medium-dice celery

½ cup medium-dice carrot

2 tbsp tomato paste

½ cup dry red wine

1 cup Beef Stock (page 38), or more as needed

1 bay leaf

Pinch dried thyme

6 tbsp Madeira or sherry

1. Preheat the oven to 275°F.

2. Season the short ribs with the salt and pepper.

3. Heat the oil in an ovenproof pot over medium-high heat until it starts to shimmer. Place the short ribs carefully in the oil and sear until deep brown on all sides. Transfer the short ribs to a pan and reserve.

4. Add the onion, celery, and carrot to the pot and cook, stirring occasionally, until golden brown. Add the tomato paste and cook until it turns a deeper color and gives off a sweet aroma, about 1 minute.

5. Add the wine to the pot, stirring to release any browned bits from the bottom of the pot. Reduce the wine by half. Return the short ribs to the pot along with any juices they may have released. Add enough stock to cover the short ribs by two-thirds. Bring to a gentle simmer over medium-low heat. Cover the pan and transfer it to the oven.

6. Braise the short ribs for 45 minutes. Add the bay leaf and thyme, and skim the liquid if necessary. Continue braising the short ribs until fork-tender, about 45 minutes more.

7. Transfer the short ribs to a pan or heatproof container and moisten with some of the cooking liquid. Set aside.

8. Return the pot to the stovetop and simmer the cooking liquid over medium-low heat until thickened, skimming as necessary. Adjust the seasoning with salt and pepper and strain. Stir in the Madeira or sherry to finish the sauce, and serve immediately with the short ribs.

Facing page: Braised Short Ribs, blanched green beans (see page 104), and mashed potatoes (see page 106)

BRAISED RED CABBAGE

1 tbsp vegetable oil or rendered bacon fat

1 cup medium-dice onion

1¼ cups medium-dice Granny Smith apples

1 cup water, plus more as needed

3 tbsp red wine

3 tbsp red wine vinegar

2 tbsp sugar

1½ oz red currant jelly

1 cinnamon stick

1 clove

1 bay leaf

2 juniper berries

1½ lb red cabbage chiffonade

½ tsp salt

¼ tsp freshly ground black pepper

1. Preheat the oven to 350°F.

2. Heat the oil or bacon fat in a large nonreactive ovenproof pot over medium-low heat. Add the onions and apples and sweat until the onions are translucent and the apples are slightly soft, about 5 minutes.

3. Add the water, wine, vinegar, sugar, and jelly. Taste; the flavor should be tart and strong.

4. Make a sachet d'épices by combining the cinnamon stick, clove, bay leaf, and juniper berries in a square of cheesecloth and tying with twine to secure. Add the sachet and cabbage to the pot. Cover and braise the cabbage in the oven until tender, 15 to 20 minutes. Check regularly to be sure the liquids have not evaporated completely. Add more water if necessary. Remove and discard the sachet.

5. Season with the salt and pepper. Serve immediately.

STEWED BLACK BEANS

2 tbsp olive oil

1 small onion, diced

2 garlic cloves, thinly sliced

1 lb black beans, soaked and drained (see page 257)

1 ham hock

Chicken Stock (page 38), as needed

Salt, as needed

1 chipotle in adobo, finely chopped

6 sun-dried tomatoes

Ground black pepper, as needed

1. Heat the oil in a large pot over medium heat. Add the onion and garlic and sweat until translucent, 4 to 5 minutes.

2. Add the beans, ham hock, and enough stock to cover the beans by 1 inch. Reduce the heat to establish a simmer and simmer for 1 hour.

3. Add the salt, chipotle, and tomatoes. Continue to simmer until the beans are tender to the bite, 20 to 30 minutes more.

4. Remove the meat from the ham hock and discard the bones. Dice the meat and add it back to the beans. Season with salt and pepper. Serve immediately.

CHICKEN TAGINE

5 chickens, each cut into 6 pieces

1 tbsp salt, plus more as needed

1½ tsp freshly ground black pepper, plus more as needed

¼ cup extra-virgin olive oil

30 cipollini onions, blanched and peeled

One ½-inch piece peeled ginger, thinly sliced

5 garlic cloves, thinly sliced

1 tsp cumin seeds, toasted and ground

¼ tsp saffron

1 to 1¼ cups water or Chicken Stock (page 38), plus more as needed

50 Picholine olives

2 preserved lemons

¼ cup chopped flat-leaf parsley

1. Season the chicken pieces with the salt and pepper.

2. Heat the oil in a large sauté pan over medium-high heat. Place the chicken pieces carefully in the oil and sauté until they turn golden brown. Transfer the chicken to a baking dish and reserve.

3. Add the onions to the pan and cook, stirring occasionally, until golden brown, 7 to 8 minutes. Add the ginger and garlic and toast until aromatic, about 1 minute more. Add the cumin and saffron and cook until the mixture turns a deeper color and gives off a sweet aroma, about 1 minute.

4. Return the chicken to the pan and add the water or stock. Adjust the seasoning with salt and pepper. Bring to a gentle simmer over medium-low heat. Cover and braise for 30 to 40 minutes, or until the chicken is cooked through, turning the pieces occasionally to keep them evenly moistened. (Maintain only a small amount of water or stock so the braising liquid will become concentrated.)

5. During the last 15 minutes of cooking, add the olives, lemons, and parsley. Simmer the mixture until the olives are tender and the aroma of the lemons is apparent.

6. Remove the lemons and serve the tagine immediately.

Osso Buco Milanese

MAKES 5 SERVINGS

5 veal shank crosscuts, each 1 lb and 1½ inches thick

1½ tsp salt, plus more as needed

1 tsp freshly ground black pepper, plus more as needed

¼ cup all-purpose flour

¼ cup olive oil

1½ cups medium-dice onion

½ cup medium-dice carrot

1 cup medium-dice celery

1 tsp minced garlic

2 tbsp tomato paste

½ cup dry white wine

1 qt Beef Stock (page 38), or more as needed

1 bouquet garni (see page 2)

½ cup Gremolata (page 91)

1. Preheat the oven to 325°F.

2. Season the veal with the salt and pepper and tie a piece of kitchen twine around the shanks to keep them together. Lightly dredge them in the flour.

3. Heat the oil in a large pot over medium-high heat until it starts to shimmer. Place the shanks carefully in the oil and sear until deep brown on all sides. Transfer the shanks to a baking dish and reserve.

4. Reduce the heat to medium-low, add the onion to the pot, and cook, stirring occasionally, until golden brown. Add the carrots and celery and cook until the celery is barely translucent. Add the garlic and tomato paste and cook until the tomato paste turns a deeper color and gives off a sweet aroma, about 1 minute.

5. Add the wine to the pot, stirring to release any browned bits from the bottom of the pot. Reduce the wine by half. Return the shanks to the pot along with any juices they may have released. Add enough stock to cover the veal by two-thirds. Bring to a gentle simmer over medium-low heat. Cover the pot and transfer it to the oven.

6. Braise the veal shanks for 45 minutes. Add the bouquet garni and skim the liquid if necessary. Continue braising the veal until fork-tender, 1 to 1½ hours more.

7. Transfer the veal shanks to a baking dish and moisten with some of the cooking liquid. Keep warm while finishing the sauce.

8. Return the pot to the stovetop and simmer the cooking liquid over medium-low heat until thickened, skimming as necessary. If needed, adjust the seasoning with salt and pepper. Strain the sauce. Serve the veal shanks immediately, topped with the sauce and the gremolata.

YANKEE POT ROAST

MAKES 10 SERVINGS

4 lb beef shoulder clod, bottom round, or eye round, trimmed

2 tsp salt, plus more as needed

½ tsp freshly ground black pepper, plus more as needed

¼ cup vegetable oil

2 cups small-dice onion

½ cup tomato purée

1 cup dry red wine

3 cups Jus de Veau Lié (page 76)

Beef Stock (page 38)

1 sachet d'épices (see page 2)

10 new potatoes

10 baby turnips

20 baby carrots

60 pearl onions, blanched and peeled

1. Preheat the oven to 350°F.

2. Season the beef with the salt and pepper and tie it with kitchen twine.

3. Heat the oil in a large pot over medium-high heat until it starts to shimmer. Place the beef carefully in the oil and sear until deep brown on all sides. Transfer the beef to a baking dish and reserve.

4. Add the onion to the pot and cook, stirring occasiionally, until golden brown, 6 to 8 minutes. Add the tomato purée and cook until it turns a deeper color and gives off a sweet aroma, about 1 minute.

5. Add the wine to the pot, stirring to loosen any browned bits from the bottom of the pot. Reduce the wine by half. Return the beef to the pot along with any juices it may have released. Add the jus lié and enough stock to come about halfway up the beef. Bring to a gentle simmer over medium to low heat. Cover the pot and transfer it to the oven.

6. Braise the beef for 1½ hours, turning occasionally to keep it evenly moistened. Add the sachet d'épices and skim the liquid if necessary.

7. Add the potatoes, turnips, carrots, and pearl onions and continue braising until the beef is fork-tender and the vegetables are fully cooked, 35 to 45 minutes more.

8. Transfer the beef to a baking dish and moisten with some of the cooking liquid. Keep it warm while finishing the sauce.

9. Return the pot to the stovetop and simmer the cooking liquid over medium-low heat until thickened, skimming as necessary. Adjust the seasoning with salt and pepper.

10. Remove the string from the beef. Slice the beef and serve immediately with the sauce and vegetables.

EGGPLANT CAPONATA

MAKES 6 CUPS

1 eggplant (about 1 lb), peeled and cut into small dice

2 tbsp salt

1 red bell pepper, seeded and cut into small dice

¾ cup minced onion

1 tsp minced garlic

¼ cup olive oil

2 cups canned diced tomatoes

2 tbsp tomato paste

2 tbsp basil chiffonade

1 tsp minced marjoram

1 tbsp balsamic vinegar

⅓ cup finely grated Parmesan

1. Preheat the oven to 250°F.

2. Place the eggplant in a large bowl and sprinkle with the salt, tossing evenly to distribute. Place the salted eggplant in a colander and allow to drain for 20 minutes.

3. Quickly rinse the eggplant under cool water, then place on paper towels to absorb excess moisture.

4. In a large bowl, combine the eggplant with the bell pepper, onion, garlic, and oil and toss to combine. Add the tomatoes and tomato paste and toss to thoroughly combine.

5. Spread the vegetable mixture evenly on a baking sheet and roast for 25 to 30 minutes, or until the vegetables are tender and lightly browned.

6. Remove the pan from the oven and add the basil, marjoram, and vinegar. Gently fold the ingredients together.

7. Transfer the caponata to a glass or stainless steel container with a lid. Let cool to room temperature, then stir in the cheese. Refrigerate the caponata in a covered glass or stainless steel container for up to 1 week. The flavor will improve if the caponata is allowed to rest for at least 24 hours before use.

Facing page, from left to right: Eggplant Caponata, Fig Compote (page 89), and Giardiniera (page 307).

GRILLING, BROILING, AND ROASTING

Grilling, broiling, and roasting are grouped together as cooking methods because they are all dry-heat cooking methods. That is, the heat source used to cook them is a direct or indirect flame, or radiant heat. No steam, water, or other liquid is added during cooking. Fats or oils added during cooking contribute flavor but do not act as the cooking medium. As a result, food that is grilled, broiled, or roasted develops a highly flavored exterior and a moist interior.

GRILLING

GRILLING IS A QUICK-COOKING TECHNIQUE used for naturally tender pieces of meat, poultry, fish, alternative proteins such as tofu or seitan, or vegetables. Grilling cooks food with radiant heat from a source located below it. Grilled foods have a slightly smoky flavor, resulting from the juices and fats that are rendered and lightly charred as the food cooks, as well as from the direct contact with the grill rack.

Items to be grilled should be of an even thickness. Meat should be trimmed of any excess fat and gristle and lightly pounded to an even thickness if necessary. Some foods are cut into strips, chunks, or cubes and then threaded onto skewers for grilling. However it is prepared, the food should be seasoned and in some cases lightly oiled before grilling.

Different parts of the grill are hotter than others. These "zones" of varying heat intensity should be identified and used to your advantage: a very hot section for cooking foods to a rare doneness, an area of moderate heat for cooking foods to a medium-rare or medium doneness, and an area of low heat for slow cooking to a medium-well or well doneness. Low heat can also be used to keep foods warm before serving. Zones could also be allocated for different types of foods, to prevent the transfer of flavors: a zone for chicken, a zone for fish, and another zone for vegetables.

> **EXPERT tip**
>
> **WOODS SUCH AS MESQUITE, HICKORY, OR APPLE** are frequently used to impart special flavors to grilled items. Hardwood chips and other aromatics can be put in a smoker box (a steel box with holes) or wrapped in aluminum foil that has been punctured with several holes. Either of these methods will allow the smoke to permeate the grill without igniting the aromatics. Try adding the following for additional flavor:
>
> Hardwood chips
>
> Herb stems
>
> Grapevine trimmings

Pan Grilling

PAN GRILLING INVOLVES COOKING FOODS ON THE STOVE over intense heat in a heavy cast-iron or other warp-resistant metal pan with a ridged interior bottom, often called a grill pan. The thick ridges create marks similar to a grill's and hold the food up and away from any juices or fat that might collect. It is important to consider, however, that pan grilling will not impart the same flavor as traditional grilling.

Basic Equipment for Grilling

GRILL. In a grill, the heat source is located below a rack. Outdoor grills burn wood, charcoal, or both, or propane, while indoor grills are either gas or electric.

WIRE GRILL BRUSH. The best results begin with a clean and well-maintained grill. A wire grill brush should be used to scour the grill rods well between uses and also between grilling different types of foods to remove any buildup of charred food particles and potential pathogens.

GRILL MOP. A mop is a small tool with a cotton head that is used for applying wet rubs (also called mops) and marinades to foods for grilling.

PASTRY BRUSHES. Brushes are a helpful tool for applying marinades and mops to foods for grilling. They may be made of flexible nylon, unbleached hog bristles, or silicone and are available in a variety of widths. After using a brush for a marinade or mop, it should be thoroughly washed and air-dried.

TONGS. Tongs are an indispensable tool for turning foods over on a grill or grill pan. A pair of heavy-duty, long-handled tongs is especially useful for grilling, so you can maintain a distance from the open flame.

OFFSET SPATULAS. Large, offset metal spatulas come in a wide variety of sizes and are a handy tool for flipping foods over on the grill. The blade may be solid or perforated, and the handle may be made of polypropylene or wood.

HAND RACK. Hand racks consist of a hinged metal cage fitted with a handle. These are the perfect tool for grilling delicate foods, such as fish and vegetables, because the metal bars trap the food, making it easier to turn over on the grill. Hand racks should be cleaned and oiled between uses to prevent meat from sticking.

SKEWERS. Many foods may be cut into pieces and threaded onto a skewer for grilling. Clean and oil metal skewers before use; soak wooden or bamboo skewers in water to prevent them from charring too much or catching fire on the grill.

GRILL PAN. A grill pan is a skillet with ridges that is used on the stovetop to simulate grilling.

Basic Preparations

There are many options for seasoning an item for grilling, including marinades and spice rubs.

MARINADES. These are typically liquid mixtures based on an acidic ingredient, such as wine, vinegar, or citrus juice, and they can add both flavor and moisture to foods (photos 1 and 2, opposite). Some marinades are cooked, while others are not. Marinades can be used to flavor an accompanying sauce or may become a dipping sauce. Marinades that have come in contact with raw meat, poultry, or seafood, however, can be used in this way if, and only if, they are boiled for several minutes to kill any lingering pathogens.

RUBS. A spice rub is a combination of spices and herbs that is applied to foods as a flavorful crust. Rubs can be either dry or wet. Either way, they create a greater depth of flavor as they are absorbed into the meat. Dry rubs are generally based on spices, while wet rubs, sometimes called mops, include moist ingredients, such as fruit juice, broth, fresh herbs, or vegetables, to give the mixture a paste-like consistency.

To use a dry rub, apply by rubbing to create a thorough coating all over the food before grilling (photos 3 and 4, opposite). To use a wet rub, use a pastry brush or small cotton mop to cover the food with the wet rub just before grilling. While the food is cooking on the grill, periodically brush or mop on additional wet rub as desired. Be very careful when mopping a wet rub onto items on the grill; too much excess could cause a flare-up.

Barbecue Sauces

BECAUSE MANY BARBECUE SAUCES CONTAIN SUGAR AND BURN EASILY, it is usually a good idea to partially cook the food before applying the sauce. That way, as the food finishes cooking, the sauce glazes and caramelizes lightly without burning. A single coat of sauce may be applied to each side of the food; to build up a thicker, slightly crusty coat of sauce, the food may be brushed repeatedly with light coats of sauce.

To use a marinade, add it to the main item and turn the food over to coat it evenly. You can do this in a shallow dish or in a resealable plastic bag.

Cover the container or seal the bag and refrigerate for the length of time indicated by the recipe and the type of food. Before grilling, brush or scrape off any excess marinade and pat dry with paper towels.

To use a dry rub, massage the spice mixture into the food. Refrigerate it overnight to allow the food to fully absorb the flavors.

Dry rubs may be left on the food during grilling or they may be removed. To remove a dry rub before grilling, rinse the food under cool running water and dry it well with paper towels.

GRILLING

1. Any tools, such as tongs, spatulas, or brushes—as well as platters, plates, or other serving items—should be placed within arm's reach before you start grilling. A wire grill brush and a damp towel should always be kept on hand for wiping the grill rods.

Preheat the grill to allow the heat to burn away any old particulates on the grill rods. Once the particulates have turned to white ash, brush them away with a wire grill brush or wipe away with a wet cloth. Rub the grates with a cloth dipped in oil.

2. Place the seasoned food on the preheated grill to start cooking. The better looking side of the food should always be the side that goes down on the grill first. Let the food cook, undisturbed, on the first side. The heated grill rods will char marks onto the surface of the food.

To make foods with a crosshatch on the grill, gently work a spatula or tongs under the food, lift, and give it a quarter turn (90 degrees).

Turn the food over (flip the food just once) and continue cooking to the desired doneness. Since most foods cooked by grilling or broiling are relatively thin and tender, they do not require much more cooking time once they have been turned over. Thicker cuts or those that must be cooked to a higher internal temperature, such as poultry, may need to be moved to a cooler portion of the grill so that they don't develop a charred exterior. Another solution is to remove the thicker cuts from the grill after they are marked on both sides and finish the cooking in the oven.

Remove meat or fish when it is still slightly underdone so it does not end up overcooked by the time it is served. Even thin pieces of meat or fish will retain some heat, causing them to continue cooking even after they have been removed from the heat.

Grilling Vegetables

The intense heat of the grill gives vegetables a rich, bold flavor. It is essential to grill only vegetables that are perfectly fresh with no softening, discoloration, or wilting. Once selected, vegetables should be properly rinsed or scrubbed. Remove the peel or skin, core, and seeds as needed. Vegetables should be cut into uniform slices (or other desired shapes) before grilling; be sure they are large enough that they will not fall through the grates. High-moisture or tender vegetables, such as onions, eggplant, and bell peppers, can be grilled raw; dense or starchy vegetables, such as sweet potatoes and carrots, may need to be partially cooked before they are grilled.

Preheat the grill before grilling vegetables. Trim and cut the vegetables as desired (see page 20). Either marinate the vegetables or brush them with oil just before grilling. Place the vegetables on the grill, and cook until they are tender and properly cooked through, turning them over as needed during grilling.

BROILING AND ROASTING

BROILING AND ROASTING are cooking techniques that rely on dry heat without the use of fats or oils and that produce food with a highly flavored exterior and a moist interior.

BROILING

EXPERT tip

AS WHEN GRILLING, marinades and spice rubs can be used to season the food before cooking.

Broiling is a technique very similar to grilling, but it uses a heat source located above the food rather than below it. The sauce served with a broiled food must be prepared separately, but foods may be marinated or seasoned with a spice rub before cooking.

Smaller or more delicate foods, such as cut vegetables and fish, are good choices for broiling. Broil tender portion-size cuts of poultry; cuts of meat from the loin, rib, or top round; and fillets of fatty fish such as tuna, swordfish, and salmon. Some less tender cuts of meat, such as hanger or flank steak, may also be used if they are cut very thin. Delicate foods like lean white fish are brushed with butter or oil and placed on the rack below the broiler's heat source. Like foods for grilling, foods for broiling should be cut into pieces of a consistent size and thickness. Meats may be pounded lightly if necessary to even out the thickness. The food should be seasoned before being broiled.

Broiling Vegetables

AS WITH GRILLING, the intense heat of the broiler gives vegetables a rich, bold flavor. Broiled vegetables have deeply browned exteriors and very tender interiors with intense flavor. The main restriction governing which vegetables can or cannot be broiled is their size.

Select perfectly fresh vegetables with no softening, discoloration, or wilting. Remove the peel or skin, core, and seeds, if appropriate. Tender vegetables, such as eggplant and zucchini, can be broiled raw; dense or starchy vegetables, such as sweet potatoes and beets, may require preliminary cooking to assure thorough cooking. Soft vegetables and pre-cooked hard vegetables may be marinated briefly before broiling.

To broil vegetables, first preheat the broiler. If the vegetables have not been marinated, brush them with oil. Arrange the vegetables on a baking sheet and place under the broiler. Cook until the vegetables are tender and properly cooked through, turning them over as needed during cooking.

Basic Equipment for Broiling

BROILER. Broilers radiate an intense heat from above and can be found as a setting in most ovens. When broiling, raise or lower the adjustable oven racks to control the heat level and cooking speed.

BROILING PAN. Broiling pans, also called broiler roasters, consist of a slotted plate that sits inside a shallow pan. The slits in the plate allow the drippings to drain away from the food as it broils, which helps to create the desired crispiness of the exterior of the food.

PASTRY BRUSHES. Brushes are a helpful tool for applying marinades to foods for broiling. They may be made of flexible nylon, unbleached hog bristles, or silicone. Pastry brushes come in a variety of widths. After applying a marinade, the brush should be thoroughly washed and air-dried.

TONGS. Tongs are an indispensable tool for turning over broiled foods.

OFFSET SPATULAS. Large, offset metal spatulas come in a wide variety of sizes and are especially useful for turning over delicate foods, for example, which tongs would break into pieces.

Chef's Lesson
BROILING

1. Preheat the broiler and broiling pan completely before adding the food. Surrounding the food with heat will prevent sticking and develop good texture and color.

2. Place the food on the broiling pan, and allow it to cook undisturbed until browned on the top side. If necessary, adjust the heat level while cooking by raising or lowering the oven or broiler rack. You may want to leave the door of the oven or broiler slightly ajar to allow steam to escape, since you want to develop a crisp exterior texture.

3. Turn the food over and continue cooking to the desired doneness. Since most broiled foods are relatively thin and tender, they do not require much more cooking time once they have been turned over. Remove meat and fish when it is slightly underdone so it does not end up overcooked by the time it is served. Even thin pieces of meat or fish will retain some heat, allowing them to continue cooking after they have been removed from the heat.

Temperatures and descriptions of degrees of doneness

DEGREE OF DONENESS	FINAL RESTING TEMPERATURE	DESCRIPTION
FRESH BEEF, VEAL, AND LAMB		
Rare	135°F	Interior appearance shiny
Medium rare	145°F	Deep red to pink
Medium	160°F	Pink to light pink
Well done	170°F	Light pink with graying on the edges for medium well; no pink for well done
FRESH PORK		
Medium	160°F	Opaque throughout; slight give; juices with faint blush
Well done	170°F	Slight give; juices clear
HAM		
Fresh ham	160°F	Slight give; juices with faint blush
Precooked (to reheat)	140°F	Already fully cooked
POULTRY		
Whole birds (chicken, turkey, duck, goose)	180°F	Leg easy to move in socket; juices with faint blush
Poultry breasts	170°F	Opaque throughout; firm throughout
Poultry thighs, legs, wings	180°F	Meat releases from bone
Stuffing (cooked alone or in a bird)	165°F	Appearance of the fully cooked stuffing will depend on the recipe
GROUND MEAT AND MEAT MIXTURES		
Turkey, chicken	165°F	Opaque throughout; juices clear
Beef, veal, lamb, pork	160°F	Opaque, may have blush of red; juices opaque, no red
SEAFOOD		
Fish	145°F	Still moist; separates easily into segments. Or until opaque
Shrimp, lobster, crab		Shells turn red, flesh becomes pearly opaque
Scallops		Milky white or opaque; firm
Clams, mussels, oysters		Shells open

ROASTING

Very similar to baking, roasting is a way of cooking food in the oven. As roasted foods are cooked through with the dry heated air inside the oven, the outer layers of the food become heated, and the food's natural juices turn to steam and penetrate the food more deeply. Well-roasted foods are tender and moist, and the skin, if left on, is crisp, creating a contrast with the juicy texture of the meat. The rendered juices, also called pan drippings or fond, are often the foundation for a sauce served with a roast.

Roasting is commonly used for cooking larger cuts of meat, whole birds, and dressed fish. Therefore, roasting requires a longer cooking time than broiling. To most fully develop flavor, season meat, poultry, and fish before roasting. A layer of fat or poultry skin helps to naturally baste foods as they roast.

The oven should be preheated for roasting. There are different techniques pertaining to oven temperatures for roasting. Some foods are roasted very quickly at high temperatures. Others are begun at low temperatures, then finished at higher temperatures. Still others are started at high temperatures, then finished at a lower temperature. Roast large cuts of meat, such as prime rib, at a low to medium temperature (300° to 325°F) throughout roasting. Start smaller or more delicate foods at a low to medium temperature (300° to 325°F), and then brown them at the very end of roasting by increasing the temperature to 350° to 375°F.

Roasted foods are often served with a pan gravy made from pan drippings. Onions, carrots, celery, garlic, or other aromatic vegetables or herbs, added to the pan during roasting, will have a deep color and will have absorbed some of the flavor from the drippings, so they will give the finished pan gravy flavor and color. Before preparing any pan gravy, be sure that the drippings are not scorched as this will produce a bitter, inedible sauce.

Vegetables are roasted for many different reasons. Thick-skinned vegetables, such as winter squashes or eggplant, can be roasted to make a richly flavored purée. Aromatic vegetables are often roasted to add an extra dimension of flavor and color to stocks, sauces, and other dishes. Tomatoes or peppers can be roasted to intensify their flavor and give them a drier texture.

Vegetables can be roasted whole, but roasting is also excellent for halved, cut, sliced, or diced vegetables, as well as vegetables that might otherwise be difficult to peel, such as bell peppers. To ensure even cooking, be sure to cut the vegetables into uniform pieces, or select ones of the same approximate size. Marinades can enhance flavor and give extra protection to vegetables as they cook in the dry heat of the oven.

Before roasting, appropriately prepare the vegetable, season it, and toss or brush with oil. Place the vegetable in a preheated baking or roasting pan. Take care not to overcrowd the vegetables. Place the pan in a medium to hot oven and roast to the desired doneness. The longer the roasting time (a factor determined by the type of vegetable, its size, thickness, and density, and the diameter of the cut), the lower the oven temperature.

There are some special considerations when roasting potatoes. Scrub or peel them and cut them into the desired shape. Since the skin adds texture and increases the nutritional value, peeling the potatoes is optional. Toss the potatoes in just enough fat to coat them lightly. The fat could be butter, olive oil, lard, goose fat, or fat and drippings from roasting meat. Season the potatoes with salt and pepper, fresh or dried herbs, and/or dried spices as desired. Arrange the potatoes in a single layer on a baking sheet or shallow roasting pan and bake in a 350°F oven, stirring often to ensure even browning, until the potatoes are tender. To test for doneness, pierce the potato with a skewer or the tines of a fork. If there is no resistance when it enters the flesh, the potato is done.

Basic Equipment for Roasting

OVEN. Ovens cook foods by surrounding them with hot air, a gentler and more even source of heat than the heat of a grill or stovetop burner. In a conventional oven, the heat source is on the bottom, whereas a convection oven has fans that force hot air to circulate all around the food, cooking it more evenly and quickly.

ROASTING PANS. A good roasting pan has relatively low sides to allow hot air to circulate freely. Select a pan that holds the food comfortably but is not so large that the pan juices scorch in the oven. When roasting, the pan should remain uncovered.

ROASTING RACK. Food to be roasted may be set on a metal rack fitted inside the roasting pan in order to elevate it from the bottom of the pan and permit hot air to contact all of the food's surfaces.

KITCHEN TWINE. Trussing large pieces of meat or whole birds with kitchen twine, also known as butcher's twine, will help hold the attractive shape during roasting.

INSTANT-READ THERMOMETER. It is important to carefully monitor the internal temperature of a roast. When the stem of an instant-read thermometer is inserted into a food, it produces an immediate temperature readout. (See the chart on page 160 for internal temperatures.)

CARVING FORK AND KNIFE. A kitchen fork with two tines approximately 4 to 6 inches long and a sharp carving knife are the appropriate tools for carving roasts as well as testing for doneness and transferring a roasted item from the pan to a carving board or platter.

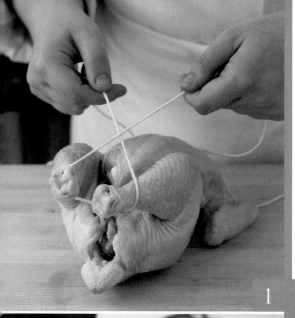

Basic Preparations for Roasting: Trussing a Chicken

The object of trussing or tying any type of bird is to give it a smooth, compact shape so that it will cook evenly and retain moisture. There are several methods for trussing poultry. This is one simple method that requires only string.

1

1. Pass the middle of a piece of kitchen twine underneath the joints at the ends of the drumsticks, and cross the ends of the twine to make an X.

2. Pull both ends of the twine tightly across the joint that connects the drumstick and the thigh and continue to pull along the body toward the bird's back, catching the wing underneath the twine.

3. Cross the ends of the twine over the backbone at the neck opening. Tie the two ends underneath the backbone with a secure knot.

2

3

IF ROASTS ARE DRASTICALLY TRIMMED, an alternative "skin" should be created in the form of a coating or crust. Different ingredients may be combined with a small amount of fat and used to form a crust, such as:

Thin sheets of fatback or bacon

Seasoned dried potato flakes

Rice flakes

Cornflakes

Cornmeal

Finely ground dried mushrooms

TO DEVELOP ADDITIONAL FLAVOR AND COLOR, sear a food before roasting it. Once the food has been seasoned and tied or trussed, it may be seared in hot fat on the stovetop, under a broiler, or in a very hot oven. Searing is an effective way to develop flavor and color in longer, slower cooking methods such as roasting.

BASTING is a technique that adds both flavor and moisture. If the food is lean and does not release enough fat of its own for basting, any one of the following may be used:

Melted butter

Oil

Glaze

Marinade

stuffings

FOODS SUCH AS WHOLE BIRDS, CHICKEN BREASTS, AND CHOPS may be stuffed before roasting. Season the stuffing and chill it to below 40°F before combining it with raw meat, poultry, or fish. Be sure to allow enough time for the flavors of the stuffing to infuse the food before roasting. If there are ingredients in the stuffing that must be cooked, like sausage or seafood, be sure that the stuffing is heated to a safe temperature before serving. For this reason, stuffings for whole roasted birds are sometimes baked separately so that the poultry isn't overcooked in an effort to cook the stuffing properly. If a stuffing is baked separately, it is called a dressing.

PREPARE A BREAD-BASED STUFFING by cubing or breaking breads (cornbread, French, or Italian-style) into small pieces. Some bread stuffings are moistened with stocks or broths. Optionally, eggs may be included to bind the stuffing. If desired, include additional flavoring ingredients, such as fresh or dried herbs, cooked sausage, seafood, or mushrooms.

PREPARE A GRAIN-BASED STUFFING by cooking a grain, such as rice, barley, or kasha, until just tender. Once cooked, cool the grain completely before the stuffing is added to meat, poultry, or fish. Grain-based stuffings can be seasoned, moistened, and bound similarly to bread-based stuffings.

Chef's Lesson
ROASTING

1. Once the food has been seasoned and tied or trussed, if necessary, it may be seared in hot fat on the stovetop, under a broiler, or in a very hot oven. Some foods are not seared, especially larger cuts, since an extended roasting time will produce a deeply colored exterior even without an initial searing.

Arrange the food on a roasting rack fitted inside a straight-sided roasting pan. There should be enough room in the pan so that food fits comfortably and has enough space around it to allow for the addition of aromatics. (If desired, arrange the aromatics in the base of the pan, and then set the rack on top.)

Place the pan in a preheated oven. Roast the food, adjusting the oven temperature as necessary. Baste as necessary throughout the cooking time. The fat and juices released by the food itself are traditionally used as the basting liquid. However, a separate basting liquid, such as a marinade or butter, may also be used, particularly if the food is lean and does not release enough fat of its own for basting.

2. Use an instant-read thermometer to determine the doneness of the roasted food. To get the most accurate reading, the thermometer must be inserted into the item's thickest part, away from any bones.

Meat, fish, poultry, and game are generally cooked to a specified internal temperature (see the chart on page 160). When the food is nearly done, remove it from the pan, cover loosely with aluminum foil to keep it moist, and place in a warm spot to rest. Resting plays a key role in carryover cooking, which should be thought of as the last stage of cooking. Allow a resting period of about 5 minutes for small items, 15 to 20 minutes for medium items, and up to 45 minutes for very large roasts. This is done because as foods roast, their juices become concentrated in the center. A resting period before cutting into the food gives the juices time to redistribute evenly throughout the roasted food. Resting also lets the temperature of the food equalize, which results in improved texture, aroma, and flavor.

3. To make a pan sauce, heat the roasting pan with the aromatic vegetables over medium heat. To prepare a jus, pour off all of the remaining fat and deglaze the pan, if desired, with wine or another flavorful liquid.

4. Add a stock that suits the roasted food and simmer until the flavor is well developed, 15 to 20 minutes. Skim the jus as it simmers to remove fat and particles from the surface. A jus may be cooked down until it thickens or thickened with a cornstarch slurry (see page 210) and served as a jus lié.

To make a pan gravy, place the roasting pan on the stovetop and cook the drippings over medium heat until any vegetables are browned and the fat is transparent and clear. The juices will have separated from the fat and reduced on the bottom of the pan. Pour off excess fat, leaving just enough to prepare a roux by cooking the fat and some flour together (see page 16 for more information on making a roux). Add a small amount of flour and continue cooking until the roux browns. Gradually add stock or broth to the pan, stirring constantly to work out any lumps. Be sure the liquid is not too hot when it is added or it may spatter. Simmer the pan gravy until it is thickened and the flavor of the flour has cooked out, a minimum of 20 minutes.

Use a fine-mesh sieve to strain the jus or pan gravy. Hold the jus or gravy in a warm pan until ready to serve.

Carving Roasted Turkey

To make the most of large roasted foods, such as turkey, they must be carved into portions correctly. After roasting a turkey and letting it rest, transfer the bird to a carving board (a cutting board with an indentation around the edges that captures the juices released during carving). If you're carving the turkey at the table, you can carve on a serving platter, but make sure the platter's edges are not so high as to obstruct the blade of your knife. Have a separate platter or stack of plates ready for the meat as you carve. A carving fork will help you steady the bird as you cut. Cut away the trussing string before you begin carving.

1

To carve a turkey, have a large cutting board, a sharp slicing knife, and a platter ready on which to place all of the carved bits ready for serving.

2

Make a cut down the keel bone, which runs lengthwise down the center of the turkey.

Working perpendicular to the table, carve down the breast meat to make slices.

Using the fork to stabilize the slices against the knife, transfer the slices to a platter. Remove the wing by cutting through the joint.

Pull the thighbone up and away from the meat. Use the knife as shown to separate the leg joint.

Shingling the slices, or overlapping them on the platter, will help prevent the meat from drying out.

MARINATED GRILLED VEGETABLES

MAKES 5 SERVINGS

1 cup vegetable oil

¼ cup soy sauce

2 tbsp fresh lemon juice

2 tbsp minced garlic

½ tsp crushed fennel seeds

1 tbsp minced rosemary

2 zucchini, cut on the diagonal into
¾-inch-thick slices

3 eggplants, cut on the diagonal into
¾-inch-thick slices

1 medium yellow onion, sliced into
¾-inch-thick rings

Salt, as needed

Freshly ground black pepper, as needed

1 green bell pepper

1 red bell pepper

¼ cup olive oil

½ cup peeled, seeded, medium-dice
tomatoes

2 tsp balsamic vinegar

1. In a large bowl, combine the vegetable oil, soy sauce, lemon juice, 1 tablespoon of the garlic, the fennel seeds, and rosemary to make a marinade. Add the zucchini, eggplant, and onion and gently toss to evenly coat. Marinate the vegetables for 1 hour. Drain any excess marinade off the vegetables before grilling. Discard the marinade.

2. Preheat the grill. Season the zucchini, eggplant, and onion with salt and black pepper. Place the vegetables on the grill and cook until browned on one side, about 2 minutes. Turn once and cook on the second side until the vegetables are tender, about 2 minutes more. Remove from the grill.

3. Grill or broil the bell peppers until evenly charred on all sides. Transfer to a stainless steel bowl, cover with plastic wrap, and let cool 30 minutes. Remove the skin, core, seeds, and ribs.

4. Heat the remaining 1 tablespoon garlic and the olive oil in a large saucepan over medium heat. Add the grilled vegetables, peppers, and tomatoes and stir gently to finish heating the vegetables through and to blend the flavors.

5. Stir in the vinegar and adjust the seasoning with additional salt and pepper. Serve immediately.

Grilled Shiitake Mushrooms with Soy-Sesame Glaze

MAKES 5 SERVINGS

SOY-SESAME GLAZE

¼ cup soy sauce

2 tbsp water

2 tbsp peanut oil or corn oil

2 tbsp tahini

1 tsp sesame oil

1½ tsp minced garlic

1 tsp peeled, minced ginger

¼ tsp red pepper flakes (optional)

1 lb 4 oz shiitake mushrooms, stems removed

5 green onions

1 tbsp toasted sesame seeds

1. To make the soy-sesame glaze, combine the soy sauce, water, peanut or corn oil, tahini, sesame oil, garlic, ginger, and red pepper flakes, if using, in a small bowl. Keep refrigerated until ready to use.

2. If desired, slice any large mushroom caps in half. Add the mushrooms and green onions to the glaze and allow to marinate for at least 15 minutes or up to 1 hour.

3. Preheat the grill.

4. Remove the mushrooms and green onions from the glaze, and drain off any excess glaze.

5. Grill the mushrooms and green onions until they have grill marks on both sides and are cooked through, about 2 minutes per side.

6. Sprinkle the mushrooms and onions with the sesame seeds and serve immediately.

NOTE *Once grilled, the mushrooms can be returned to the marinade, allowed to cool to room temperature, and then used to garnish salads or other dishes.*

GRILLED SEITAN SKEWERS

MAKES 4 SERVINGS

1 tbsp olive oil

1 shallot, diced

½ jalapeño, seeded and minced

2 garlic cloves, minced

2 tsp peeled, minced ginger

3 tbsp soy sauce

3 tbsp fresh lime juice

1 tbsp sesame oil

2 tbsp honey

1 tbsp cilantro, roughly chopped

12 oz seitan, cut into ¼-inch-thick strips

1. Heat the oil in a small skillet over low heat. Add the shallot and jalapeño and sauté until softened, about 2 minutes. Add the garlic and ginger and sauté until aromatic, about 1 minute more. Transfer the mixture to a blender or food processor.

2. Add the soy sauce, lime juice, sesame oil, honey, and cilantro to the blender or food processor and pulse until smooth. If the mixture is too thick and pastelike, add water 1 tablespoon at a time to thin it to a marinade consistency.

3. Transfer the jalapeño mixture to a shallow dish and use it to coat each piece of seitan. Allow the seitan to marinate, refrigerated, for at least 1 hour or up to overnight.

4. Preheat the grill. Soak 12 wooden skewers in water for 30 minutes.

5. Thread the marinated seitan onto the skewers and grill the seitan until browned on both sides and cooked through, 3 to 4 minutes per side. Serve immediately.

Flatbread with Roasted Peppers, Oven-Dried Tomatoes, Eggplant, and Jack Cheese

MAKES 4 SERVINGS

4 plum tomatoes, thinly sliced

1 tbsp chopped basil

2 tsp chopped thyme

1 tsp chopped oregano

Salt, as needed

1 tbsp extra-virgin olive oil

8 slices eggplant, ⅓-inch thick

4 pita breads

1½ cups Pesto (page 79)

2 cups roasted red bell peppers (see page 26)

¾ cup grated mozzarella

¾ cup grated pepper Jack

Freshly ground black pepper, as needed

1. Preheat the oven to 225°F.

2. Place the tomatoes on a baking sheet. Season the tomatoes with the basil, thyme, oregano, salt, and a drizzle of the oil. Roast the tomatoes until they have dried slightly, about 45 minutes. Cool the tomatoes and reserve.

3. Preheat the grill. Lightly brush each eggplant round with the remaining oil.

4. Preheat the oven to 400°F.

5. Grill the eggplant until browned and tender, 3 to 4 minutes per side.

6. Heat each pita in a warm pan on the stovetop. Spread an even layer of the pesto on each pita and top evenly with tomatoes, eggplant, roasted peppers, and cheeses.

7. Bake the flatbread until the crust is crisp and the cheeses are bubbly on the surface. Let cool slightly before serving. Finish with freshly ground black pepper.

GRILLED TOFU WITH EGGPLANT AND PARMESAN

MAKES 4 SERVINGS

One 14-oz package extra-firm tofu, sliced lengthwise into 4 sheets about ¼ inch thick

1 eggplant, peeled and cut into ½-inch-thick slices

Salt, as needed

RED WINE MARINADE

¼ cup red wine vinegar

1 cup olive oil

¼ tsp salt

¼ tsp freshly ground black pepper

1 tsp Italian seasoning

3 garlic cloves, minced

1 tbsp olive oil

1 green bell pepper, seeded and cut into medium dice

1 small onion, cut into medium dice

2 garlic cloves, chopped

Tomato Sauce (page 73)

Grated Parmesan, as needed

1. Press the tofu slices between paper towels to remove excess water.

2. Layer the eggplant slices in a colander resting in a bowl, sprinkling salt on each layer as it is placed in the colander. Allow to drain for 20 minutes.

3. Rinse the eggplant thoroughly under cool water, then place on paper towels to absorb excess moisture. Cut eggplant slices into cubes.

4. To make the marinade, whisk together the vinegar, olive oil, salt, pepper, Italian seasoning, and minced garlic in a medium bowl until combined.

5. Add the tofu and eggplant to the bowl with the marinade and marinate for at least a 30 minutes.

6. Preheat the grill.

7. Heat the olive oil in a medium skillet over medium heat. Sauté the bell pepper, onion, and chopped garlic. Add the eggplant and brown slightly. Add the tomato sauce and bring to a simmer.

8. Grill the tofu slices until heated through, about 2 minutes per side. Top with cheese and serve the tofu slices on top of the eggplant sauce.

GRILLED CHICKEN BREASTS WITH FENNEL

MAKES 5 SERVINGS

⅓ cup olive oil

2 garlic cloves, crushed

¼ tsp cracked fennel seeds

Salt, as needed

Freshly ground black pepper, as needed

5 boneless, skinless chicken breasts (5 to 6 oz each)

2 tbsp butter

2 tbsp minced shallots

2½ cups julienned fennel

1 tbsp Pernod

1. Preheat the grill.

2. Combine the oil, garlic, fennel seeds, a pinch of salt, and a pinch of pepper in a large bowl. Add the chicken, toss to coat, and cover. Marinate in the refrigerator for 30 minutes. Drain any excess marinade from the chicken before grilling; blot the chicken with paper towels if necessary.

3. Place the chicken on the grill with the best looking side down. Grill, undisturbed, for about 2 minutes. Brush with the marinade and turn the chicken over. Continue to cook the chicken, brushing with the marinade periodically, until opaque and cooked through, 6 to 8 minutes more.

4. Melt the butter in a saucepan over medium-high heat. Add the shallots and sauté until translucent, about 1 minute.

5. Add the julienned fennel and cover the pan. Cook until the fennel is tender, about 10 minutes. Add the Pernod and season with salt and pepper. Serve each chicken breast on a bed of the fennel.

Beef Teriyaki

MARINADE

½ cup light soy sauce

1½ cups sake

⅓ cup mirin

¼ cup sugar

¼ cup peeled, grated Granny Smith apple

5 beef skirt steaks (about 6 oz each)

3⅔ cups snow peas

1 tbsp vegetable oil

10 medium white mushroom caps

2½ cups bean sprouts

1 tsp salt

1. Combine the soy sauce, sake, mirin, and sugar in a saucepan and bring to a boil over high heat. Remove from the heat and stir in the apple. Allow the marinade to cool completely. Pour the marinade over the steaks in a large bowl, cover, and refrigerate for 8 hours or up to overnight.

2. Preheat the grill.

3. Cut each snow pea into 2 or 3 pieces on the diagonal.

4. Heat the oil in a sauté pan or wok over medium-high heat. Add the mushroom caps, bean sprouts, and snow peas and cook just until tender, about 3 minutes. Season with the salt. Keep warm while you grill the steaks.

5. Drain any excess marinade from the steaks before grilling; blot with paper towels if necessary.

6. Place the steaks on the grill with the best looking side down. Grill, undisturbed, for about 2 minutes.

7. Turn the steaks over and cook to the desired doneness. (For doneness indicators and temperatures, see the chart on page 160.)

8. Remove the steaks from the grill and allow to rest in a warm place for 5 minutes. Slice each steak into 5 pieces on the diagonal. Serve immediately with the vegetables.

BARBECUED STEAK WITH HERB CRUST

MAKES 5 SERVINGS

HERB CRUST

1 tsp minced garlic

2 tbsp chopped flat-leaf parsley

¾ cup bread crumbs

5 tbsp butter, melted

½ tsp salt

¼ tsp freshly ground black pepper

5 sirloin steaks (about 10 oz each)

2 tsp salt

½ tsp freshly ground black pepper

2 tsp minced garlic

2 tbsp plus 1 tsp vegetable oil

¾ cup Barbecue Sauce (page 80)

1. Preheat the grill.

2. To make the herb crust, combine the garlic, parsley, bread crumbs, butter, salt, and pepper in a small bowl. Stir to blend well, and reserve.

3. Season the steaks with the salt and pepper. Rub the garlic into the meat, and lightly brush each steak with the oil.

4. Place the steaks on the grill with the best looking sides down. Grill, undisturbed, for about 2 minutes. Turn the steaks over and cook to the desired doneness. (For doneness indicators and temperatures see the chart on page 160.)

5. Meanwhile, preheat the broiler.

6. Arrange the steaks on a baking sheet and top each with a portion of the herb crust mixture. Place under the broiler for about 2 minutes to brown the crust. Serve the steaks immediately with the barbecue sauce on the side.

GRILLED LAMB CHOPS WITH ROSEMARY, ARTICHOKES, AND CIPOLLINI ONIONS

`MAKES 5 SERVINGS`

MARINADE

3 black peppercorns

1 bay leaf

1 cup flat-leaf parsley

2 tbsp thyme

2 tbsp rosemary

2 garlic cloves, smashed

½ tsp salt

¼ tsp freshly ground black pepper

1½ cups olive oil

10 lamb rib chops (about 4 oz each)

ARTICHOKES

2 qt cold water

Juice of 1½ lemons

15 baby artichokes

½ cup extra-virgin olive oil, plus more as needed

Salt, as needed

Freshly ground black pepper, as needed

15 cipollini onions

¼ cup sliced garlic

1 tbsp chopped oregano

2 tbsp chopped flat-leaf parsley

1½ cups Chicken Stock (page 38)

5 tbsp butter, cubed

1. To make the marinade, place the peppercorns, bay leaf, parsley, thyme, rosemary, garlic, salt, and pepper in a blender. Add ¼ cup of the oil and blend until the mixture is smooth. Gradually add the remaining 1¼ cups oil, blending after each addition. Pour the marinade over the lamb chops and refrigerate in a covered container for at least 45 minutes or up to overnight.

2. For the artichokes, combine the cold water with the lemon juice in a large bowl. Peel the stems and remove the tough outer leaves of the artichokes. Split each artichoke in half lengthwise. Using a spoon, remove and discard the fibrous choke from the center of each half. Cut the halves into quarters and submerge in the lemon water to prevent browning.

3. Heat 3 tablespoons (or a little more if needed) of the oil in large sauté pan over medium-high heat. Working in batches, as necessary to avoid overcrowding the pan, cook the artichokes until light golden brown, about 15 minutes. Season the artichokes with salt and pepper, remove them from the pan, and transfer to a plate or pan lined with paper towels to drain. Reserve.

4. Prepare a large bowl of ice water. Bring a large pot of water to a boil and boil the onions until tender, 8 to 10 minutes. Immediately transfer the onions to the bowl of ice water. When cool enough to handle, peel the onions and cut them in half.

5. Heat 2 tablespoons of the oil in a large sauté pan over medium heat. Cook the onions until lightly caramelized, about 5 minutes. Remove from the pan, let cool, and reserve.

6. In a separate pan, heat 1 tablespoon of the oil over medium-high. Add the garlic and sauté until the edges just begin to brown. Add the onions, artichokes, oregano, parsley, salt, and pepper. Add the stock and continue cooking until reduced by three-quarters. Stir in the butter and continue cooking, stirring occasionally, until the vegetables are covered with the glaze. Keep warm while you prepare the lamb.

7. Preheat the grill. Drain any excess marinade from the lamb chops and season each chop with salt and pepper. If desired, wrap the bones with aluminum foil.

8. Place the lamb chops on the grill with the best looking side down. Grill, undisturbed, for about 2 minutes. Turn the lamb chops over and continue grilling to the desired doneness, about 4 minutes more for rare, 7 minutes for medium rare, 9 minutes for medium, 11 minutes for medium well, and 14 minutes for well done. (For doneness indicators and temperatures, see the chart on page 160.)

9. To serve, place a mound of glazed vegetables in the middle of each plate and top with 2 lamb chops.

GRILLED SIRLOIN STEAK WITH MUSHROOM SAUCE

MAKES 5 SERVINGS

5 sirloin steaks (about 10 oz each)

2 tsp salt

½ tsp freshly ground black pepper

3 tbsp vegetable oil

1¼ cups Mushroom Sauce (page 77), warm

1. Preheat the grill.

2. Season the steaks with the salt and pepper and brush lightly with the oil. Place the steaks on the grill with the best looking side down. Grill, undisturbed, until the steak is cooked halfway through.

3. Turn the steaks over and cook to the desired doneness. (For doneness indicators and temperatures, see the chart on page 160.)

4. Serve each steak with ¼ cup of the mushroom sauce.

GRILLED PORK CHOPS WITH SHERRY VINEGAR SAUCE

MAKES 5 SERVINGS

5 bone-in pork chops, 2 inches thick (about 12 oz each)

2 tsp salt

½ tsp freshly ground black pepper

2 tbsp olive oil

1¼ cups Sherry Vinegar Sauce (page 70), plus more as needed

1. Preheat the grill.

2. Season the pork with the salt and pepper and brush it lightly with the oil. Place the pork chops on the grill with the best looking side down. Grill, undisturbed, for 8 to 10 minutes. Turn the pork chops over and grill to the desired doneness. (For doneness indicators and temperatures, see the chart on page 160.)

3. Remove the pork chops from the grill and allow them to rest, loosely covered with aluminum foil, for about 5 minutes.

4. Meanwhile, heat the sherry vinegar sauce. Top each pork chop with about ¼ cup of the sauce and serve immediately.

Facing page: Grilled Pork Chops with Sherry Vinegar Sauce, Potatoes au Gratin (page 129), and Roasted Brussels Sprouts (page 195)

GRILLED GARLIC SHRIMP AND RADISH SALAD

MAKES 4 SERVINGS

15 shrimp (16/20, about 5 oz), peeled and deveined

2 garlic cloves, minced

Juice of 1 lime

VINAIGRETTE

1½ tsp olive oil

2 garlic cloves, minced

1 tbsp diced shallots

2 tbsp tomato paste

1 tbsp brandy

¾ cup Chicken Stock (page 38)

Arrowroot slurry: ¾ tsp arrowroot, plus cold water as needed (see page 210)

1 tbsp apple cider vinegar

1 tbsp rice vinegar

1 tbsp tahini

2 tsp reduced-sodium soy sauce

2 tsp minced jalapeños

1 tsp sesame oil

1 tsp peanut oil

⅔ cup daikon radishes, thinly sliced

⅔ cup radishes, thinly sliced

½ cup carrots, thinly sliced

1 tbsp minced celery

2 oz soba noodles, cooked

¼ tsp white sesame seeds

1. Soak 4 wooden skewers in water for 30 minutes.

2. In a small bowl, toss the shrimp with the garlic and lime juice. Thread 4 shrimp onto each skewer and refrigerate until needed.

3. To make the vinaigrette, heat the oil in a medium saucepan over medium heat. Add the reserved shrimp shells and sauté until opaque, 2 to 3 minutes. Add the garlic and shallots and sweat until the shallots are translucent, about 2 minutes more.

4. Add the tomato paste and sauté until rust-colored. Deglaze the pan with the brandy and reduce until the liquid has evaporated. Add the stock and simmer until the mixture has reduced by half. Remove the pan from the heat.

5. Strain the mixture into a bowl and transfer to a clean pan. Bring to a boil.

6. In a small bowl, combine the arrowroot with the cold water to make a slurry with the consistency of heavy cream. Stir the arrowroot mixture into the boiling stock.

7. Remove the pan from the heat, add the vinegars, and cool completely. Stir the tahini, soy sauce, and jalapeños into the vinaigrette mixture. Whisk in the oils.

8. Preheat the grill.

9. Combine the daikon, radishes, carrots, celery, noodles, and sesame seeds and toss with the vinaigrette.

10. Grill the shrimp skewers until the shrimp are cooked, about 3 minutes per side. Serve immediately over the salad.

Squash Gratin

3 cups sliced shallots

4 tbsp butter, at room temperature

2 cups panko bread crumbs

2 tbsp chopped flat-leaf parsley

5½ cups (about 5 lb) sliced yellow squash

3 cups shredded cheddar

2 cups heavy cream

Salt, as needed

Freshly ground black pepper, as needed

1. Preheat the oven to 350°F.

2. In a small sauté pan over medium heat, sweat the shallots in 1 tablespoon of the butter until translucent. Set aside.

3. Butter a 9 x 13-inch baking dish with 1 tablespoon of the butter.

4. In a medium sauté pan over medium heat, add the remaining 2 tablespoons butter, the bread crumbs, and parsley. Cook until the bread crumbs are lightly toasted, about 5 minutes.

5. Arrange alternating layers of shallots, squash, bread crumbs, and cheese in the prepared baking dish, reserving some bread crumbs for the top.

6. Meanwhile, in a small saucepan over medium heat, bring the cream to a quick boil. Season with salt and pepper. Pour over the layered vegetables until they are covered halfway. Sprinkle the reserved bread crumbs over the top of the vegetables.

7. Cover the pan with aluminum foil and bake until the squash is tender, 30 to 45 minutes.

8. Preheat the broiler. Remove the foil from the baking dish, and broil until the top of the gratin has browned, about 3 minutes. Let rest for 15 minutes before serving.

Broiled Shrimp with Garlic

½ cup dried bread crumbs

2 tsp minced garlic

1½ tsp chopped flat-leaf parsley

1½ tsp chopped oregano

5 tbsp butter, melted

½ tsp salt

⅛ tsp freshly ground black pepper

32 oz shrimp (16/20 count), peeled, deveined, and butterflied

1. Combine the bread crumbs, garlic, parsley, oregano, and 4 tablespoons of the butter in a small bowl. Season with the salt and pepper.

2. Preheat the broiler to high and position the rack 3 to 4 inches from the heat source.

3. Arrange the shrimp in an oven-safe dish and brush them lightly with the remaining 1 tablespoon butter.

4. Sprinkle the bread crumb mixture evenly onto the shrimp. Broil until the shrimp are very hot and cooked through, 2 to 3 minutes. Serve immediately.

Broiled Sardines with Shaved Fennel and Orange Salad

MAKES 6 SERVINGS

1½ lb fresh sardines, cleaned

CRUMB TOPPING

¾ cup plain fresh bread crumbs

2 tbsp chopped flat-leaf parsley

1 tbsp grated Parmesan

2 tsp olive oil

1 tsp minced garlic

SALAD

1½ cups very thinly shaved fennel

1 navel orange, peeled, sectioned, and diced

½ cup thinly sliced red onion

¼ cup pitted black olives

⅛ tsp salt

⅛ tsp freshly ground black pepper

1. Preheat the broiler to high and position the rack 3 to 4 inches from the heat source.

2. Rinse the sardines inside and out and blot dry with paper towels. (If desired, cut away the head, tail, and fins.) Open each sardine, spreading it flat, and place in a 9 x 13-inch baking dish, skin side up. The fish should not be touching or overlapped; use a second dish if necessary.

3. To make the crumb topping, combine the bread crumbs, parsley, cheese, olive oil, and garlic in a bowl and work them together until blended. Top each sardine with some of the crumb topping.

4. To make the salad, combine the fennel, orange, onion, olives, salt, and pepper in a large bowl and set aside to marinate while the sardines cook.

5. Broil the sardines until the crumb topping is golden and crisp and the fish is cooked through, 12 to 15 minutes. If necessary, lower the rack to prevent the crust from scorching. Serve the sardines on a heated platter or on individual plates with the salad on the side.

FILLET OF MAHI MAHI WITH PINEAPPLE-JÍCAMA SALSA

MAKES 5 SERVINGS

1 lb 14 oz mahi mahi fillets, cut into five 6-oz servings

1½ tsp salt

½ tsp freshly ground black pepper

2 tbsp plus 2 tsp fresh lime juice

2 tbsp plus 2 tsp vegetable oil

2½ cups Pineapple-Jícama Salsa (page 86)

1. Preheat the grill or broiler.

2. Season the fillets with the salt, pepper, and lime juice. Lightly brush the fillets with the oil.

3. Place the fillets, with the best looking side down, on the grill or broiler rack. Grill or broil the fillets, undisturbed, for about 2 minutes. (If desired, give each piece of fish a quarter-turn to achieve grill marks.)

4. Turn the fillets over and continue cooking until the flesh is opaque and firm, 3 to 5 minutes more. Serve immediately with the salsa on the side.

Broiled Fish with Mint Chutney

MAKES 5 SERVINGS

MARINADE

½ cup sour cream

2 tbsp cashew butter

¼ cup chickpea flour

1 tsp ajwain seeds, crushed

1 tsp finely chopped Thai chiles

1½ tsp ground fennel

Salt, as needed

2¼ tsp ground white pepper

1 tbsp plus 1½ tsp fresh lemon juice

½ tsp ground ginger

1½ tsp garlic paste

KEBABS

1 lb 14 oz black cod fillets, cut into 3-inch cubes

Salt, as needed

Fresh lemon juice, as needed

2 tbsp butter, melted

1¼ cups Mint and Yogurt Chutney (page 87)

1. To make the marinade, combine the sour cream, cashew butter, flour, ajwain seeds, chiles, and fennel in a large bowl. Season with salt, the white pepper, lemon juice, ginger, and garlic paste.

2. Season the fish with salt and lemon juice and let stand for 15 minutes. Place the fish in the marinade and transfer to the refrigerator. Marinate for about 1 hour.

3. Preheat the broiler to high and position the rack 3 to 4 inches from the heat source.

4. Place the fish on a baking sheet fitted with a rack. Each piece of fish should be moist and coated with the marinade. Brush the fish lightly with the butter.

5. Broil until the top of the fish is dark brown with spots of black, 12 to 15 minutes. Serve immediately with the chutney.

BAKED KALE CHIPS

MAKES 4 SERVINGS

1 head kale, rinsed and dried thoroughly, ribs removed

2 tbsp extra-virgin olive oil

2 tsp salt

Grated parmesan, as needed

1. Preheat the oven to 350°F.

2. Cut the kale into bite-size pieces and toss with the oil and salt in a large bowl to evenly coat. Arrange the kale in a single layer on a baking sheet. Bake for 10 minutes. Turn the pieces over, and continue to bake until the kale is crispy, about 10 minutes more.

3. Sprinkle the kale chips with the cheese and serve immediately.

BAKED POTATOES WITH CHIVE SOUR CREAM

MAKES 5 SERVINGS

5 russet potatoes

2 tsp vegetable oil

Salt, as needed

Freshly ground black pepper, as needed

½ cup plus 2 tbsp sour cream

1 tbsp minced chives

1. Preheat the oven to 425°F.

2. Scrub the potatoes and blot them dry. Using a paring knife or the tines of a fork, pierce the skins in a few places. Rub the potatoes lightly with the oil and season with salt and pepper.

3. Place the potatoes on a baking sheet and bake until very tender and cooked through, about 1 hour.

4. Meanwhile, in a small bowl, mix together the sour cream and chives until well combined. Season with salt and pepper.

5. When the potatoes are done, cut halfway through each potato lengthwise and pinch the ends to create a gap in between. Garnish each potato with 2 tablespoons of the chive sour cream.

TUSCAN-STYLE ROASTED POTATOES

MAKES 5 SERVINGS

1 lb 10 oz russet potatoes, peeled and cut into large dice

1 tbsp olive oil

2 tsp minced garlic

2 tsp minced rosemary

Salt, as needed

Freshly ground black pepper, as needed

1. Preheat the oven to 375°F.

2. Toss the potatoes with the olive oil, garlic, rosemary, salt, and pepper.

3. Place the potatoes on an oiled baking sheet and roast until tender and brown, 40 to 45 minutes. Season with additional salt and pepper if needed. Serve immediately.

WHIPPED SWEET POTATOES WITH GINGER

MAKES 5 SERVINGS

1½ lb sweet potatoes

2 tbsp butter

¼ cup heavy cream

1 tsp peeled and minced ginger

Salt, as needed

Freshly ground black pepper, as needed

1. Preheat the oven to 425°F.

2. Scrub the potatoes and blot them dry with paper towels. Using a paring knife or the tines of a fork, pierce the skins in a few places.

3. Place the potatoes in a pan fitted with a roasting rack and bake until very tender and cooked through, about 45 minutes.

4. While the potatoes are still hot, slice them in half lengthwise and scoop out the flesh. Using a food mill or potato ricer, purée the potatoes into a heated bowl.

5. In a small pot over medium heat, bring the butter, cream, and ginger to a simmer. Pour the mixture over the puréed sweet potatoes and stir gently until the mixture is well combined. Season with salt and pepper and serve immediately.

CITRUS-ROASTED BEETS

1 lb beets (about 6 small beets)

Salt, as needed

Freshly ground black pepper, as needed

Zest of 1 orange

2 tbsp olive oil

2 tbsp fresh orange juice

3 tbsp chopped cilantro, flat-leaf parsley, or mint

1. Preheat the oven to 350°F.

2. Trim the stem ends of the beets, leaving about 1 inch intact; leave the root ends untouched.

3. Place the beets in a 9 x 9-inch baking dish with enough cold water to come halfway up the side of the beets. Scatter salt, pepper, and half of the orange zest over the top. Cover tightly with aluminum foil and bake until the beets are tender enough to pierce easily with the tip of a paring knife, about 1 hour.

4. When the beets are cool enough to handle, trim the ends and slip off the skins. Cut each beet into quarters lengthwise. Cut each quarter into ½-inch-thick slices.

5. In a serving bowl, whisk together the olive oil, remaining orange zest, the orange juice, and the cilantro, parsley, or mint. Add the beets and toss well. Season with additional salt and pepper, if needed, and serve warm.

ROASTED BRUSSELS SPROUTS

2 qt Brussels sprouts

¼ cup olive oil

1½ tsp salt

¾ tsp freshly ground black pepper

1. Preheat the oven to 400°F.

2. Slice each Brussels sprout in half and remove any loose outer leaves.

3. Toss the Brussels sprouts in the olive oil and spread them in a single layer on a large baking sheet or, if necessary, two baking sheets. Do not overcrowd.

4. Roast until the Brussels sprouts have browned edges and are tender to the bite. Toss with the salt and pepper and serve.

BAKED ACORN SQUASH WITH CRANBERRY-ORANGE COMPOTE

1 acorn squash (about 24 oz), quartered and seeded

1 tbsp honey or maple syrup, or 2 tbsp plus 1 tsp brown sugar

4 tbsp butter

½ tsp salt, plus more as needed

¼ tsp freshly ground black pepper, plus more as needed

1 cup Cranberry-Orange Compote (page 88)

1. Preheat the oven to 400°F.

2. Place the squash sections, cut side up, on a baking sheet. Sprinkle each piece with the honey, maple syrup, or sugar. Divide the butter into 4 pieces and place 1 piece onto each quarter. Season with the salt and pepper.

3. Cover the squash with aluminum foil and bake for 30 minutes. Remove the foil and continue baking, basting periodically with the pan juices, until tender, about 15 minutes more.

4. To serve, transfer squash to a heated platter and top with the compote.

Roasted Autumn Vegetables with Spinach Pesto

ROASTED VEGETABLES

2 cups peeled, large-dice beets

1 medium parsnip, trimmed and cut into large dice

½ medium fennel bulb, cored and cut into ¼-inch-thick slices

1 small butternut squash (about 12 oz), peeled, seeded, and cut into large dice

¾ cup medium-dice carrot

½ lb mushrooms, quartered

1 cup medium-dice red onion

1 cup medium-dice celery

1 red bell pepper, seeded and cut into medium dice

2 tbsp extra-virgin olive oil

1 tbsp chopped thyme

1 tbsp chopped rosemary

Salt, as needed

Freshly ground black pepper, as needed

SPINACH PESTO

¾ lb spinach

½ bunch fresh basil, leaves only, chopped

2 tbsp extra-virgin olive oil, plus more as needed

3 roasted garlic cloves (see Note)

4 green onions, white and green parts, chopped

¼ cup pine nuts

Salt, as needed

Freshly ground black pepper, as needed

1. To make the roasted vegetables, preheat the oven to 350°F.

2. In a large bowl, toss the beets, parsnip, fennel, squash, carrot, mushrooms, onion, celery, and bell pepper with the oil to coat. Sprinkle with the thyme, rosemary, salt, and pepper and toss again.

3. Spread the mixture in a roasting pan or baking dish and roast until tender, about 1 hour. Remove from the oven and keep warm.

4. To make the spinach pesto, combine the spinach and basil in a blender or food processor. With the machine running, slowly add the oil and process until fully blended. Add the garlic, green onions, and pine nuts and process until the mixture forms a thick paste. Add more oil if necessary to reach the desired consistency. Season with salt and pepper. Serve the warm roasted vegetables topped with the pesto.

NOTE *To roast garlic, cut the tip off a whole head of garlic (or multiple heads, as desired) and place the unpeeled head in a small baking dish. Roast the garlic in a 350°F oven for 30 to 45 minutes. Separate the cloves and squeeze the roasted garlic from the skins. Reserve any extra garlic for another use; it is excellent spread onto bread or sandwiches or whisked into a vinaigrette.*

ROAST CHICKEN WITH PAN GRAVY

MAKES 4 SERVINGS

One 3- to 3½-lb roasting chicken

Salt, as needed

Freshly ground black pepper, as needed

2 sprigs thyme

2 sprigs rosemary

¼ cup vegetable oil or butter, melted (optional)

½ cup medium-dice yellow onion

¼ cup medium-dice carrot

¼ cup medium-dice celery

1 tbsp all-purpose flour

1½ cups Chicken Broth (page 40)

1. Preheat the oven to 400°F.

2. Season the chicken with salt and pepper and place the thyme and rosemary in the cavity. Rub the skin with oil and truss the chicken (see page 164). Place the chicken, breast side up, in a roasting pan fitted with a roasting rack. Roast, basting the chicken occasionally with the oil or butter, if using, or the juices that accumulate in the bottom of the pan, for 40 minutes.

3. Remove the pan from the oven and lift out the chicken. Scatter the onion, carrot, and celery on the bottom of the pan and replace the rack with the chicken. Return to the oven and continue to roast, basting occasionally, until an instant-read thermometer inserted in the thickest part of the thigh registers 170°F, 30 to 40 minutes more.

4. Remove the chicken and rack from the roasting pan and let the chicken rest for 15 minutes before carving.

5. Meanwhile, place the roasting pan on the stovetop over medium-high heat and cook the vegetables until browned, about 5 minutes. Pour off all but 2 tablespoons of the fat. Add the flour and cook, stirring frequently with a wooden spoon, to make a blond roux (see page 16), about 5 minutes. Pour in the broth, whisking until completely smooth. Simmer the gravy until it reaches a sauce-like consistency, 10 to 12 minutes. Taste and adjust the seasoning with salt and pepper if needed. Strain the gravy through a fine-mesh sieve.

6. Carve the chicken (see page 168) and serve with the pan gravy.

ROAST TURKEY WITH CHESTNUT DRESSING AND PAN GRAVY

1 turkey (about 15 lb)

1 apple, quartered

1 bay leaf

1 large sprig thyme

½ bunch flat-leaf parsley

1 to 2 tbsp fresh lemon juice

Salt, as needed

Freshly ground black pepper, as needed

CHESTNUT DRESSING

½ cup (8 tbsp/1 stick) butter

¾ cup minced yellow onion

1½ lb day-old bread, cubed

1 cup Chicken Stock (page 38), warm

1 egg

2 tbsp chopped parsley

1 tsp chopped sage

2¼ cups shelled, peeled and roasted chestnuts, chopped (about 8 oz)

1 tsp salt

½ tsp freshly ground black pepper

PAN GRAVY

¾ cup small-dice yellow onion

½ cup small-dice carrot

½ cup small-dice celery

5 cups Chicken Broth (page 40)

Cornstarch slurry: ⅓ cup cornstarch combined with ⅓ cup cold water (see page 210)

Salt, as needed

Freshly ground black pepper, as needed

1. Preheat the oven to 450°F.

2. Stuff the turkey with the apple, bay leaf, thyme, and parsley. Rub the lemon juice over the entire surface of the bird and season with salt and pepper.

3. Place the turkey, breast side up, in a roasting pan fitted with a roasting rack. Transfer to the oven and immediately reduce the oven temperature to 350°F. Roast for 3 hours, basting occasionally with the drippings that accumulate in the bottom of the pan.

4. Remove the turkey from the oven and decrease the oven temperature to 350°F. Transfer the turkey, on the roasting rack, to a baking sheet. Degrease the pan drippings by skimming away any excess fat from the surface with a paper towel. Return the turkey on the rack and any juices that have accumulated on the baking sheet to the roasting pan. Continue to roast until an instant-read thermometer inserted in the thickest part of the thigh registers 180°F, 30 to 60 minutes more.

5. To prepare the chestnut dressing, melt the butter in a sauté pan over medium heat. Add the onion and cook until tender, about 3 minutes.

6. Combine the bread cubes, stock, and egg and add to the pan with the onion. Add the parsley, sage, chestnuts, salt, and pepper and mix well.

7. Transfer the dressing to a buttered baking dish and cover with parchment paper. Bake until browned and heated through, about 45 minutes. Reserve in a warm place until ready to serve.

8. Remove the turkey and the rack from the roasting pan, cover the bird with aluminum foil, and allow it to rest for 45 minutes.

9. While the turkey is resting, make the pan gravy: Combine the pan drippings with the onion, carrot, and celery in a saucepan. Add ½ cup of the broth to the roasting pan and stir to deglaze the pan, scraping up any browned bits from the bottom of the pan. Add to the saucepan along with the remaining 4½ cups broth. Simmer over medium heat until flavorful and slightly reduced, skimming away any fat that rises to the surface, 20 to 25 minutes. Gradually add the slurry to the simmering broth, whisking constantly, until the gravy has a sauce-like consistency. Simmer for 2 minutes more and then strain through a fine-mesh sieve. Season with salt and pepper, if needed.

10. Remove and discard the apple, bay leaf, thyme, and parsley from inside the turkey. Carve the turkey (see page 90) and serve with the pan gravy and dressing.

CAROLINA BARBECUE

MAKES 5 SERVINGS

6 lb pork butt

1 tbsp salt

2 tbsp freshly ground black pepper

5 sandwich buns, split in half and toasted

¾ cup North Carolina Piedmont Sauce (page 89)

¾ cup Barbecue Sauce (page 90)

¾ cup Mustard Barbecue Sauce (page 90)

1. Preheat the oven to 300°F.

2. Season the pork butt with the salt and pepper. Place it in a roasting pan and roast until tender, about 5 hours.

3. Remove the pork from the oven and allow it to cool slightly. When cool enough to handle, shred or chop the pork.

4. For each portion, serve about 6 ounces of the pork on a toasted bun with the sauces served on the side.

ROAST DUCK WITH ORANGE SAUCE

MAKES 4 SERVINGS

4 duck breast halves (8 to 10 oz each)

Salt, as needed

Freshly ground black pepper, as needed

2 tbsp golden raisins

¾ cup brandy

2 tbsp sugar

3 tbsp fresh orange juice

¼ cup apple cider vinegar

1 tbsp currant jelly

2 cups Chicken Broth (page 40)

2 tsp grated orange zest

1. Trim the duck breasts of excess fat and season with salt and pepper.

2. Combine the raisins with the brandy in a small saucepan and warm over low heat. Allow the raisins to plump for about 10 minutes.

3. Meanwhile, combine the sugar and 1 tablespoon of the orange juice in a sauté pan and cook over medium heat without stirring. Once the sugar has begun to melt, stir occasionally until the sugar has completely melted and the mixture is golden brown, about 8 minutes. Immediately add the vinegar and continue to cook until reduced by half, 2 to 3 minutes more. Add the remaining 2 tablespoons orange juice to the reduced sugar mixture. Stir in the raisins, along with any unabsorbed brandy, and the currant jelly.

4. Heat an ovenproof sauté pan over high heat. Add the duck breasts, skin side down. Reduce the heat to medium-low and sauté until the skin is browned and crisp, about 15 minutes. Turn the breasts over and sauté on the opposite sides for 10 minutes more (for medium doneness). Transfer the duck breasts to warmed plates and cover loosely with aluminum foil to keep warm while finishing the sauce.

5. Pour the duck fat out of the sauté pan and discard. Return the pan to medium heat. Add the broth and stir to deglaze the pan, scraping up any browned bits from the bottom of the pan. Bring the broth to a rapid simmer, and continue simmering until reduced by half, 4 to 5 minutes. Add the raisin and orange sauce and stir to combine. Taste and season with salt and pepper if necessary.

6. Serve the duck breasts with the orange sauce, garnished with the orange zest.

BAKED STUFFED PORK CHOPS

5 center-cut pork chops, 1½ inches thick
(about 9 oz each)

STUFFING

2 tbsp vegetable oil

½ cup minced onion

½ cup minced celery

1 tsp minced garlic

3½ cups dried bread crumbs

2 tsp chopped flat-leaf parsley

½ tsp rubbed sage

1 tsp salt, plus more as needed

½ tsp freshly ground black pepper, plus
more as needed

⅓ cup Chicken Stock (page 38), plus
more as needed

1. Cut a pocket in the side of each pork chop and refrigerate the chops until the stuffing is ready.

2. Heat 1 tablespoon of the oil in a pan over medium heat. Add the onion and cook until golden brown, 8 to 10 minutes. Add the celery and garlic and cook until the celery is soft, 8 to 10 minutes more. Remove the mixture from the pan, spread it on a baking sheet, and allow to cool completely.

3. When cool, combine the onion mixture with the bread crumbs, parsley, and sage. Season with the salt and pepper. Add just enough of the stock to make a stuffing that is moist but not wet. Chill the stuffing until it reaches 40°F.

4. Preheat the oven to 350°F.

5. Divide the chilled stuffing mixture into 5 equal portions and place 1 portion into the pocket cut into each pork chop. If desired, secure the pocket closed using presoaked wooden skewers.

6. Season the chops with salt and pepper. Heat the remaining 1 tablespoon oil in a sauté pan over high heat. Add the pork chops and sear until golden brown on both sides, about 4 minutes per side. Place the chops in a baking dish, transfer to the oven, and bake until the chops reach an internal temperature of 160°F, about 20 minutes. Serve immediately.

Salmon Fillets with Smoked Salmon and Horseradish Crust

MAKES 5 SERVINGS

1 lb 14 oz salmon fillets, cut into five 6-oz portions

2 tbsp fresh lime juice

1 tsp minced shallots

1 tsp minced garlic

1 tsp crushed black peppercorns

SMOKED SALMON AND HORSERADISH CRUST

3 tbsp butter

½ tsp minced shallots

½ tsp minced garlic

¾ cup fresh bread crumbs

2½ oz minced smoked salmon

1 tbsp prepared horseradish

1¼ cups Beurre Blanc (page 75), warm

1. Preheat the oven to 350°F.

2. Rub the salmon fillets with the lime juice, shallots, garlic, and peppercorns. Place the fillets in a baking dish and reserve.

3. To make the smoked salmon and horseradish crust, melt the butter in a pan over medium heat. Add the shallots and garlic and sauté until they are aromatic, about 1 minute.

4. Combine the sautéed shallots and garlic, the bread crumbs, smoked salmon, and horseradish in a food processor and process to a fine texture.

5. Place some of the crumb mixture on top of each fillet. Bake the salmon until it is opaque pink on the outside and just beginning to flake, 6 or 7 minutes.

6. To serve, pool ¼ cup of the beurre blanc on each plate and place the salmon on top.

Ancho-Crusted Salmon with Yellow Pepper Mole

MAKES 5 SERVINGS

1 ancho chile, chopped stem and seeds removed

2 tsp cumin seeds

2 tsp fennel seeds

2¼ tsp coriander seeds

2 tsp whole black peppercorns

2 tsp dried thyme

2 tsp dried oregano

2 tsp salt

2 tsp dry mustard powder

1 lb 14 oz salmon fillets, cut into five 6-oz portions

1 tbsp plus 2 tsp vegetable oil

1¼ cups Yellow Mole (page 82), warm

1. Preheat the oven to 300°F.

2. Spread the chile, cumin, fennel, and coriander seeds on a baking sheet and toast in the oven until fragrant, about 5 minutes. Remove and cool to room temperature.

3. Increase the oven temperature to 350°F.

4. In a spice grinder, combine the toasted chile and spices with the peppercorns, thyme, and oregano. Grind to a coarse powder. Stir in the salt and dry mustard.

5. Lightly coat each portion of salmon with the crust.

6. Heat the oil in an ovenproof sauté pan over medium-high heat. Sauté the salmon fillets on the best-looking side until the spices start to brown, 1 to 2 minutes. Flip the salmon over and sauté for 1 to 2 minutes more.

7. Flip the salmon over once more, transfer the pan to the oven, and bake the fillets until they reach the desired doneness, 4 to 6 minutes, depending on the thickness of the fish. Serve immediately with the mole.

SAUTÉING, PAN FRYING, AND DEEP FRYING

To sauté something is to cook it rapidly over high heat in relatively little fat. Pan-fried and deep-fried foods use considerable amounts of fat. Pan-fried foods should be partially submerged during cooking, while deep-fried foods are fully submerged. Both of these methods have similar results, including a crisp, browned exterior and a moist, flavorful interior.

Sautéing and the closely related technique of stir-frying are methods of quickly cooking food in a little fat over high heat. Derived from the French word *sauté*, meaning "jump," sautéing refers to the motion of food tossed in a hot pan as it is cooked. Culinarily, to sauté a food is to cook a food in an open pan over medium to high heat using relatively little oil or fat. For this method, it is of particular importance not to overcrowd the pan to ensure that the high temperature of the cooking surface is maintained and that foods can be moved easily in the pan in a single layer to ensure uniform browning. When sautéing meat, the meat is typically turned only once, after a crust has formed. Stir-frying, a similar method, is used in many Asian cuisines. Like sautéing, it uses naturally tender foods, little fat, and high heat. In both methods, the juices released during cooking are most often used as the base for a sauce made in the same pan.

SAUTÉING

THE AIM OF SAUTÉING is to produce a flavorful, golden brown exterior on foods. Only naturally tender items should be sautéed, and after sautéing they should remain tender. Shellfish, poultry or game bird breasts, and tender cuts of beef, veal, lamb, and pork (from the rib, loin, or parts of the leg) are excellent options for sautéing. Firm and moderately textured fish are easier to sauté than very delicate fish.

Sautéed dishes often include a sauce made with the drippings left in the pan. The base liquid that is used for a pan sauce should suit the main item being sautéed. Depending on the main item, the base could be a vegetable purée or coulis, reduced stock, or a prepared sauce, such as tomato sauce.

SEARING

Searing is often the first step in roasted, braised, or stewed dishes. Searing and sautéing are very closely related. The difference is not how the technique is performed but that sautéed foods are cooked through, while searing is intended to be used in conjunction with longer, slower cooking methods as an effective way to develop flavor and color, but not to finish cooking the food.

EXPERT tips

A DUSTING OF ALL-PURPOSE FLOUR can help to absorb excess moisture and prevent some foods from sticking to the pan during sautéing. It will also produce a good surface color for light or white meats, poultry, and fish. If you decide to dust a food, be sure to coat it evenly and shake off any excess flour.

ALWAYS SEASON THE FOOD before sautéing, because it is more effective than adding seasonings at the end of the cooking time.

ADDING BUTTER, glazes, or pan sauces to a main item after sautéing will add to the flavor and presentation of the dish.

FOR A HEALTHIER OPTION, use healthier fats, such as olive oil, to sauté the main item. The more natural marbling or fat present in the food, the less fat you will need to add to the pan; well-seasoned or nonstick pans may not require any fat beyond that which is already present in the food.

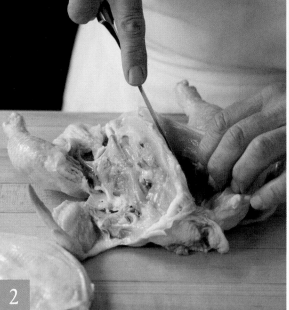

Chef's Lesson
FABRICATING A CHICKEN

1. Although it may seem intimidating at first, fabricating a chicken, or cutting it into smaller parts for cooking, is actually a very simple technique. First, cut from the neck opening down the center of the bird, following the keel bone.

2. Cut away the breast, following the contour of the rib cage with the knife. Repeat with the other breast.

3. Turn the chicken over. Cut around the wing bone and remove the wings.

4. Separate the leg and thigh, following the contour of the carcass and cutting through the joint.

5. Separate the drumstick from the thigh by cutting through the joint.

Basic Equipment for Sautéing

SAUTÉ PAN. Also called a sauteuse, a sauté pan has short, sloped sides and is wider than it is tall to encourage rapid evaporation. It is made of a metal that responds quickly to rapid heat changes. Select a pan that is large enough so that all pieces of the item you are sautéing will just cover the bottom of the pan without overlapping.

TONGS. Tongs are the ideal tool for turning foods over during sautéing and for removing them from the pan.

WOODEN SPOON. A wooden spoon is useful when preparing a pan sauce for a sautéed dish due to its ability to effectively withstand high temperatures. The back of a wooden spoon can also be used to test the consistency of a sauce.

TASTING SPOONS. Pan sauces should be tasted during cooking to monitor flavor and seasoning.

Basic Preparations

PURE STARCH SLURRY. Cornstarch, arrowroot, tapioca, and other pure starches have great thickening power, and starch slurries are commonly used to thicken pan sauces. Dissolving a starch in liquid helps keep it from forming lumps as it thickens the sauce, so slurry consists of a pure starch that has been dissolved in a cold liquid, such as water or stock, yielding a mixture with a consistency similar to heavy cream. Pure starch slurries can be blended in advance, but the starch may settle out of the liquid and fall to the bottom of the container if it is not used immediately; to recombine the slurry, simply stir it just before use.

USING A PURE STARCH SLURRY. To prepare a pure starch slurry, first consult the recipe for how much starch is needed to thicken a particular sauce. Stir cold water into the starch 1 tablespoon at a time until the mixture resembles the consistency of heavy cream. Pour or ladle the slurry into the simmering sauce while whisking constantly. Bring the liquid back to a boil and cook just until the sauce reaches the desired thickness. Be sure to whisk constantly to prevent lumping and scorching. When added in this way, the slurry will quickly thicken the liquid, making it easy for you to control the final consistency of the sauce.

Chef's Lesson
SAUTÉING

1. Season the food just before cooking. Heat the pan before adding the fat. (This is referred to as conditioning the pan.) Allow the fat to get hot before adding any food to the pan. To sauté red meats or very thin pieces of meat, heat the cooking fat until its surface ripples and looks hazy. Less intense heat is required for white meats, fish, shellfish, and thicker cuts of red meat. Immediately add the food to the pan. The better looking side of the food should always be the side that goes down first. Let the food cook, undisturbed, for several seconds and up to 1 to 2 minutes. The food may stick to the pan at first, but it will release itself by the time it is ready to be turned.

2. When the first side has browned, turn the food over and repeat on the other side. To develop the best flavor and color, it's best to turn most sautéed foods over only once. Sautéed shrimp or vegetables are exceptions to this rule and may be repeatedly tossed or turned. When the food is cooked through and browned on both sides, remove it from the pan and reserve it in a warm place while you prepare a sauce in the sauté pan, if desired.

3. Before making a sauce, remove any excess fat from the sauté pan, being careful not to remove the browned drippings, called fond, that

have accumulated in the bottom of the pan. If you're including any aromatic ingredients that need to be cooked, such as onions or garlic, cook them in the pan at this point. Then, add a liquid, such as stock or wine, to release the fond and give the sauce flavor. Reduce the liquid until the pan is nearly dry. Add the sauce base (such as a separately prepared sauce, reduced stock, or vegetable purée) to the pan and bring to a simmer. If it is called for, add any cream along with the sauce base so that it can be reduced. If the sauce needs to be thickened, add a small amount of a pure starch slurry (see opposite page) until the desired consistency is reached. Remember that, in order to thicken properly, the sauce must be brought to a boil after the slurry is added. A pan sauce may be finished in several ways. It may be strained through a fine-mesh sieve for a very smooth texture. Garnishing ingredients, such as herbs, juices, or purees, may be simmered in the sauce long enough for them to be heated through. Or, a small amount of butter may be added just before serving to add flavor and body to the sauce.

After a final check of the seasoning, you may choose to return the main item (for example, a chicken breast or veal scallop) to the finished sauce in the pan briefly to coat and gently reheat it. Alternatively, the sauce may be spooned in a pool on the plate and the food set on top, or the sauce may be spooned over or around the food.

Sautéing Vegetables

SAUTÉED VEGETABLES HAVE A DISTINCT FLAVOR that is influenced by the type of cooking fat and garnishing ingredients used.

RINSE, trim, and peel the raw vegetable and cut it into the desired shape. Arugula, spinach and other leafy greens, mushrooms, summer squash, and onions may be sautéed or stir-fried from their raw state. Thoroughly drain greens and other vegetables that can hold excess moisture. This important step assures the best flavor, texture, and color in the finished dish. Some vegetables will not cook completely when sautéed unless they are parcooked by a separate method first. In this case, partially or wholly cook the vegetable by boiling, steaming, or roasting it first.

SELECT a cooking fat that complements the flavor of the vegetable. Oils such as olive, peanut, canola, corn, or safflower can be used, as well as butter or rendered animal fat (lard, duck fat, or bacon fat). Optional seasonings and aromatics (salt, pepper, and lemon juice) can adjust or heighten the flavor. Finely mince or chop fresh herbs and add them at the last moment.

RIGHT, ABOVE:
Sauté vegetables in a small amount of fat, taking care not to overcrowd the pan.

RIGHT, BELOW:
When vegetables are sautéed, they soften and their color intensifies. Immediately add the food to the pan. Let the food cook, undisturbed, for several seconds and up to a minute or two. The food may stick to the pan at first, but it will release itself by the time it is ready to be turned. When the first side has browned, turn the food over and repeat on the other side.

ABOVE, LEFT:
Sauté the aromatics, if using, until they just begin to release their aroma before adding the leafy greens.

ABOVE, RIGHT:
Leafy greens can be mounded loosely in the pan, as they lose volume quickly while sautéing.

LEFT:
The finished sautéed greens will be bright in color and soft in texture.

STIR-FRYING

TYPICALLY ASSOCIATED WITH ASIAN COOKING, stir-frying is a technique that shares many similarities with sautéing. Foods are customarily cut into small pieces—usually strips, dices, or shreds—and cooked rapidly in a small amount of oil. The foods must be added to the pan in sequence; those items requiring the longest cooking times are added first, those that cook quickly only at the last moment. The sauce for a stir-fry, like that of a sauté, is made or finished in the pan. A properly prepared stir fry has a complex combination of flavors, textures, and colors. While a sauté pan is used for sautéing, stir-frying is typically done in a specialty pan called a wok. During stir-frying, the ingredients are kept moving almost constantly, and the wok's unique shape allows the ingredients to be tossed easily for even cooking.

Basic Equipment for Stir-Frying

WOK. A thin-walled, round-bottomed pan called a wok is typically used for stir-frying, because the unique shape allows for even heat distribution and easy tossing of the ingredients.

LADLE. Use a small ladle to add the oil to the hot wok for stir-frying.

WOK SPATULAS OR TONGS. Ideally, a set of specialty stir-frying tools known as wok spatulas are used for cooking stir-fries, but tongs can serve the same purpose if necessary.

EXPERT tip

ADDITIONAL INGREDIENTS or garnishes, such as any of the folllowing, may be added to stir-fried dishes for extra flavor. These ingredients may be added as soon as the wok is hot or at the very end of the cooking time, depending on the ingredient and the desired result.

Garlic

Fresh herbs

Grated ginger

1. Heat the wok over high heat. When the wok is hot, add the oil by ladling it around the upper edge of the pan. Once the oil in the bottom of the pan is hot, add the main ingredients to the center of the pan in sequence, starting with the items that take the longest time to cook. Add vegetables such as carrots and broccoli near the beginning of the cooking time, more tender vegetables such as zucchini and yellow squash at the midpoint, and delicate vegetables such as green onions or fresh herbs at the last moment.

2. Once the ingredients are in the wok, keep them in constant motion by stirring or tossing with a wok spatula or tongs. As the ingredients become hot, push them up onto the sides of the wok; this allows the wok to recover its heat before you make the next addition of ingredients. Continue to stir-fry until each addition is hot.

3. Serve stir-fries very hot, directly from the wok.

PAN FRYING AND DEEP FRYING

PAN-FRIED FOODS have many of the same characteristics of deep-fried foods, including a crisp, browned exterior and a moist, flavorful interior, but very different effects are produced by the different amount of fat or oil that is used for pan frying versus deep frying.

PAN FRYING

IN PAN FRYING, the food is cooked more by the oil's heat than by direct contact with the pan. The hot oil seals the food's coated surface, locking in the natural juices. Because no juices are released and a larger amount of oil is involved, sauces accompanying pan-fried foods are usually made separately.

TO DEVELOP ADDITIONAL FLAVOR, season the food with fresh or dried herbs and/or spices prior to pan frying or add the flavorful ingredients to the breading or batter that will be used to coat the item.

DIFFERENT CRUSTS CAN BE ACHIEVED depending on the type of coating that is used on a pan-fried food. These coatings include:

- Fresh or dry bread crumbs
- Panko (Japanese bread crumbs)
- Flour
- Cornmeal
- Cornstarch
- Nuts or seeds
- Shredded coconut
- Cornflakes
- Potato flakes or shredded potatoes

The object of pan frying is to produce a flavorful exterior with a crisp, brown crust that acts as a barrier to hold in juices and flavor. Select cuts of meat that are naturally tender for pan frying, as you would for sautéing. Rib or loin cuts, top round, or poultry breasts are all good choices. Lean fish, such as sole or flounder, are also well suited to pan frying. Remove the skin and bones of poultry and fish fillets if necessary or desired. You may want to pound cutlets with a mallet to give them an even thickness and to shorten cooking time.

Pan-fried food is usually portion-size or smaller, and the food is almost always coated—either dredged in flour, breaded, or coated with a batter. (See opposite page for more information on breading.)

The fat for pan frying must be able to reach high temperatures without breaking down or smoking, and the oil can make a difference in the flavor of the finished dish. Vegetable oils, olive oil, and shortenings are good options for pan frying. Lard, goose fat, and other rendered animal fats also have a place in certain regional and ethnic dishes.

When pan frying, arrange the food pieces in the pan in a single layer without touching. If the food is crowded inside the pan, the temperature of the fat will drop quickly and a good crust will not form on the food.

Pan Frying Vegetables

IN ADDITION TO TENDER PROTEINS, vegetables are well suited to pan frying. To prepare vegetables for pan frying, rinse, peel, trim, and cut them into uniform pieces. If the vegetable is particularly tough, it may be necessary to wholly or partially cook it before it is pan fried. Once the vegetable is prepared, coat it with flour, breading, or batter as desired (see opposite page). Most vegetable oils, shortening, and rendered animal fat (duck fat or lard) can be used for pan frying vegetables. Aromatics and seasonings may be added to the vegetable before or after cooking, or they may be included in the breading or batter, if appropriate. In addition, a specific recipe may call for a sauce, relish, or salsa to finish the pan-fried vegetables.

Basic Equipment for Pan Frying

PAN. Pans for pan frying should be made of heavy-gauge metal and should be able to transmit heat evenly. The sides should be higher than those appropriate for sautés, to avoid splashing hot oil out of the pan as food is added to the oil or turned during cooking.

CONTAINERS. Select wide, shallow containers for holding breading, batters, and other coating ingredients.

TONGS OR SLOTTED SPATULA. Use tongs or a slotted spatula to turn foods over during pan frying and to remove the pan-fried food from the pan.

PAPER TOWELS. Have paper towels on hand to blot away any surface fat from the pan-fried food.

BREADING

BREADING IS DONE TO CREATE a crisp crust on pan-fried foods. It is prepared by coating foods with flour, egg, and bread crumbs or other coatings. The following method is the most efficient way to bread a number of foods:

Make an egg wash by blending eggs (whole, yolks, or whites) with water or milk. The general guideline is to use ¼ cup of milk or water for every 2 whole eggs. Sometimes the food is dipped in milk or buttermilk rather than egg wash, so consult each specific recipe.

Blot the food dry with paper towels and season it before applying any coating. Use flour or a similar meal or powder, such as cornstarch, to lightly dredge or dust the food. Shake off any excess. Dip the food in the egg wash and make sure it is coated on all sides. Transfer the food to the container of bread crumbs. Use your dry hand to pack the bread crumbs evenly around the food. Shake off any excess. Arrange the breaded food in a single layer on a clean baking sheet or tray until you're ready to pan fry.

Discard any unused flour, egg wash, and bread crumbs. The presence of juices, drippings, or particles of the raw food you just coated make these products unsafe to use for other foods.

The standard breading procedure first dips an item in flour, then egg wash, then bread crumbs for the best coating.

1

2

3

Chef's Lesson
PAN FRYING

1. Blot the food dry with a paper towel and coat it with the desired breading, batter, or other coating. Heat the cooking fat until a faint haze or slight shimmer is noticeable (about 350°F over medium heat). Very carefully add the food to the hot fat with the best looking side down. Be sure not to overcrowd the pan, or the food will not develop good color and texture. The fat should come one-third to one-half of the way up the main item. If the fat is at the correct temperature, it will bubble up around the food and start to brown the coating within 45 seconds.

2. Turn the food and continue to cook until the other side is also evenly browned and the food is cooked through. It is difficult to give precise instructions for determining the doneness of pan-fried foods. In general, the thinner and more delicate the meat, the more quickly it will cook. Some foods, because they are thick or include bones or a stuffing, may need to be removed from the fat and placed in a preheated oven to finish cooking. If they do need to go into the oven, be sure that they are not covered, because a lid would trap steam and soften the crisp, pan-fried coating.

3. When the item is cooked through, remove it from the pan and drain on paper towels. Do not hold fried foods for more than a very brief period before serving, because they tend to get soggy. If you do need to hold a pan-fried food for a short period of time before serving, place it on an open rack and do not cover it. Serve sauces for pan-fried foods under the food or separately to avoid them moistening the food's crisp coating.

DEEP FRYING

SIGNIFICANTLY MORE OIL IS USED FOR DEEP FRYING than for pan frying. The food is completely submerged in fat or oil to develop a crisp, brown exterior while maintaining a juicy interior. Food for deep frying is almost always coated with a breading, a batter such as a tempura or beer batter, or a simple flour coating. The coating acts as a barrier between the fat and the food and also contributes flavor and texture.

To cook rapidly and evenly, foods for deep frying must be trimmed and cut into a uniform size and shape. Select cuts that are naturally tender; some typical choices include poultry, seafood, and vegetables. Remove the skin and bones of poultry and fish fillets if necessary or desired. Be certain to season the food before adding a coating.

A batter or plain flour coating is applied immediately before deep frying the food. Ideally, breading should be done as close to the time you're going to serve the food as possible, but if necessary, it can be done 20 to 25 minutes ahead and the items refrigerated before frying. (For breading instructions, see page 217.)

The fat will lose temperature for a brief time when food is added. The more food, the more the temperature will drop and the longer it will take to come back to the proper level.

DIFFERENT CRUSTS can be achieved depending on the type of coating used. Possible coatings include:

> Fresh or dry bread crumbs
>
> Panko (Japanese bread crumbs)
>
> Flour
>
> Plain batter
>
> Beer batter
>
> Tempura batter

EXPERT tip

Basic Equipment for Deep Frying

ELECTRIC OR GAS DEEP FRYER. Versions for home cooking are made to be used on your countertop, with capacities ranging from 1 to 3 quarts. They have safety features, such as locking covers that protect you from the spattering of hot oil. They also come with thermostats for setting precise temperatures.

POT. It is also possible to deep fry foods in a pot on the stovetop. Choose a pot with sides high enough to prevent fat from foaming over or splashing out and wide enough to allow you to add and remove the food easily.

DEEP-FAT FRYING THERMOMETER. Maintaining the proper temperature is vital to success when deep frying. Whether using a fryer or a pot, use a deep-fat frying thermometer to frequently check the fat's temperature.

TONGS OR FRYING BASKET. Many fryers have a wire basket that fits inside to lower the food into the oil, hold the food as it deep fries, and easily remove it from the fryer. If you're using a pot, you can use a skimmer or tongs to add and remove the food.

PAPER TOWELS. Have clean paper towels ready to receive deep-fried foods as they come out of the fryer or pot. Use the paper towels to drain or blot away any excess fat on the food's surface.

Deep Frying Vegetables

WHEN VEGETABLES ARE DEEP FRIED, the results can range from crisp, fragile chips to hearty croquettes. Choose fresh and flavorful vegetables and prepare them for deep frying according to the specific recipe's requirements. All vegetables for deep frying must be thoroughly rinsed and in some cases scrubbed. Trim away tough or inedible skins, peels, cores, seeds, and roots. Cut or slice as required. Some fried vegetable preparations call for a breading or batter. If so, the breading or batter should be applied to the vegetable just before it is fried.

The most popular vegetable for deep frying is the potato. To ensure that the finished potato has good color, texture, and flavor and that it fries properly without becoming greasy or scorched, potatoes are often blanched before being fried (see page 104 for more information on blanching). Very thinly cut potatoes (for example, matchstick potatoes) can usually be cooked in a single step, without blanching first.

Low-moisture potatoes are best for deep frying. Scrub and peel them, and remove the eyes. Cut the potatoes into even slices, sticks, wedges, or other desired shape. If the potatoes are peeled and cut in advance of cooking, hold them submerged in cold water. Rinse the potatoes in several changes of cold water if indicated, and drain and dry them thoroughly to prevent splattering when they are added to the oil. Potatoes that are to be deep fried for such preparations as straw or matchstick potatoes, in particular, should be rinsed so they don't clump together as they cook.

Choose a neutral oil with a high smoke point for frying the potatoes. Deep-fried potatoes are customarily seasoned with salt after frying and served with condiments such as ketchup or malt vinegar.

Electric or gas deep fryers are excellent for frying potatoes because they maintain even temperatures. They are also put together in such a way that it is relatively easy to clean them and care for the oil properly.

DEEP FRYING

1. Blot the food dry with a paper towel and coat it with the desired breading, batter, or other coating. Fill the pot or fryer with the cooking fat and heat to 325° to 375°F. The fat must maintain the proper temperature in order to prepare crisp, flavorful, non-greasy fried foods. Carefully add the main item to the hot fat. It should be completely submerged. Do not crowd the pan or fryer.

2. There are two methods of deep frying. The choice depends on the food, the coating, and the intended result. The swimming method of frying is generally used for battered food. Carefully lower the battered food into the hot oil using tongs. When the oil starts to bubble, release the food; it will not sink. If needed, flip the food during cooking to ensure even browning on all sides.

The basket method is generally used for breaded items. Place the breaded food in a frying basket and then lower the basket into the hot fat. Once the food is cooked, lift the basket and the food back out of the fat. Foods that tend to rise to the surface too rapidly can be held down by setting a second basket on top of the food; this is known as the double-basket method.

3. Drain the fried food on paper towels or on a wire rack set over paper towels before serving. Foods served very hot, directly from the fryer, have a better, less greasy taste.

Sautéed Squash Noodles

MAKES 3¾ QUARTS NOODLES

3 cups julienned yellow squash

3 cups julienned zucchini

3½ cups blanched, julienned leeks

3 cups blanched green beans, split lengthwise

3 tbsp butter

Salt, as needed

Freshly ground black pepper, as needed

1 tbsp chopped flat-leaf parsley

1. In a medium bowl, toss together the squash, zucchini, leeks, and green beans.

2. In a sauté pan over medium heat, melt the butter. Add the vegetables. Sauté until the vegetables are cooked through, 4 to 5 minutes.

3. Season with salt and pepper, add the parsley, and serve.

ITALIAN-STYLE SAUTÉED SPINACH

1 tbsp olive oil

2 tbsp diced pancetta, or 1 strip bacon, diced

¼ cup minced yellow onion

1 garlic clove, minced

8 cups spinach

Salt, as needed

Freshly ground black pepper, as needed

¼ cup grated Parmesan

1. Heat the oil in a large sauté pan over medium heat. Add the pancetta or bacon and sauté until the fat renders and the pancetta is translucent, about 1 minute. Increase the heat to high, add the onion and garlic, and sauté until the garlic is aromatic, about 1 minute more.

2. Add the spinach by the handful, sautéing just until the leaves wilt before adding more. Once all the leaves are added to the pan, sauté until they are deep green, tender, and softened, 3 to 4 minutes more. Drain the mixture if necessary, and season generously with salt and pepper.

3. Remove from the heat and stir in the cheese. Serve immediately.

GINGERED SNOW PEAS AND YELLOW SQUASH

1 tbsp peanut oil

1 tbsp minced ginger

1 tbsp peeled, minced shallots

1 tsp minced garlic

12 oz snow peas

1½ cups medium-dice yellow squash

Salt, as needed

Ground white pepper, as needed

1. Heat the oil in a large sauté pan over medium heat. Add the ginger, shallots, and garlic, and sauté until fragrant, about 1 minute.

2. Add the snow peas and squash and cook until tender, 2 to 3 minutes. Season with salt and white pepper and serve immediately.

SAUTÉED BRUSSELS SPROUTS WITH BROWN BUTTER

MAKES 10 SERVINGS

2 qt Brussels sprouts

2 tbsp olive oil

¾ cup chopped onion

3 tbsp water

4 tbsp butter

1½ tsp salt

¾ tsp freshly ground black pepper

1. Slice each Brussels sprout in half lengthwise and remove the core. Gently pull the layers of leaves apart.

2. Heat the oil in a medium sauté pan over medium heat, add the onion, and cook until translucent, about 5 minutes.

3. Add the Brussels sprouts leaves and the water to the pan, and cook until the leaves are tender. Remove from the heat.

4. In a small saucepan over medium heat, melt the butter and cook until it has a nutty smell and is a medium-dark brown color. Season with salt and pepper.

5. Add the brown butter to the cooked Brussels sprouts leaves and toss to coat.

MINI MUSHROOM BURGERS WITH CARAMELIZED ONIONS

MAKES 20 MINI BURGERS

MUSHROOM PATTIES

1 lb 4½ oz cremini mushrooms

¼ cup olive oil

1 cup minced shallots

2 roasted garlic cloves (see Note page 198)

Salt, as needed

¼ cup plus 1 tbsp white wine

Freshly ground black pepper, as needed

1 tbsp plus 1 tsp chopped flat-leaf parsley

1 tbsp plus 1 tsp chopped chives

⅓ cup grated Parmesan

2 tbsp shredded Gruyère

¾ cup panko bread crumbs

2 eggs, beaten

CARAMELIZED ONIONS

1 tbsp balsamic vinegar

1 tbsp vegetable oil

½ large sweet onion, cut into slices ⅛ inch thick

1 tbsp plus 1 tsp brandy

1 red bell pepper, roasted, peeled, seeded, and cut into julienne

20 mini hamburger buns, sliced in half horizontally

1. To make the mushroom patties, clean the mushrooms and trim off any bad stems. Working in batches, quarter the mushrooms and place them in a food processor. Pulse until the mushrooms are minced but not wet or pasty.

2. In a medium sauté pan, heat 1 tablespoon of the olive oil over medium heat. Add the shallots and sauté until translucent, about 5 minutes.

3. Crush the roasted garlic with the flat edge of a knife and work it into a paste. Add the garlic paste to the pan with the shallots and sauté for 1 minute.

4. Add the minced mushrooms to the pan and season with salt. Sauté the mixture until the mushrooms release their liquid, then continue to cook over medium heat to reduce the liquid until the mixture is dry.

5. Deglaze the pan with the wine and continue cooking until the mixture is dry again. Season as needed with salt and black pepper. Remove from the heat and allow to cool.

6. Add 2 tablespoons of the olive oil, the parsley, chives, cheeses, panko, and eggs to the mushroom mixture and allow to rest until the bread crumbs have absorbed all excess moisture, about 15 minutes.

7. To make the caramelized onions, place the balsamic vinegar in a small pot over medium-high heat. Cook until the liquid has reduced to about 1 teaspoon. Remove from the heat and reserve.

8. Heat the vegetable oil in a sauté pan over medium-high heat. Add the sliced onions and cook, stirring frequently, until the onions are a deep caramel color. Deglaze the pan with the brandy and continue cooking until the liquid evaporates. Remove the onions from the heat and allow to cool. Add the reduced balsamic vinegar to the onions and mix well to combine.

9. Form the mushroom mixture into patties, using about 1 ounce per patty. Season the patties lightly with salt and pepper. Heat the remaining 1 tablespoon olive oil in a sauté pan over medium heat. Cook the patties until they have formed a golden brown crust on both sides, 2 to 3 minutes per side.

10. To assemble the burgers, place some roasted red bell pepper on each of the bottom buns, followed by a patty topped with a small stack of caramelized onions. Complete the sandwiches with the top buns. Serve warm.

Chicken Breast with Fines Herbes Sauce

4 boneless, skinless chicken breast halves (about 8 oz each)

Salt, as needed

Freshly ground black pepper, as needed

All-purpose flour, as needed

2 tbsp vegetable oil

2 tsp minced shallots

½ cup dry white wine

½ cup Chicken Broth (page 40)

¼ cup heavy cream

Cornstarch slurry (optional): 1 tsp cornstarch combined with 1 tsp cold water (see page 210)

1 tsp finely chopped tarragon

1 tsp finely chopped flat-leaf parsley

1 tsp finely chopped chives

1 tsp finely chopped chervil

1. Season the chicken breasts with salt and pepper and dredge in the flour, shaking off any excess.

2. Heat the oil in a large sauté pan over medium-high heat. Add the chicken breasts and sauté on the first side until light golden, about 5 minutes. Turn the chicken over and continue to sauté until opaque throughout, 7 to 8 minutes more. Transfer to warmed plates and cover loosely with aluminum foil to keep warm while preparing the sauce.

3. Pour off all but 1 tablespoon of oil from the pan and place the pan over medium-high heat. Add the shallots and sauté until translucent, 1 to 2 minutes.

4. Add the wine and stir to deglaze the pan, scraping up any browned bits from the bottom of the pan. Continue cooking over medium-high heat until the liquid has nearly cooked away. Add the broth, bring to a simmer, then add the cream and simmer until the mixture is flavorful and has reduced to a sauce-like consistency, about 5 minutes. If needed, add the slurry to the sauce, stirring constantly, and bring to a simmer to thicken the sauce slightly.

5. In a small bowl, combine the tarragon, parsley, chives, and chervil (the fines herbes). Add them to the sauce, and season with salt and pepper. Pour the sauce over the chicken and serve immediately.

Chicken Breast with Fines Herbes Sauce, Wild Rice Pilaf (page 274), and Broccoli and Toasted Garlic (page 118)

CHICKEN PROVENÇAL

5 chicken breasts (about 8 oz each)

1 tsp salt

½ tsp freshly ground black pepper

⅓ cup all-purpose flour (optional)

2 tbsp vegetable oil

PROVENÇAL SAUCE

1 tsp minced garlic

1½ anchovy fillets, mashed to a paste

1 cup tomato concassé (see page 24)

⅔ cup dry white wine

1½ cups Jus de Veau Lié (page 76)

⅓ cup sliced Niçoise olives

¾ cup basil chiffonade

1. Blot the chicken dry with paper towels. Season with salt and pepper and dredge in flour, if desired.

2. Heat the oil in a large sauté pan over medium-high heat until it is almost smoking. Add the chicken and sauté on the first side until golden brown, about 3 minutes. Turn the chicken over and continue to sauté until cooked through, 3 to 4 minutes more. Transfer the chicken to warmed plates and cover with aluminum foil to keep warm while preparing the sauce.

3. To make the Provençal sauce, pour any excess fat from the pan. Add the garlic and anchovies and sauté to release their aroma, 30 to 40 seconds. Add the tomatoes and continue to sauté until any juices they release have cooked down. Add the wine and deglaze the pan, then continue simmering until the wine has nearly cooked away.

4. Add the jus de veau lié to the pan and simmer until the mixture has reduced to a sauce-like consistency.

5. Strain the sauce into a clean pan, return it to the stovetop, and bring it to a simmer over medium heat. Add the olives and basil, bring the sauce back to a simmer, and adjust the seasoning with additional salt and pepper if needed.

6. Return the chicken to the pan and turn to coat it with the sauce. Serve immediately.

NOTE *You may choose to experiment with the flavoring of the sauce. Try using different kinds of olives, add some capers, or use other herbs, either in addition to or as a replacement for the basil. Oregano, marjoram, chives, chervil, and thyme are all good choices.*

MINI HAMBURGERS

12 oz finely ground lean beef

1 cup finely chopped shallots or onion

3 garlic cloves, minced

1 red chile, seeded, and finely chopped

1 egg, beaten

3 tbsp panko bread crumbs

Salt, as needed

Freshly ground black pepper, as needed

20 mini hamburger buns, sliced in half horizontally

Barbecue Sauce (page 80) or other prepared sauce, as needed

20 thin slices plum tomatoes

20 thin slices cipollini onion

2 cups mixed baby greens

20 baby gherkins (optional)

1. Mix together the beef, shallots or onion, garlic, chile, egg, panko, salt, and pepper. Shape tablespoonfuls of the mixture into 20 round, flat patties, until all of the mixture has been used.

2. In a large sauté pan over medium heat, sauté the patties until browned on each side and cooked through, about 3 minutes per side.

3. To assemble the burgers, spread the top of each bun with some barbecue sauce, and place 1 slice of tomato, 1 slice of onion, and some greens on top. Place a hamburger patty on the bottom bun and sandwich the buns together.

4. If desired, secure each sandwich with a toothpick skewered with a baby gherkin.

VEAL SCALOPPINE MARSALA

8 veal top-round cutlets (about 3 oz each)

Salt, as needed

1 tsp freshly ground black pepper, plus more as needed

All-purpose flour, as needed

2 tbsp vegetable oil

¼ cup minced shallots

¼ cup dry red wine

1 sprig thyme

1 bay leaf

½ cup Chicken Broth (page 40)

½ cup Marsala

2 tbsp butter

1. Place each cutlet between two sheets of parchment paper and pound to a ¼-inch thickness. Season with salt and pepper and dredge in the flour.

2. Heat the oil in a sauté pan over medium-high heat. Add the veal and sauté until golden brown and cooked through, about 2 minutes on each side. Transfer to a warmed plate and cover loosely with aluminum foil to keep warm.

3. Add the shallots to the pan and sauté over medium heat, stirring often, until translucent, about 1 minute. Add the red wine, thyme, bay leaf, and 1 teaspoon pepper and stir to deglaze the pan, scraping up any browned bits from the bottom of the pan. Simmer until the wine has nearly cooked away, about 3 minutes. Add the broth and simmer for 5 to 6 minutes more. Add the Marsala and simmer until the liquid has reduced by half, 2 to 3 minutes more.

4. Discard the bay leaf, or strain the sauce through a fine-mesh sieve, if desired.

5. Reduce the heat to low and whisk in the butter. Season with additional salt and pepper, if needed. Spoon the sauce over the veal, and serve immediately.

SHRIMP IN ACHIOTE SAUCE

1 lb 12 oz shrimp (16/20 count), peeled and deveined

2 tsp minced garlic, plus 2 garlic cloves

2 tsp salt, plus more as needed

3 tbsp achiote paste

1 cup chopped onion

1 dried pequín chile

2 cloves

2 allspice berries

¼ cup fresh orange juice

¼ cup fresh lime juice

2 tbsp white vinegar

Freshly ground black pepper, as needed

2 tbsp vegetable oil

1. Rub the shrimp with the minced garlic and salt and refrigerate in a covered container for up to 2 hours.

2. Combine the achiote paste, onion, garlic cloves, chile, cloves, allspice, orange juice, lime juice, and vinegar in a blender and blend until very smooth, 2 to 3 minutes. Season with salt and pepper. Pour over the shrimp, cover, and allow to marinate for 20 minutes in the refrigerator.

3. Drain the shrimp and reserve the marinade. Heat the oil in a sauté pan over high heat. Working in batches, if necessary, add the shrimp and sauté until golden brown, 3 to 4 minutes. Pour the reserved marinade over the shrimp and let the contents boil for 1 to 2 minutes more. Adjust the seasoning with salt and pepper, if necessary.

4. Transfer the shrimp to a warm serving platter. Cook the sauce for 1 to 2 minutes more. Pour the sauce over the shrimp and serve immediately.

MINI BACON-CRUSTED SCALLOP BURGERS

15 oz bay scallops

1 egg

¾ cup heavy cream

1 tsp salt, plus more as needed

7 strips bacon (about 7 oz)

2 tbsp olive oil

Freshly ground black pepper, as needed

AVOCADO SPREAD

3 roasted garlic cloves (see Note page 198)

3 tbsp fresh lime juice

2 avocados, halved, pitted, peeled, and mashed

3 tbsp chopped cilantro

Salt, as needed

Freshly ground black pepper, as needed

18 mini hamburger buns, sliced in half horizontally

¾ cup alfalfa sprouts

1. Put the scallops in a strainer over a mixing bowl to allow any excess moisture to drain off. Cover and refrigerate the scallops, egg, and cream so that they are all well chilled.

2. Transfer the scallops to a food processor fitted with a sharp blade. Process for about 5 seconds, until the scallops are coarsely ground. Scrape down the bowl. Add the egg and salt and process until they are just incorporated, about 5 seconds. Scrape down the sides of the bowl. Process no longer than 15 seconds more, adding the cream in a steady stream. To ensure even mixing, scrape the sides of the bowl every 5 seconds.

3. Remove the scallop mixture from the food processor and force it through a fine-mesh sieve. Cover the bowl and reserve the scallop mixture in the refrigerator.

4. Preheat the oven to 350°F.

5. Place the bacon slices in a single layer in a baking sheet fitted with a wire rack. Cook the bacon in the oven until it is firm and crisp but not darkened, 15 to 20 minutes. Remove from the oven and set aside until cool enough to handle. Mince the bacon and reserve.

6. Line a baking sheet with parchment paper. Prepare a 2-inch round cutter or ring mold by spraying the inside with cooking spray. Place the cutter on the parchment paper. Pack 2 teaspoons of minced bacon inside the cutter and top with about 1½ tablespoons of the scallop mixture. Press the scallop mixture down onto the bacon to make sure that it is well-packed. Add another 2 teaspoons bacon to the top of the scallop patty and press it gently into the scallop mixture. Remove the cutter to unmold the patty. Repeat the process until all of the bacon and scallop mixtures are used.

7. Heat the oil in a small sauté pan over medium heat. Season the scallop patties with salt and pepper and gently place them in the sauté pan using a metal spatula. Cook the patties until they are golden brown and the bacon is crisp, 2 to 3 minutes per side. Remove from the pan and transfer to paper towels.

8. To make the avocado spread, combine the garlic, lime juice, avocado, cilantro, salt, and pepper in a bowl and mix until the mixture is smooth and spreads easily.

9. To assemble the scallop burgers, spread about 1½ teaspoons of the avocado spread onto the top half of each bun, and top with 1 tablespoon of alfalfa sprouts. Place the scallop burgers on the bottom halves of the buns and sandwich together. Serve immediately.

Sautéed Trout à la Meunière with Sautéed Squash Noodles (page 222)

Sautéed Trout à la Meunière

5 whole trout, boned (about 9 oz each)

1 tsp salt

½ tsp freshly ground black pepper

¼ cup all-purpose flour

2 tbsp vegetable oil

11 tbsp butter

2 tbsp fresh lemon juice

2 tsp chopped flat-leaf parsley

1. Blot the trout dry with paper towels. Season with the salt and pepper and dredge in the flour.

2. Heat the oil in a large sauté pan over medium heat. Working in batches, as necessary, sauté the trout until lightly browned on each side and cooked through, 3 to 4 minutes per side. Transfer the trout to a warmed dish and cover with aluminum foil to keep warm while preparing the sauce.

3. Pour any excess grease from the pan. Add the butter, and cook over medium-high heat until lightly browned with a nutty aroma, 2 to 3 minutes.

4. Add the lemon juice and swirl it around the pan to deglaze it. Stir in the parsley and pour or spoon the sauce over the trout. Serve immediately.

Red Snapper with Grapefruit Salsa

1 lb 14 oz red snapper fillets, skin on, cut into five 6-oz portions

½ tsp salt

Pinch freshly ground black pepper

½ cup all-purpose flour, plus more as needed

2 tbsp olive oil, plus more as needed

1¼ cups Grapefruit Salsa (page 86)

1. Season the snapper with the salt and pepper and dredge in the flour, shaking off any excess.

2. Heat the oil in a sauté pan over medium-high heat. Add the snapper and sauté until golden brown and cooked through, 2 to 3 minutes per side, depending on the thickness of the fillets. Top with the grapefruit salsa and serve immediately.

Sautéed Squid and Steamed Mussels with Cannellini Beans, Spinach, and Pancetta

MAKES 4 SERVINGS

8 oz squid

¾ cup white wine

16 mussels, scrubbed and debearded

3 slices pancetta

½ cup sliced red onion

2 garlic cloves, thinly sliced

½ cup sliced fennel

⅔ cup cooked cannellini beans

4 cups spinach

¾ cup plum tomatoes, peeled, seeded, and diced

2 tsp basil chiffonade

2 tsp chopped oregano

Salt, as needed

Freshly ground black pepper, as needed

2 tsp olive oil

1 tbsp grated Parmesan

2 tsp chopped flat-leaf parsley

1. Using a sharp knife, thinly slice the bodies of the squid into rings. Leave the tentacles whole. Refrigerate until ready to cook.

2. In a medium pan over low heat, bring the wine to a simmer. Add the mussels and steam until they open, about 3 minutes. Transfer the mussels to a plate and reserve the cooking liquid.

3. In a large sauté pan over medium heat, cook the pancetta until the fat has rendered and the pancetta is crisp. Add the onion, garlic, and fennel and sauté until the fennel is tender, 4 to 6 minutes. Add the beans, spinach, tomatoes, basil, oregano, and enough of the reserved cooking liquid to wilt the spinach. Season with salt and pepper.

4. In a medium pan, heat the oil over medium heat. Add the squid and sauté until opaque, about 2 minutes. Add the cooked mussels to the bean mixture and toss to heat through. Serve the squid with the mussel and bean mixture, topped with the cheese and parsley.

Ma Po Dofu

MAKES 4 SERVINGS

Grapeseed oil or canola oil, as needed

1 lb firm tofu, cut into ¼-inch-thick triangles

3 tbsp peanut oil

2 tsp peeled, minced ginger

2 garlic cloves, minced

1 green onion, white and green parts, thinly sliced

1 tbsp hot bean paste

1 tbsp black bean sauce

2 tsp Korean chili powder

1 cup stemmed, thinly sliced shiitake mushrooms

1 cup halved snow peas

1 cup seeded, thinly sliced red bell peppers

½ cup bean sprouts

1 tbsp oyster sauce or vegetarian oyster sauce

1 tbsp toasted sesame oil

1 tbsp chopped cilantro

1 tsp ground Sichuan peppercorns

Salt, as needed

1. Fill a deep pot half-full with the grapeseed or canola oil. Heat the oil over medium heat until it registers 350°F on a deep-fry thermometer. Working in batches, as necessary, deep fry the tofu until golden brown. Drain well on paper towels and reserve.

2. Heat the peanut oil in a wok or large sauté pan over high heat. Add the ginger, garlic, and green onion and stir-fry until fragrant, 2 to 3 minutes.

3. Add the bean paste, bean sauce, and chili powder. Stir well until combined, about 1 minute. Add the mushrooms, snow peas, bell peppers, and bean sprouts, and stir-fry until the vegetables are tender, 3 to 4 minutes.

4. Add the tofu, oyster sauce, sesame oil, cilantro, and Sichuan peppercorns, and season with salt. Stir-fry until heated through, about 2 minutes. Serve immediately.

PAN-FRIED ZUCCHINI

MAKES 5 SERVINGS

2 cups vegetable oil

BEER BATTER

1 cup all-purpose flour

¼ tsp baking powder

½ tsp salt

1 egg, separated

1 cup lager beer

1 lb 4 oz zucchini, cut into ½-inch-thick slices on the diagonal

2 tsp salt, plus more as needed

½ cup all-purpose flour

1. Heat the oil in a medium sauté pan or cast-iron skillet over medium heat until it registers 325°F on a deep-fry thermometer.

2. Meanwhile, to make the beer batter, whisk together the flour, baking powder, and salt. Add the egg yolk and the beer all at once and whisk until very smooth. Reserve in the refrigerator.

3. Using a mixer fitted with the whisk attachment, whip the egg white on high speed to soft peaks. Gently fold the egg white into the batter and use the batter immediately.

4. Season the zucchini slices with the salt, dredge in flour, shake off the excess, and dip into the batter to coat evenly on both sides. Allow any excess batter to drain back into the bowl.

5. Carefully lay each zucchini slice in the hot oil. Pan fry on the first side until browned, 1 to 2 minutes. Turn the zucchini over carefully and fry until the second side is golden brown, 1 to 2 minutes more.

6. Using a slotted spoon or skimmer, transfer the zucchini to paper towels to drain. Adjust the seasoning with additional salt, if necessary. Serve immediately.

SOUTHERN-STYLE FRIED CHICKEN WITH COUNTRY GRAVY

MAKES 4 SERVINGS

1 fryer chicken (2½ to 3½ lb)

Salt, as needed

Freshly ground black pepper, as needed

1 cup buttermilk

1 tbsp Dijon mustard

2 tsp chopped tarragon

2 tsp all-purpose flour, plus more as needed

Vegetable oil, as needed

1 cup whole milk, warmed

1. Cut the chicken into serving pieces (see page 209). Trim the pieces of excess fat and season well with salt and pepper.

2. Whisk together the buttermilk, mustard, and tarragon in a large bowl. Put the buttermilk marinade and chicken pieces in a resealable plastic bag, squeeze to remove excess air, and close. Massage the bag to coat the chicken evenly. Marinate in the refrigerator for at least 4 hours and up to 12 hours, turning occasionally.

3. Preheat the oven to 300°F.

4. Remove the chicken from the marinade, allowing any excess to drip off. Dredge the chicken in flour.

5. Pour oil into a skillet to a depth of ½ inch. Heat the oil over medium heat until it registers 350°F on a deep-fry thermometer. Add the chicken legs and thighs to the hot oil, in batches as needed, and pan fry until golden brown on the first side, 6 to 7 minutes. Turn and fry on the second side until golden, 7 to 8 minutes more. Transfer to a wire rack set over a baking sheet and keep warm in the oven. Using a slotted spoon or skimmer, remove any browned bits from the oil and let the oil return to 350°F. Fry the breast pieces in the same way, then transfer them to the pan in the oven. Bake until the chicken is opaque throughout and an instant-read thermometer inserted into the thickest parts registers 180°F for the thigh and leg portions, about 25 minutes, and 170°F for breast portions, about 10 minutes.

6. Meanwhile, make the gravy. Using the slotted spoon or skimmer, remove any browned bits from the oil in the pan and pour off all but 2 to 3 teaspoons of the oil.

7. Add 2 teaspoons of flour and cook, stirring frequently with a wooden spoon, to make a blond roux, 2 minutes. Add the milk, stirring well to break up any lumps. Cook the gravy over low heat, stirring and skimming as necessary, until thickened to a saucelike consistency, 5 to 10 minutes. Season with salt and pepper. Strain the gravy and serve it with the chicken.

PAN-FRIED VEAL CUTLETS

1 lb 14 oz boneless veal top round, cut into five 6-oz cutlets

1 egg

2 tbsp whole milk

½ tsp salt

¼ tsp freshly ground black pepper

½ cup all-purpose flour, plus more as needed

1¾ cups bread crumbs, plus more as needed

Vegetable oil, as needed

1. Place each cutlet between two sheets of parchment paper or plastic wrap and pound to a thickness of about ¼ inch.

2. In a small bowl, gently whisk the egg together with the milk.

3. Blot the veal dry with paper towels and season with salt and pepper. Dredge in the flour, shaking off any excess. Dip the veal in the egg mixture, and then roll in the bread crumbs.

4. Heat about ⅛ inch of oil in a high-sided pan over medium heat until it registers 350°F on a deep-fry thermometer. The oil should reach about halfway up the side of the veal cutlets when the cutlets are added. Working in batches as needed to avoid overcrowding the pan, add the breaded veal to the hot oil and pan fry on the first side until golden brown and crisp, about 2 minutes. Turn the veal over and pan fry on the second side, 1 to 2 minutes more.

5. Transfer the veal to paper towels to drain briefly. Serve immediately.

WIENER SCHNITZEL *Prepare the pan-fried cutlets as directed above. Heat ½ cup butter in a large sauté pan until it sizzles, about 2 minutes. Add the pan-fried veal to the hot butter and turn to coat on both sides. Serve immediately on heated plates, garnished with lemon wedges or slices and parsley sprigs.*

BREADED PORK CUTLETS *Substitute an equal amount of boneless pork loin for the veal and prepare as directed above.*

Pan-fried Chicken Breast with Prosciutto

6 boneless, skinless chicken breasts

Salt, as needed

Freshly ground black pepper, as needed

6 thin slices prosciutto

1½ cups mushrooms, sliced and sautéed

6 thin slices fontina

2 egg whites, lightly beaten, as needed

All-purpose flour, as needed

Eggs, beaten, as needed

Bread crumbs, as needed

Extra-virgin olive oil, as needed

1. Place each breast between two sheets of parchment paper or plastic wrap and pound with a mallet to a thickness of between ¼ and ½ inch.

2. Season the chicken breasts with salt and pepper. Top each breast with 1 slice of prosciutto, ¼ cup mushrooms, and 1 slice of cheese, leaving a border of 1 inch uncovered. Brush the edges with egg white, fold half of the pounded breast over the filling to meet the opposite edge, and then gently pound the edges with a mallet to seal.

3. Dredge the chicken breasts in the flour, shaking off any excess. Coat in the beaten eggs and then roll in the bread crumbs.

4. In a sauté pan, heat enough oil to come one-third to one-half of the way up the sides of the chicken breasts. When the oil is shimmering, place 3 chicken breasts in the pan, seam side down, and cook until the bottom is golden brown, 3 to 5 minutes. Turn the breasts over, and cook the second side until golden brown. Remove the breasts from the pan and transfer to a dish lined with paper towels. Repeat with the remaining 3 breasts. Let the chicken rest for 20 minutes before serving.

Zucchini Fritters with Feta

MAKES 18 FRITTERS

2½ cups coarsely grated zucchini

2½ tsp salt, plus more as needed

¾ cup crumbled feta

1 cup chopped flat-leaf parsley

½ cup chopped green onions

1 tbsp chopped dill

1 egg

1 egg yolk

½ cup all-purpose flour, plus more as needed

1 tsp freshly ground black pepper, plus more as needed

1 cup olive oil

Yogurt, as needed for serving (optional)

1. In a bowl, toss the zucchini with ½ teaspoon of the salt and let stand for 5 minutes. Transfer to a strainer and press out excess moisture. Retun to the bowl.

2. Add the feta, parsley, green onions, dill, egg and egg yolk, ½ cup flour, 2 tsp salt and the pepper to the zucchini. Mix well, adding additional flour, if necessary, to achieve a batterlike consistency.

3. Heat the oil in a skillet over medium-high heat until it is shimmering. Drop batter by the heaping tablespoon into the oil and fry until golden brown. Using a spatula, flip the fritters and cook until brown on the other side. Adjust the consistency of the batter by adding more flour as needed.

4. Transfer fritters to a baking sheet or plate lined with paper towels to drain. Sprinkle with additional salt and pepper, if needed. Serve warm or at room temperature, with dollops of yogurt, if desired.

Yucca Tots with Buttermilk Dipping Sauce

MAKES 4 SERVINGS

YUCCA TOTS

2½ to 3 lbs yucca, peeled and diced, woody core removed (about 6 cups)

¼ grated dry Monterey Jack

2 tbsp butter, cubed

¼ cup buttermilk powder

2 tsp onion powder

1 tsp garlic powder

½ tsp sugar

Salt, as needed

Freshly ground black pepper, as needed

BUTTERMILK DIPPING SAUCE

2 tbsp sour cream

2 tbsp buttermilk

½ cup mayonnaise

⅓ cup chopped chives

¼ cup thinly sliced green onions, white and green parts

¼ cup chopped flat-leaf parsley

Peanut oil, as needed

1. To make the yucca tots, cook the yucca in a large pot of salted boiling water until tender, 15 to 20 minutes. Drain very well and allow the steam to dissipate. Using a food mill fitted with a coarse screen, purée the yucca into a large bowl.

2. Mix the cheese, butter, buttermilk powder, onion powder, garlic powder, and sugar into the warm yucca. Season with salt and pepper.

3. Form the yucca purée into balls approximately 1 inch in diameter. Cover and refrigerate until well chilled, at least 3 hours or up to overnight.

4. To make the buttermilk dipping sauce, combine the sour cream, buttermilk, mayonnaise, chives, green onions, and parsley in a bowl and mix well. Cover and refrigerate until needed.

5. Pour the oil into a medium pot that is taller than it is wide to a depth of 4 inches. Heat the oil over medium heat until it registers 350°F on a deep-fry thermometer.

6. Working in batches as needed, fry the tots until they are golden brown on all sides and rise to the surface of the oil, 4 to 6 minutes. Using a slotted spoon or skimmer, transfer the tots to paper towels to drain. Serve immediately with the dipping sauce.

FRENCH-FRIED POTATOES

MAKES 4 SERVINGS

1½ lb russet potatoes, peeled and sliced into matchsticks ⅜ inch thick

2½ cups vegetable oil

Salt, as needed

1. Rinse, drain, and dry the potatoes thoroughly. (Alternatively, the potatoes may be held in cold water until ready to cook. Dry them thoroughly before cooking, or the oil will splatter when they are added to it.)

2. Heat the oil in a large cast-iron skillet or a 14-inch wok, preferably one with a handle, over high heat. Add the potatoes, and reduce the heat to medium. Cook for 25 minutes, gently jiggling the pan from time to time. Do not stir, to avoid breaking the fries.

3. Increase the heat to high and cook the fries, stirring occasionally, until golden brown, 10 to 15 minutes more. Transfer to paper towels to drain briefly. Season with salt and serve immediately.

HERBED FRENCH FRIES *Prepare the potatoes as described above. Rather than seasoning with salt, place the fries in a bowl and toss with minced fresh herbs. Try using fennel, basil, rosemary, thyme, savory, chives, dill, oregano, or a combination.*

FLOUNDER À L'ORLY

MAKES 5 SERVINGS

2 cups vegetable oil, plus more as needed

2 lb flounder fillets, cut into five 6-oz portions

2 tbsp fresh lemon juice

½ tsp salt

¼ tsp freshly ground black pepper

All-purpose flour, as needed

Beer Batter (page 241)

1½ cups Tomato Sauce (page 73)

10 parsley sprigs

5 lemon wedges

1. Heat the oil in a deep fryer or tall pot until it registers 350°F on a deep-fry thermometer.

2. Blot the fillets dry with paper towels and season with lemon juice, salt, and pepper. Dredge in the flour, shaking off any excess, then dip into the beer batter. Working in batches, place the fillets in a fryer basket, lower it into the oil, and deep fry the fish until golden brown and cooked through, 3 to 4 minutes.

3. Transfer to paper towels to drain briefly and serve immediately with the tomato sauce, parsley sprigs, and lemon wedges.

Fried Fish Cakes

1 Thai chile

¼ cup chopped shallots

2 garlic cloves, peeled

3 tbsp chopped cilantro root or stem

1 tbsp minced galangal

1 kaffir lime leaf, or the zest of 2 limes

½ tsp salt

¾ lb white-fleshed fish fillets, minced

1 tbsp fish sauce

2 oz long beans, sliced into paper-thin rounds

4 cups peanut oil

1. Purée the chile, shallots, garlic, cilantro, galangal, lime leaf or zest, and salt to a paste in a food processor.

2. Combine spice paste, fish, fish sauce, and beans in a bowl and knead until well combined and the consistency is slightly tacky. Shape the mixture into 3-inch round, flat cakes. Refrigerate until ready to cook.

3. Heat the oil in a large pot or deep fryer until it registers 350°F on a deep-fry thermometer. Deep fry the cakes, working in batches if necessary, until they are golden brown on the outside and float to the top of the oil, about 3 minutes.

4. Transfer the cakes to paper towels to drain briefly. Serve immediately.

Fried Fish Cakes with Onion and Cucumber Salad (page 304)

Vegetable Tempura

MAKES 5 SERVINGS

1 cup vegetable oil

½ cup peanut oil

½ cup sesame oil

TEMPURA BATTER

2 eggs, beaten

1 cup water

½ cup ice, crushed

1½ cups all-purpose flour, plus more as needed

1 red bell pepper, seeded and cut into ¼-inch strips

10 medium shiitake mushrooms, stems removed

20 green beans

20 small broccoli florets

1 small sweet potato, cut into ¼-inch-thick slices

1 medium onion, cut into ¼-inch-thick slices

Tempura Dipping Sauce (recipe follows)

1. Combine the vegetable, peanut, and sesame oils in a deep pot or fryer and heat until it registers 350°F on a deep-fry thermometer.

2. Meanwhile, make the tempura batter. Combine the eggs, water, ice, and flour and mix gently. Do not overmix.

3. Lightly dredge the vegetables in flour, dip in the batter, and then immediately deep fry until crispy and white or light golden brown. Work in batches if necessary, frying a single variety of vegetable at a time.

4. Transfer the tempura to paper towels to drain. Serve immediately with the dipping sauce.

TEMPURA DIPPING SAUCE

MAKES 1¾ CUPS SAUCE

1 cup light soy sauce

½ cup mirin

2 tsp toasted sesame oil

¼ cup peeled, finely grated daikon radish

1 tbsp peeled, grated ginger

Combine all of the ingredients in a small saucepan and warm slightly over low heat. Serve immediately, or cool and refrigerate for later use.

COOKING PASTA, GRAINS, AND LEGUMES

Pasta, grains, and legumes are all highly adaptable items that may be used in appetizers and small bites, soups, salads, main dishes, and even desserts. On today's table, specialty grains such as quinoa, wheat berries, and amaranth, and unusual legumes such as flageolets and borlotti beans are becoming more and more common, and everyday grains, legumes, and pastas are being presented in interesting new ways.

COOKING PASTA

PASTA AND NOODLES, BOTH FRESH AND DRIED, should be boiled in a large amount of salted water to ensure the best flavor and texture. Some pastas and noodles cook very rapidly, while others take several minutes to cook properly. If you are working with an unfamiliar shape or style of dried pasta, be sure to consult the instructions on the package.

Water is the most common cooking liquid, although some recipes may call for stock. Add salt to the water as it comes to a boil to keep the pasta from sticking together as it cooks; the water should be noticeably salty, but not unpleasantly so. Add the pasta, boil until it is tender, and drain immediately in a colander. Pasta should be served as soon as possible after cooking.

Al dente is the most desired doneness for the majority of pastas and noodles. The phrase *al dente* is Italian for "to the tooth" and refers to pasta that is just slightly firm and pleasantly chewy, instead of mushy or overcooked. It should be able to be bitten easily but still offer a slight resistance and a sense of texture.

Basic Equipment for Cooking Pasta, Grains, and Legumes

POT WITH LID. Boiling pasta and simmering grains and legumes requires a pot large enough to allow for the expansion of the pasta, grain, or legume. For making a pilaf, be sure that the pot has a tight-fitting lid.

WIDE SAUCEPAN. A wide saucepan or straight-sided sauté pan is best for making risotto.

COLANDER OR STRAINER. Use a colander or strainer to drain cooked pasta, grains, or legumes as needed.

WOODEN OR HEATPROOF SILICONE SPOON. A heatproof spoon is an essential tool when simmering grain cereal and meals or preparing a pilaf or risotto.

COOKING GRAINS AND LEGUMES

GRAINS AND LEGUMES ARE DRIED FOODS that must be properly rehydrated before they can be eaten. Legumes and most grains are generally combined with the liquid before bringing it to a boil, but some grains, like quinoa, are added to the liquid only after it has come to a boil. Refer to specific recipes for details. Although grains and legumes are often referred to as being boiled, they are actually simmered, because the higher heat of a boiling liquid would toughen them.

Be sure to carefully sort grains and legumes before cooking them. Spread them out in a single layer on a baking sheet and, working from one end of the pan to the other, remove any dirt, stones, or moldy beans.

Most legumes and some grains must also be soaked prior to cooking. Whole grains, such as wheat and rye berries, benefit from soaking because it softens the outer layer of bran. Imported basmati and jasmine rice should be soaked to remove excess starch from the surface and prevent clumping; domestic basmati and jasmine rice does not need to be soaked. If you choose to soak a grain or legume, there are two methods that are commonly used (described below): the long-soak method (photo 1) and the short-soak method (photo 2). Except for time, there is no appreciable difference between them.

LEFT:

For the long-soak method, place the sorted and rinsed legumes or grains in a container and add enough cool water to cover them by about 2 inches. Let soak in the refrigerator for 4 hours or up to overnight, depending on the type of legume or grain.

RIGHT:

For the short-soak method, place the sorted and rinsed legumes or grains in a pot and add enough water to cover them by about 2 inches. Bring the water to a simmer, then immediately remove the pot from the stovetop and cover. Let the legumes or grains steep, off the heat, for about 1 hour.

Water, stock, and broth are common choices for the cooking liquid. Each type of grain or legume absorbs a different amount of liquid, so see the package or specific recipe for instructions. Grains are done when they are tender to the bite. They should be fluffy, with a sweet, nutty flavor. Legumes are done when they are completely tender and creamy on the inside but still retain their shape. They should be soft and easy to mash with a fork or spoon.

PILAF

Pilaf is a grain dish in which the grain, usually rice, is first heated in a pan, either dry or with a little fat, and then combined with a hot liquid and simmered, covered, on the stovetop or in the oven. A neutral-flavored vegetable oil is most often used to cook the aromatics and sauté the grain for pilaf. Stock or broth is generally the preferred cooking liquid. A member of the onion family, such as shallots, onions, green onions, garlic, or leeks, is usually required for a pilaf. In addition to onions, bay leaves and thyme are commonly used for flavor, but other spices and herbs may be added.

Chef's Lesson
MAKING PILAF

1. To make a pilaf, first heat the fat in a pot over medium heat. Add the aromatic vegetables and cook until tender.

2. Add the rice or other grains and sauté, stirring frequently, until the grains are well coated with the fat. Add the simmering cooking liquid and bring the mixture to a simmer, stirring once or twice to prevent the rice from sticking to the pot. Add any additional flavoring ingredients, cover the pot, and complete the cooking in a moderate oven or over low heat on the stovetop. Test a few grains for doneness by biting into them. They should be tender, but with a noticeable texture, not soft and mushy. The individual grains should separate easily.

3. When all of the liquid has been fully absorbed, remove the pot from the heat and let the pilaf rest, covered, for 5 minutes. Uncover the pot and fluff the pilaf with a fork before serving.

RISOTTO

Like pilaf, risotto is a grain dish that requires a special cooking method. Risotto is a creamy, porridgelike grain dish traditionally made with Italian varieties of medium-grain round rice, such as Arborio or Carnaroli. Other grains, including other long-grain or brown rices, barley, and wheat berries, may also be prepared following the same method. The cooking time will be longer for brown rice and whole grains, and the amount of liquid required may be greater.

The cooking liquid most often suggested for risotto is stock or broth. Wine may replace a portion of the stock or broth in some recipes. Minced leeks, shallots, or onions are traditionally included in a risotto. Other aromatic vegetables, including garlic, mushrooms, fennel, or carrots, or spices such as saffron may also be added. Butter contributes a sweet, rich flavor to risotto, but other fats or oils may also be used. If adding a cheese, it should be stirred in just before serving for the best flavor.

Chef's Lesson
MAKING RISOTTO

1. To make risotto, first heat some butter in a heavy-bottomed straight-sided sauté pan or other heavy saucepan over medium heat. Add any aromatic vegetables and cook until tender. Add the rice and cook in the butter until it develops a toasted aroma. Add one-quarter to one-third of the simmering cooking liquid to the rice and stir constantly over medium heat until all of the liquid is absorbed. Stir the risotto constantly as it absorbs the liquid. After the rice absorbs the first addition of liquid, the grains appear firm and quite distinct, and no real creaminess is evident yet.

2. Continue adding portions of the cooking liquid, a little at a time, until all of the liquid has been absorbed. The rice grains will begin to have a creamy, saucelike consistency. Continue cooking, stirring constantly, until the rice is fully cooked and the risotto is creamy and thick without becoming mushy. The average cooking time for risotto prepared with Arborio rice is 20 minutes.

3. As soon as the rice is fully cooked, reduce the heat to low and vigorously stir the butter, grated cheese, or other finishing ingredients into the risotto until well blended.

COOKING GRAIN CEREALS AND MEALS

EXPERT
tips

FOR A HEALTHIER OPTION, use whole grains whenever possible, as they have increased health benefits. Brown rice, quinoa, wheat berries, kasha, millet, and barley are just few options.

ANY GARNISHING INGREDIENTS should be added to risotto near or at the end of cooking. The timing for additional ingredients is important and will depend on the required cooking time of each individual ingredient. Garnishing ingredients for risotto may include:

  Cut or whole vegetables (broccoli, peas, asparagus)

  Fresh herbs

  Seafood (shrimp, scallops, squid)

  Cheese (Parmesan or Romano)

ADDING BROWN OR GREEN LENTILS to a rice pilaf makes a heartier dish. The lentils will cook in the same amount of time that it takes to cook the rice or similar grains, so the resulting pilaf will be fluffy and dry, not mushy.

WATER, STOCK, BROTH, OR MILK may be used as the liquid for cooking cereal or meal. Depending on the desired result, sweeteners, such as any of the following, can be added to achieve a different flavor.

  Sugar

  Honey

  Agave syrup

  Maple syrup

CEREALS AND MEALS ARE PRODUCED BY MILLING A WHOLE GRAIN into smaller pieces. Cereals and meals vary widely according to the way they are processed. The bran and germ may be left intact or removed. Some grains are treated before milling; for example, bulgur wheat is steamed and dried before it is crushed. Depending on the grain, the final result might be quite coarse, like cracked wheat or groats, or fine, like cornmeal. Coarser cereals produce a dense, porridgelike texture. Finer meals produce a smooth, even silky texture similar to a pudding.

All cereals and meals should have a fresh, appealing aroma. As they age, the natural oils can become rancid. Storing grains, cereals, and meals in the freezer can prevent this spoilage. Some cereals and grains should be rinsed before cooking, while others must be dry so that they can be added gradually to the cooking liquid. Cereals and meals are generally cooked in only as much liquid as it is possible for them to absorb. Each type will absorb a different amount of liquid, so refer to the package or recipe directions for details.

Salt is generally added to the cooking liquid, and sometimes spices or herbs are added as well. Taste and adjust the seasoning at the end of the cooking time. Cereals and meals tend to need considerable salt, or they can taste flat.

COOKING GRAIN CEREALS AND MEALS

1. Bring the cooking liquid to a full boil in a heavy-bottomed pot and add the cereal or meal in a thin stream, stirring constantly, or combine the cereal and liquid first and bring to a boil, depending on the type of cereal or meal. Refer to the package or recipe for instructions. Add salt, along with any other desired seasoning, as the liquid comes to a boil.

2. Reduce the heat to establish a simmer and cook, stirring as necessary to prevent scorching. Drag the spoon across the bottom of the pot and into the corners to release the cereal or meal.

3. Cook the cereal or meal to the proper doneness. The mixture will thicken noticeably during cooking. Some meals or cereals may become stiff enough to pull away from the sides of the pot; others will remain fluid enough to pour easily. Meals should have a relatively smooth, creamy texture.

Cooking Polenta

POLENTA IS A VERSATILE GRAIN MEAL that may be eaten firm or soft, hot or chilled, baked or fried. It is cooked in a simmering liquid until the grains soften and the liquid is absorbed. Ingredients such as vegetables or cheese are often added to just-cooked polenta while it is still hot. Vegetables should be cut into small pieces, sautéed, and seasoned properly before being added to polenta.

After simmering polenta to the desired doneness, it may be served immediately, chilled and served cold, or prepared to be finished with another method. To do this, spread the polenta out in an even layer on a baking sheet, cover it with plastic wrap, and place it in the refrigerator. Once the polenta is thoroughly chilled, it can be cut into shapes as desired and baked, grilled, sautéed, or pan fried until the exterior is crispy and the interior is heated through.

COOKING GRAINS

GRAIN (1 CUP DRY)	LIQUID (cups)	APPROXIMATE YIELD (cups)	COOKING TIME	COOKING METHOD
PEARL BARLEY	2	4	35–45 minutes	Boil or follow pilaf method (see page 258)
BARLEY GROATS	2½	4	50 minutes–1 hour	Boil or follow pilaf method (see page 258)
BUCKWHEAT GROATS (KASHA)	1½–2	2	12–20 minutes	Boil or follow pilaf method (see page 258)
BULGUR	4	2	2 hours (soaked), or 5–10 minutes (simmered)	Soak in hot liquid for 2 hours, then drain, or simmer 5–10 minutes, then drain
COUSCOUS	As needed (steaming), or 2 (pilaf method)	2–3 cups	60 minutes, fluffing every 20 minutes (steamed), or 10–15 minutes (pilaf method)	Steam or follow pilaf method (see page 258)
CRACKED WHEAT	2	3	20 minutes	Boil or steam
HOMINY GRITS	4	3	25 minutes	Follow polenta method (see page 261)
MILLET	2	3	30–35 minutes	Boil or follow pilaf method (see page 258)
OAT GROATS	2	2	45 minutes–1 hour	Boil
POLENTA, COARSE GRIND CORNMEAL	4	3–4	35–45 minutes	Follow polenta method (see page 261)
QUINOA	2	2	10–12 minutes	Follow pilaf method (see page 258)
RICE, BASMATI	1½	3	25 minutes	Simmer, boil, or follow pilaf method (see page 258)
RICE, LONG-GRAIN, BROWN	3	4	40 minutes	Boil, steam, or follow pilaf method (see page 258)
RICE, LONG-GRAIN, WHITE	1½–1¾	3	18–20 minutes	Boil, steam, or follow pilaf method (see page 258)
RICE, SHORT-GRAIN, WHITE	1–1½	3	20–30 minutes	Boil or steam
RICE, WILD	3	4	30–45 minutes	Boil or steam
WHEAT BERRIES	3	2	1 hour or more	Boil or steam

Cooking Dried Legumes

LEGUME	SOAKING TIME	COOKING TIME (add liquid to cover and simmer)	USES	FLAVORING SUGGESTIONS
BLACK BEANS	4–8 hours	1½ hours	Chilis, stews, soups, stuffings	Onion, garlic, cumin, oregano, Mexican herbs such as epazote and hoja santa
BLACK-EYED PEAS	Overnight	45 minutes–1 hour	Chilis, stews, soups, stuffings, especially in Southern U.S. cuisine	Onion, garlic, smoky flavors, mushrooms
CHICKPEAS	12–18 hours	2–2½ hours or more	Hummus, falafel, salads, pasta dishes	Lemon, rosemary, garlic, onion, fennel, cumin, coriander, curry
FAVA BEANS	12 hours	3 hours	Purées, succotash, salads, pasta dishes, falafel, stews	Olive oil, tarragon, chervil, chives, fennel, mushrooms, roasted peppers
GREAT NORTHERN BEANS/CANNELLINI	4–8 hours	1 hour	Tuscan-style beans, purées, soups	Garlic, onion, rosemary, oregano, basil, tarragon, herbes de Provence
KIDNEY BEANS (RED OR WHITE)	4 hours	1 hour	Chilis, stews, salads, soups, stuffings	Latin and Mexican spice combinations, vinaigrettes
LENTILS	None	30–40 minutes	Soups, purées, green lentils in salads or pilaf	Middle Eastern spice blends, curry, herbes de Provence, onion, garlic, walnuts, mushrooms, goat cheese
LIMA/BUTTER BEANS	4–8 hours	1–1½ hours	Succotash, soups, salads, stuffings	Butter, olive oil, herbs, onion, green onion, chives
NAVY BEANS	4 hours	2 hours	Chilis, stews, soups, stuffings, baked beans	Molasses, brown sugar, onion, garlic, all types of herbs and vegetables
SPLIT PEAS	None	30 minutes	Soups, purées	Carrots, onion, leek, garlic, smoky flavors, cumin, mint, tarragon
PINK BEANS	4–8 hours	1 hour	Chilis, stews, soups, stuffings, combined with rice	Latin and Mexican spice combinations, vinaigrettes
PINTO BEANS	4–8 hours	1½–2 hours	Chilis, stews, soups, refried, mashed, especially in Southwestern and Southern U.S. cuisine	Latin and Mexican spice combinations, vinaigrettes, garlic, onions, smoky flavors

Fresh Egg Pasta

MAKES 1 POUND 8 OUNCES PASTA

1 lb all-purpose flour, plus more as needed

Pinch salt

4 eggs

1 to 2 tbsp water, plus more as needed

2 tbsp vegetable oil or olive oil (optional)

1. Combine the flour and salt in a large bowl and make a well in the center. Place the eggs, water, and oil, if using, in the center of the well. Using a fork, gradually pull the dry ingredients into the egg mixture in the center of the well and stir until a loose mass forms. As the dough is mixed, adjust the consistency with additional flour or water as needed. The dough should be tacky but minimally moist.

2. Turn the dough out onto a floured work surface and knead until the texture is smooth and elastic, 4 to 5 minutes. Gather and smooth the dough into a ball, cover lightly with plastic wrap, and let the dough relax at room temperature for at least 1 hour.

3. Roll out the pasta dough into thin sheets and cut into the desired shape by hand or using a pasta machine. Cook the pasta immediately, or cover and refrigerate for up to 2 days.

HERBED PASTA *Add 2 to 3 oz chopped fresh herbs to the eggs; adjust the dough with additional flour as needed.*

WHOLE WHEAT PASTA *Substitute whole wheat flour for half of the all-purpose flour.*

BUCKWHEAT PASTA *Substitute 3¼ oz buckwheat flour for an equal amount of the all-purpose flour.*

BLACK PEPPER PASTA *Add 2 tsp cracked black peppercorns to the flour.*

RED PEPPER PASTA *Sauté 6 oz puréed roasted red pepper in an open sauté pan until reduced and dry. Cool the purée and add to the eggs; adjust the dough with additional flour as needed.*

Butternut Squash and Sage Ravioli

MAKES 4 SERVINGS

1 butternut squash, halved lengthwise

7 tbsp butter

2 tbsp chopped sage, plus 16 sage leaves

1⅓ cups plus ¼ cup grated Parmesan

2 tbsp lemon zest

½ tsp freshly grated nutmeg

Salt, as needed

Freshly ground black pepper, as needed

Fresh Pasta Dough (opposite page)

1. Preheat the oven to 350°F.

2. Place the butternut squash halves onto a baking sheet, cut side up, cover the sheet with aluminum foil, and roast until the flesh is tender, 45 minutes to 1 hour. Let cool slightly.

3. In a small sauté pan over medium heat, melt 3 tablespoons butter with the chopped sage. Continue to cook until very hot and lightly browned, 3 to 4 minutes. Remove the pan from the heat and set aside.

4. Scoop the flesh out from the squash. Discard the seeds. Using a blender or food processor, combine the squash, butter mixture, 1⅓ cups cheese, the lemon zest, and nutmeg and process until smooth. Season with salt and pepper.

5. Using a pasta machine, roll out the pasta dough into thin sheets about ⅛ inch thick. Cut the sheets into 40 even squares and cover with plastic wrap until ready to be filled.

6. To assemble the ravioli, brush the edges of a pasta square lightly with water. Spoon some of the squash filling in the center of the square.

7. Top with another square, keeping the edges of the dough lined up. Lightly press the edges of the dough together. Crimp the edges with a fork to seal them. Repeat with the remaining pasta squares.

8. Bring a large pot of salted water to a boil. Add the ravioli and simmer until tender, 5 to 7 minutes. Drain in a colander.

9. Heat the remaining 4 tablespoons butter in a large sauté pan over medium heat. Add the ravioli and toss lightly to coat with the butter. Add the sage leaves and remaining ¼ cup cheese and toss to coat and heat through, about 1 minute. Serve immediately.

Classic Mac and Cheese

MAKES 6 TO 8 SERVINGS

8 oz elbow macaroni

3 tbsp butter

5 tbsp flour

3 cups milk

½ tsp sweet or smoked Spanish paprika

1 bay leaf

5 cups shredded sharp cheddar

¼ tsp Tabasco sauce

½ tsp freshly cracked black pepper

2 tsp salt

¼ cup panko bread crumbs

1. Preheat the oven to 375°F.

2. Bring a pot of salted water to a boil over high heat. Add the pasta and boil until just tender, 7 to 9 minutes. Drain the pasta in a colander.

3. While the pasta is cooking, melt the butter in a large sauté pan or saucepan over medium heat. Add the flour, stirring until there are no lumps and the mixture has cooked through but not browned, about 5 minutes. Add the milk, paprika, and bay leaf. Increase the heat to medium-high to establish a simmer. Simmer for 10 to 15 minutes, until the sauce is thick enough to coat the back of a spoon. Remove and discard the bay leaf.

4. Reduce the heat to medium-low. Add 4½ cups of the cheese to the sauce in batches of about 1 cup, waiting until most of the cheese is melted before adding the next batch. Do not allow the sauce to boil while you add the cheese. Season with the Tabasco, pepper, and salt.

5. Combine the pasta with the cheese sauce and mix well to coat. Pour the mixture into a 2-quart baking dish and sprinkle with the remaining ½ cup cheese. Sprinkle the bread crumbs over the cheese. Bake until the cheese begins to bubble around the edges and the bread crumbs turn golden brown and crisp, 20 to 30 minutes. Allow the mac and cheese to rest for 5 to 10 minutes before serving.

NOTE *This basic recipe is a great starting point for endless variations, so feel free to experiment. Try adding chopped smoked ham, the "burnt ends" from a pork butt or beef brisket, or cooked lobster meat. You can also replace some of the cheddar with another cheese, such as blue cheese.*

Gnocchi di Ricotta

MAKES 5 SERVINGS

1 lb 6 oz ricotta

2 cups all-purpose flour, sifted

3 eggs

¼ cup plus 2 tbsp olive oil

1¼ tsp salt

3 tbsp butter

2 cups Chicken Stock (page 38), hot

8 oz grated Parmesan

½ tsp freshly ground black pepper

1. Put the ricotta, flour, eggs, oil, and salt into the bowl of a food processor. Process until the ingredients come together to form a smooth dough, about 1 minute. Transfer the dough to a bowl.

2. Bring a large pot of salted water to a boil. Using two spoons, shape the dough into oval quenelles and then drop them one by one into the boiling water. When all the dough has been used, return the water to a boil for 1 minute. Using a slotted spoon, transfer the gnocchi carefully to a bowl.

3. Heat the butter in a medium skillet over medium heat. Add the gnocchi and hot stock and cook to heat through, 1 to 2 minutes.

4. Using a slotted spoon, transfer the gnocchi to a serving bowl. Garnish with the cheese and pepper. Serve immediately.

NOTE *Ricotta gnocchi are very delicate and can break easily, so take care when removing them from the water and when transferring them to the serving plate.*

Spätzle

MAKES 5 SERVINGS

3 eggs

¼ cup whole milk

½ cup water

Salt, as needed

Ground white pepper, as needed

Freshly grated nutmeg, as needed

1 tbsp fines herbes, plus more as needed (optional)

2 cups all-purpose flour

¼ cup (4 tbsp/½ stick) butter

1. In a large bowl, combine the eggs, milk, and water and season with salt, white pepper, and nutmeg. Add the fines herbes, if using. Work in the flour by hand and then beat with a wooden spoon until smooth. Cover the bowl with plastic wrap and allow the mixture to rest for 1 hour.

2. Bring a large pot of salted water to a simmer. Press the dough through a spätzle maker into the simmering water. When the spätzle float to the top of the pot, remove them with a spider. (If not using immediately, cool the spätzle in ice water, drain well, and refrigerate for later use.)

3. Heat the butter in a large sauté pan over medium-high heat. Add the spätzle and sauté until very hot. Season with additional salt, pepper, and fines herbes, if using, and serve immediately.

NOTE *Although the browning of späetzle is not traditional, some cooks prefer to allow it extra time in the pan to get brown and slightly crispy.*

Pasta alla Carbonara

MAKES 5 SERVINGS

1 lb spaghetti

2 tbsp butter or olive oil, plus more as needed

8 oz minced pancetta or bacon

¾ cup heavy cream

4 egg yolks

½ cup grated Parmesan, plus more as needed

Salt, as needed

Freshly ground black pepper, as needed

2 tbsp chopped flat-leaf parsley

1. Bring a large pot of salted water to a rolling boil. Add the spaghetti and stir a few times to separate the strands. Cook the spaghetti until it is tender to the bite but still retains some texture, about 8 minutes.

2. Drain the spaghetti in a colander. (Note: If the spaghetti is prepared in advance, rinse it with cold water, drain well, and rub a small amount of oil through the strands. Refrigerate until ready to serve. Reheat the pasta in boiling salted water and drain well while preparing the sauce.)

3. Heat the butter or oil in a large sauté pan, add the pancetta or bacon, and sauté over medium heat until the fat has rendered, 3 to 4 minutes. Add the drained, cooked spaghetti and sauté until the spaghetti is very hot. Add half of the cream to the pan and bring it to a simmer.

4. In a small bowl, blend the egg yolks with the remaining cream and the cheese. Add the egg mixture to the pasta and cook gently over low heat, stirring constantly, until the sauce is heated through. Do not overheat, or the sauce will curdle. Season with salt and pepper.

5. Garnish with the parsley and additional cheese, if desired. Serve immediately.

Orecchiette with Italian Sausage, Broccoli Rabe, and Parmesan Cheese

MAKES 5 SERVINGS

1 lb broccoli rabe

½ cup olive oil

1 lb Italian sausage

1 cup minced onion

1 cup Tomato Sauce (page 73)

1 lb orecchiette

2 garlic cloves, sliced

¼ tsp red pepper flakes

2 tbsp water

¼ cup chopped parsley

¼ cup basil chiffonade

¼ cup chopped oregano

¼ cup minced chives

½ cup grated Parmesan

1. Bring a large pot of salted water to a boil over medium heat. Trim the broccoli rabe by cutting off 1 inch from the bottom of each stem. Prepare a bowl of ice water. Add the broccoli rabe to the pot of boiling water and blanch until it is almost cooked, about 4 minutes. Shock the broccoli rabe in the ice water. Drain well and set aside.

2. Heat ¼ cup of the oil in a large sauté pan over medium heat. Add the sausage and cook until nearly cooked through. Using a whisk, crumble the sausage in the pan. Add the onion and cook until tender, about 4 minutes. Add the tomato sauce. Let the mixture cook until it resembles a Bolognese-style sauce, about 5 minutes. Remove from the heat and set aside.

3. Bring another large pot of salted water to a boil. Add the pasta and cook until al dente, about 6 minutes. Drain in a colander.

4. While the pasta is cooking, heat the remaining ¼ cup oil in another large sauté pan over medium heat. Add the garlic, red pepper flakes, water, and sausage mixture. Cook for 1 minute, stirring to combine. Add the parsley, basil, oregano, chives, and broccoli rabe. Add the pasta and half of the cheese and toss to mix. Serve immediately, garnished with the remaining cheese.

PAD THAI

MAKES 5 SERVINGS

1 lb rice noodles

1 tbsp dried shrimp

4 tbsp Thai chili paste (nam prik pao), plus more as needed

2 tbsp fish sauce, plus more as needed

2 tbsp rice vinegar

2 tbsp palm sugar, plus more as needed

2 tbsp vegetable oil, plus more as needed

¼ cup chopped garlic

1 leek, white and green parts, julienned

1 lb extra-firm tofu, pressed (see Note) and cut into medium dice

3 eggs, beaten slightly

2 green onions, thinly sliced into 1-inch strips

8 oz bean sprouts

1 cup roughly chopped cilantro

5 lime wedges

½ cup peanuts, pan-roasted and coarsely chopped

1. Soak the noodles in a bowl of warm water for 30 minutes. Drain well.

2. Soak the dried shrimp in a small bowl of cool water for 30 minutes. Drain and finely chop.

3. Whisk together the chili paste, fish sauce, vinegar, and sugar.

4. Heat the oil in a wok over medium-high heat. Add the shrimp, garlic, leek, and tofu. Stir-fry until the leeks brighten in color and soften slightly. The garlic should begin to turn golden, but not brown.

5. Add the noodles and stir to coat with the oil. Stir-fry for 30 seconds. Push the noodles to the upper edge of one side of the wok. Add a drizzle of oil to the space created in the wok, then add the beaten eggs and spread with a spatula to begin cooking. Allow the eggs to cook for 10 seconds before beginning to stir-fry the noodle-egg mixture again.

6. Stir in the fish sauce mixture and the green onions. Stir-fry until the noodles are soft, adding water as necessary to facilitate softening.

7. Fold in the sprouts and cilantro. Adjust the seasoning with additional chili paste, fish sauce, and sugar, as needed.

8. Garnish with the lime wedges and peanuts and serve immediately.

NOTE *To press tofu, place it in a roasting pan. Place a flat plate or baking sheet on top of the tofu and weight it with a heavy object such as a small pot filled with water. Let sit for about 1 hour. Discard the liquid and use the tofu as directed.*

COCONUT RICE

1 cup long-grain white rice

1 tbsp vegetable oil or melted butter

1 cup water

1 cup unsweetened coconut milk

Salt, as needed

Freshly ground black pepper, as needed

1. Rinse the rice under cold water in a strainer until the water runs clear, if desired. Drain the rice well before using.

2. Heat the oil or butter in a heavy-bottomed medium pot over medium heat. Add the rice and sauté, stirring frequently, until coated with oil or butter and heated through.

3. Add the water and coconut milk and season with salt and pepper. Bring to a simmer, reduce the heat, cover, and cook for 12 to 15 minutes.

4. Allow the rice to rest for 5 minutes, fluff it with a fork, and serve immediately.

SAFFRON RICE

MAKES 5 SERVINGS

1½ cups basmati rice

3 cups water

1 tsp salt

1 tbsp butter

2 tbsp whole milk

½ tsp saffron threads, crumbled

1. Preheat the oven to 400°F. Lightly butter a medium sauté pan.

2. Rinse the rice under cold water in a strainer until the water runs clear, if desired. Drain the rice well before using. Bring the water to a boil in a saucepan and add the salt.

3. Melt the butter in a small sauce over medium heat. Add the milk and saffron to steep.

4. Add the rice to the boiling water, cover with a lid, and cook for 7 minutes. Drain the rice in a colander and transfer it to the buttered sauté pan.

5. Ladle the milk mixture over the rice and toss lightly with a fork to combine. Do not stir.

6. Tightly cover the pan with parchment paper and then aluminum foil. Transfer to the oven and bake for 15 minutes.

7. Remove from the oven and allow the rice to rest for 5 minutes, uncovered, then fluff with a fork and serve immediately.

RICE PILAF

2 cups long-grain white rice

2 tbsp butter or vegetable oil

1 cup minced onion

4 cups Chicken Stock (page 38), hot

1 bay leaf

2 thyme sprigs

Salt, as needed

Freshly ground black pepper, as needed

1. Preheat the oven to 350°F.

2. Rinse the rice under cold water in a strainer until the water runs clear, if desired. Drain the rice well before using.

3. Heat the butter or oil in a heavy-bottomed medium ovenproof pot over medium heat. Add the onion and cook, stirring frequently, until tender and translucent, 5 to 6 minutes.

4. Add the rice and sauté over medium-high heat, stirring frequently, until coated with butter or oil and heated through, 2 to 3 minutes.

5. Add the hot stock and bring to a simmer, stirring to prevent the rice from clumping together or sticking to the bottom of the pot.

6. Add the bay leaf and thyme, and season with salt and pepper. Cover the pot and place it in the oven (or leave it over low heat on the stovetop). Cook until the grains are tender to the bite, 16 to 20 minutes. Remove and discard the bay leaf.

7. Allow the rice to rest for 5 minutes, fluff with a fork, and serve immediately.

WILD RICE PILAF *Substitute an equal amount of wild rice for the long-grain rice. Increase the stock to 6 cups. Increase the cooking time to 45 to 60 minutes.*

BROWN RICE PILAF WITH PECANS AND GREEN ONIONS

MAKES 5 SERVINGS

1½ cups long-grain brown rice

1 tbsp butter or vegetable oil

½ cup minced onion

3 cups Chicken Stock (page 38), **hot**

1 bouquet garni (see page 2)

Salt, as needed

Freshly ground black pepper, as needed

¼ cup toasted pecans, chopped

¼ cup sliced green onions

1. Preheat the oven to 350°F.

2. Rinse the rice under cold water in a strainer until the water runs clear, if desired. Drain the rice well before using.

3. Heat the butter or oil in a heavy-bottomed medium ovenproof pot over medium heat. Add the onion and cook, stirring frequently, until tender and translucent, 5 to 6 minutes.

4. Add the rice and sauté over medium-high heat, stirring frequently, until coated with butter or oil and heated through, 2 to 3 minutes.

5. Add the hot stock and bring to a simmer, stirring to prevent the rice from clumping together or sticking to the bottom of the pot.

6. Add the bouquet garni, and season with salt and pepper. Cover the pot and transfer it to the oven (or leave it over low heat on the stovetop). Cook until the grains are tender to the bite, 35 to 40 minutes.

7. Allow the rice to rest for 5 minutes, uncover, and then use a fork to fold in the pecans and green onions while separating the grains and releasing the steam. Serve immediately.

Paella Valenciana

10 shrimp (16/20 count), peeled and deveined, shells reserved

¼ cup extra-virgin olive oil

1 tsp crushed saffron threads

4½ cups Chicken Stock (page 38), plus more as needed

5 chicken legs, separated

Salt, as needed

Freshly ground black pepper, as needed

1 cup large-dice onion

1 cup large-dice red bell peppers

1 cup large-dice green bell peppers

2 tbsp minced garlic

3 oz dry Spanish chorizo, sliced ¼ inch thick

1½ cups rice

1 cup peeled, seeded, large-dice tomatoes

10 littleneck clams, thoroughly scrubbed

1½ lb mussels, scrubbed and debearded

1 cup green peas, cooked

¼ cup thinly sliced green onions

2 piquillo chiles, julienned

1. In a medium pot, sauté the shrimp shells in 2 tablespoons of the oil until they turn pink. Add the saffron and stock and simmer, covered, for 30 minutes. Strain the liquid into a pot and keep hot.

2. Season the chicken with salt and pepper. Add 1 tablespoon of the oil to a paella pan over medium heat and heat until just smoking. Add the chicken and brown on all sides. Remove the chicken from the pan and reserve.

3. Add the remaining 1 tablespoon oil to the pan. Add the onion and bell peppers and sauté over medium heat for 2 to 3 minutes. Add the garlic, and sauté for 1 minute more. Add the chorizo and rice, stirring to coat the rice with the oil.

4. Add the tomatoes, the reserved hot stock, the browned chicken, and clams. Cover, reduce the heat, and cook for 5 minutes, or until all the clams have opened. Do not stir the rice.

5. Add the mussels and shrimp. Cover and cook for 5 to 7 minutes, adding more stock during cooking, if necessary, so that the rice does not dry out.

6. During the last minute of cooking, add the peas. Serve immediately, garnished with the green onions and piquillo chiles.

Risotto

2 tbsp butter

1 cup minced onion

1 cup Arborio rice

4 cups Chicken Stock (page 38), hot

Salt, as needed

Freshly ground black pepper, as needed

1. Heat the butter in a heavy-bottomed, straight-sided sauté pan or a saucepan over medium heat. Add the onion and sweat until softened and translucent, 6 to 8 minutes.

2. Add the rice and mix thoroughly to coat with butter. Cook, stirring constantly, until a toasted aroma rises from the pan, about 1 minute.

3. Add one-third of the stock to the rice and cook, stirring constantly, until the rice has absorbed the stock. Repeat, adding the remaining stock in 2 more additions, allowing each addition to be absorbed before adding the next. Cook the risotto until the rice is just tender and most of the liquid has been absorbed; the dish should be creamy, not mushy. Season with salt and pepper and serve immediately.

PARMESAN RISOTTO *Prepare the risotto, replacing up to one-quarter of the stock with a dry white wine. Add the wine to the stock as it heats to a simmer for the best flavor. Finish the risotto by adding ½ cup grated Parmesan and 8 tbsp butter.*

WILD MUSHROOM RISOTTO *Soak 1 oz dried wild mushrooms in ½ cup warm water for 30 minutes to 1 hour. Drain the mushrooms and add to the pan with the onions. Strain the soaking liquid through a cheesecloth-lined strainer to remove any sediment, measure it, and use it to replace an equal amount of the stock in the risotto.*

BASIC POLENTA

7½ cups water

Salt, as needed

1 cup coarse yellow cornmeal

2 tbsp butter

Freshly ground black pepper, as needed

1. Bring the water to a boil in a heavy-bottomed medium saucepan and season with salt.

2. Pour the cornmeal into the water in a steady stream, stirring constantly until it has all been added. Reduce the heat to low and simmer, stirring often, until the polenta pulls away from the sides of the pot, about 45 minutes. It should not taste starchy or gritty.

3. Remove the pot from the heat and stir in the butter. Season with salt and pepper. Serve immediately.

NOTE *For firm polenta, decrease the amount of water to 5 cups. After stirring in the butter, spread the polenta onto a greased or plastic-lined baking sheet that has ½-inch-high sides, and refrigerate until cool enough to cut into the desired shapes. Finish by sautéing, pan frying, grilling, or baking.*

BOILED EDAMAME

1 qt water

1 tbsp sea salt

1 lb edamame

1. Bring the water and 2 teaspoons of the salt to a boil in a heavy-bottomed medium stockpot.

2. Add the edamame and simmer until tender, 4 to 5 minutes. Drain the edamame and season with the remaining 1 teaspoon salt. Serve hot or at room temperature.

Broccoli Rabe and Cannellini Beans

1 tbsp olive oil

2 tbsp diced pancetta or 1 strip bacon, diced

¼ cup minced yellow onion

1 garlic clove, minced

½ cup **Chicken Broth** (page 40)

6 cups trimmed broccoli rabe

1 cup cooked cannellini beans

Salt, as needed

Freshly ground black pepper, as needed

¼ cup grated Parmesan

¼ tsp freshly grated nutmeg

1. Heat the oil in a large sauté pan over medium heat. Add the pancetta or bacon and sauté until the fat renders and the pancetta is translucent, about 1 minute.

2. Increase the heat to high, add the onion and garlic, and sauté until the garlic is aromatic, about 1 minute more.

3. Add the broth and bring to a simmer. Add the broccoli rabe and the beans and cook until the broccoli rabe is bright green and tender, 4 to 5 minutes. Season generously with salt and pepper.

4. Remove from the heat and stir in the cheese and nutmeg. Serve immediately.

RED BEANS AND BOILED RICE

1 cup dried red kidney beans, soaked
(see page 257)

2 oz andouille sausage, sliced

1 tbsp vegetable oil

⅓ cup minced onion

¼ cup medium-dice celery

¼ cup medium-dice green bell peppers

1 garlic clove, minced

1 tsp salt, plus more as needed

Freshly ground black pepper, as needed

1⅓ cups long grain white rice

3 cups water

Tabasco sauce, as needed

1. Drain the soaked beans and transfer them to a medium stockpot. Add the sausage and cover with cool water by 3 inches. Simmer the beans over medium heat until they are completely tender, 20 to 25 minutes. If necessary, add additional water, keeping enough liquid to cover the beans as they cook. Reserve the beans in their cooking liquid.

2. Heat the oil in a large pot over medium heat. Add the onion, celery, bell peppers, and garlic and cook until they begin to turn golden brown, 5 to 7 minutes. Add the cooked beans and their liquid and simmer for 30 minutes. Season with salt and pepper. The beans should remain brothy. If necessary, add additional water.

3. While the beans are cooking, rinse the rice under cold water in a strainer until the water runs clear, if desired. Drain the rice well before using. Bring the water to a boil in a medium pot and add 1 teaspoon salt.

4. Add the rinsed rice to the boiling water and simmer until tender, stirring, 10 to 15 minutes.

5. Mash the beans with the back of a wooden spoon until creamy. Season with additional salt and pepper, if needed, and the Tabasco. Serve the beans immediately on a bed of the rice.

BLACK BEANS WITH BELL PEPPERS AND CHORIZO

MAKES 4 SERVINGS

1 cup dried black beans, soaked for 4 to 12 hours (see page 257)

1 tsp salt, plus more as needed

¼ cup vegetable oil

2 strips bacon, minced

1 yellow onion, cut into medium dice

2 garlic cloves, minced

¼ lb chorizo, sliced

1 red or green bell pepper, seeded and cut into medium dice

½ cup thinly sliced green onions, white and green parts

1 tbsp minced basil

1 tbsp minced cilantro

2 tsp minced oregano

Freshly ground black pepper, as needed

Sour cream, as needed (optional)

1. Drain the soaked beans and transfer them to a large pot. Add cool water to cover by 3 inches. Bring to a boil over high heat, reduce the heat to medium, and simmer, stirring occasionally and adding water as necessary to keep the beans completely covered, until barely tender to the bite, about 70 minutes.

2. Add 1 teaspoon salt and continue simmering until the beans are very tender, 15 to 20 minutes more. Drain the beans and reserve the cooking liquid.

3. Heat the oil in a large pot over medium heat. Add the bacon and sauté until crisp, 2 to 3 minutes. Add the yellow onion and garlic and sauté until lightly browned, 6 to 8 minutes. Add the sausage and bell pepper and sauté until the bell pepper is tender, about 5 minutes.

4. Add the drained beans and enough of the reserved cooking liquid to keep them moist; the consistency should be that of a thick stew. Simmer until all the flavors have developed and all the ingredients are heated through, 20 to 25 minutes. Add the green onions, basil, cilantro, and oregano. Season with additional salt and pepper.

5. Serve immediately, topped with sour cream, if using.

Refried Beans

2 cups dried pinto beans, soaked overnight (see page 257)

2½ qt water or Chicken Broth (page 40), plus more as needed

½ cup bacon fat or lard

1½ cups minced onion

1 garlic clove, minced

1 cup peeled, seeded, and small-dice tomatoes

1½ tsp salt

¼ tsp freshly ground black pepper

½ tsp chili powder

Pinch ground cumin

1. Drain the soaked beans and combine them with the water or broth in a heavy-bottomed saucepan. Bring to a boil.

2. Reduce the heat to medium-low to establish a simmer. Simmer the beans, covered, for about 1 hour, or until tender. Add heated water or broth as needed to keep the beans covered. Once the beans are tender, drain them and reserve the cooking liquid.

3. Heat the bacon fat or lard in a sauté pan over medium heat until hot but not smoking. Add the onion and garlic and sauté until translucent, 3 to 4 minutes. Add the tomatoes and cook until just softened, about 2 minutes. Add the cooked beans to the vegetables and stir thoroughly with a wooden spoon, mashing the beans with the back of the spoon as you stir. If desired, leave some of the beans whole to provide additional texture.

4. Season with the salt, pepper, chili powder, and cumin. If the beans are too thick, thin them with a little of the reserved cooking liquid.

MIDDLE EASTERN CHICKPEAS

12 oz dried chickpeas, soaked (see page 257)

SACHET D'ÉPICES

1½ tsp cumin seed

1 tsp coriander seed

¼ tsp mustard seed

One 1-inch piece ginger, peeled and sliced

½ tsp cracked pink peppercorns

½ tsp cracked black peppercorns

5 cardamom pods

1 cinnamon stick

2 tbsp vegetable oil

1 cup medium-dice onion

2 tbsp minced garlic

3 qts Chicken Stock (page 38)**, plus more as needed**

Salt, as needed

Fresh lemon juice, as needed

Freshly ground black pepper, as needed

1. Drain the soaked beans and reserve.

2. To make the sachet d'épices, place the cumin, coriander, mustard, ginger, pink and black peppercorns, cardamom, and cinnamon in a square of cheesecloth and tie it into a pouch with baking twine (see page 2).

3. Heat the oil in a medium pot over medium heat. Add the onion and sweat until tender and translucent, 5 to 6 minutes. Add the garlic and cook for 1 minute more.

4. Add the soaked chickpeas, stock, and sachet and bring to a simmer. Simmer for 1 hour.

5. Season with salt and continue to simmer until the beans are tender to the bite, 20 to 30 minutes more. Season with fresh lemon juice, additional salt, and pepper.

6. Drain the beans and serve immediately, or let cool in their liquid and refrigerate for later use.

SALADS AND SANDWICHES

Salads and sandwiches are staples in every kitchen. While we may often think of them as casual foods, if assembled with creativity and precision, salads and sandwiches can be quite sophisticated.

SALADS

FRESH CONCOCTIONS OF HERBS AND LETTUCES have been relished in every part of the world from the beginning of recorded culinary history. Today salads go far beyond simple greens, encompassing composed salads, warm salads, fruit salads, potato and other prepared vegetable salads, pasta and grain salads, and legume salads. Salads have traditionally been served as a first course or side dish, but a heartier salad containing protein, grains, or legumes can be a great option as a main course.

COMPOSED SALADS

These consist of components carefully arranged on a plate, rather than being tossed together. When making a composed salad, consider flavor, texture, and how well each element combines with the others. There are no specific rules governing composed salads, but it is best if each item on the plate enhances the flavor of the other items but is beautifully prepared enough to stand on its own.

WARM SALADS

These are made by tossing the ingredients in a warm dressing in a warm pan over low to medium heat. The salad should be just warmed through. Another approach is to use a chilled green salad as the bed for a hot main item, such as grilled meat or fish.

FRUIT SALADS

Some fruit salads are fairly sturdy, while others lose quality very rapidly. Fruits that turn brown, such as apples, pears, and bananas, can be soaked in citrus juice before adding them to the salad as long as the juice doesn't compete with the other ingredients in the salad and the fruit is not prepared too far in advance. Fresh herbs such as mint or basil may be added to fruit salads for flavor and garnish. Try experimenting to see which herbs work best with the fruits in a specific salad. Before working with any fruit, it must be properly rinsed.

POTATO AND OTHER PREPARED VEGETABLE SALADS

The classic American potato salad is a creamy salad, dressed with mayonnaise. Other potato salads enjoyed around the world, like German Potato Salad (page 320), are dressed with vinaigrette. Potatoes for potato salads must be cooked completely but not overcooked, and they should be dressed before they are completely cool for better absorption of the flavors of the dressing.

In addition to potato salad, there are numerous other types of prepared vegetable salads. Prepare vegetables for this type of salad as required in a specific recipe. Some vegetables may be served raw, while others must be blanched or fully cooked before going into the salad.

PASTA AND GRAIN SALADS

Grains and pastas for salads should be fully cooked. However, care should be taken to avoid overcooking, because cooked grains and pasta will still be able to absorb some of the liquid in the dressing and can quickly become soggy. Salt and pepper are important seasonings, but others such as vinegars, herbs, and citrus juices can give grain and pasta salads a brighter flavor.

LEGUME SALADS

Unlike grains and pastas, which have a tendency to become soft as they sit in a dressing, beans and other legumes will not soften any further. The acid in salad dressings can actually make the beans tougher, even if they are fully cooked. Therefore, bean salads should not be dressed and allowed to sit for an extended period of time. If a salad is going to be composed of several different types of beans, it is important that beans with different cooking times be cooked separately to the proper doneness before they are combined into the salad.

PREPARING GREENS

Commercially prepared salad blends are available today for convenience, but you can also create your own by combining lettuces from within one group or by selecting from among two or more groups. When preparing a green salad, separate the leaves from the head or bunch. Loose heads and bunching greens will separate into individual leaves easily. If necessary, trim away coarse ribs or stem ends, and use a paring knife to remove the core. Greens and herbs used for salads are often quite sandy and gritty, and nothing is worse than a gritty salad. All greens, including prepackaged salad mixes, must be washed before serving. Wash greens thoroughly in plenty of cool water to remove all traces of dirt or sand. Dry the greens completely, because salad dressings cling best to well-dried greens. Once greens are cleaned and dried, keep them refrigerated until you are ready to dress and serve them. Use cleaned salad greens within a day or two. Cut or tear the lettuce into bite-size pieces. Traditional salad recipes have always called for lettuces to be torn rather than cut to avoid discoloring, bruising, or crushing the leaves, but the choice to either cut or tear lettuce is primarily a matter of personal style and preference.

GARNISHES

Choose garnishes according to the season and your desired presentation. Either toss these ingredients with the greens as they are being dressed or marinate them separately in a little vinaigrette and use them to top or place around the salad.

DRESSINGS

The dressing's flavor should be appropriate to the salad ingredients, because the dressing serves to pull all the flavors together. Use delicate dressings with delicately flavored greens and more robust dressings with more strongly flavored greens.

VINAIGRETTE. A basic component of many different types of salads is vinaigrette. A vinaigrette is made by blending oil, an acidic ingredient like vinegar, and other flavoring ingredients until they form a homogenous sauce. The sauce remains emulsified only a short time, quickly separating back to oil and vinegar. Both the oil and the vinegar may be infused with flavor, or the flavoring ingredients can be added directly to

EXPERT tip

GOOD-QUALITY OILS and vinegars can be infused with spices, aromatics, herbs, and fruits or vegetables. They can be used on their own as a dressing for vegetables, pastas, grains, or fruits and, of course, they can be used in vinaigrettes and other dressing recipes for a very special effect.

Wilting

Salads and other preparations sometimes call for greens such as spinach or arugula to be wilted, or cooked briefly in a pan. Wilting is a technique similar to sautéing, but it is generally done over lower heat, and the greens are just heated through, not fully cooked. When wilting heartier greens, a small amount of cooking liquid, such as stock or broth, is sometimes added to the pan in addition to the fat. As vegetables are wilted, their color intensifies, their texture softens, and their volume greatly decreases.

the vinaigrette. The challenge of making a good vinaigrette is in achieving a balance between the acidic ingredient and the oil, so that the flavor of the acid comes through and is not dominated by the oil.

Basic Equipment for Salads

SALAD SPINNER. This hand-operated tool uses centrifugal force to spin the water away from the greens so that they have a better flavor and dressing clings evenly to them. Clean and sanitize the spinner carefully after each use. If a spinner is not available, drain the greens well, spread them out in thin layers on sheet pans, and air-dry inside a refrigerator.

POT. Use an appropriate-size pot to blanch or boil vegetables that will be included in a salad.

BOWL. Choose an appropriate-size bowl whenever coating salad ingredients with the dressing or tossing a green salad.

TONGS OR SPOON. Tongs or a spoon can be used to toss or stir the salad, coating the ingredients with the dressing.

WHISK. A whisk is a necessary tool for preparing a vinaigrette. The shape and motion of the whisk allow the oil and vinegar to be combined into a homogenous mixture.

MEASURING SPOONS AND CUPS. Accurate measuring is essential to properly preparing vinaigrettes and other dressings.

MAKING A VINAIGRETTE

1. To make a vinaigrette, first add the desired flavoring ingredients to the vinegar. Adding mustard, salt, pepper, herbs, or other flavorings to the vinegar is the best way to ensure that they will be evenly dispersed in the dressing.

2. While constantly whisking the vinegar, gradually add the oil in a thin stream to create a thick, emulsified vinaigrette.

3. If desired, crumbled cheese, fresh or dried fruits, vegetables, or other garnishes can be added to the vinaigrette at this point. Cover and refrigerate vinaigrettes when not in use. As the vinaigrette sits, it can begin to separate. Whisk or stir the vinaigrette before each use to recombine the oil and vinegar.

croutons

CROUTONS ARE OFTEN USED as a garnish for salads, as well as for soups and stews. Croustades, crostini, rusks, and bruschetta are all types of croutons. Some are cut into slices, others into cubes or disks. Some are toasted, some deep fried, some grilled, and some broiled. Good croutons are light in color, relatively greaseless, and well seasoned with a crisp, crunchy texture throughout.

- To make croutons, cut bread into the desired size. (Removing the crust is optional.) Rub, spray, or toss the cubes or slices lightly with oil or melted butter, if desired. Add salt and pepper.

- To toast croutons, spread them out in a single layer on a baking sheet. Bake at 400°F or toast them in the broiler. Turn them from time to time while in the oven to toast them evenly and to avoid scorching.

- To fry croutons, add the prepared bread to hot butter or oil in a sauté pan, fry until evenly browned, and drain well on paper towels.

- While the croutons are still hot, add any herbs or grated cheese as desired.

SANDWICHES

A SANDWICH CAN BE OPEN OR CLOSED, SMALL OR LARGE, HOT OR COLD. A sandwich constructed with a top and bottom slice of bread is known as a closed sandwich, while a sandwich built on only one slice of bread is known as an open-faced sandwich. Cold sandwiches include standard deli-style versions made from sliced meats or mayonnaise-dressed salads and club sandwiches, also known as triple-decker sandwiches. Hot sandwiches may feature a freshly cooked or heated filling, such as a hamburger or pastrami. Others are grilled, like a Reuben sandwich, melt, or Italian panini. Sometimes a hot filling is mounded on bread and the sandwich is topped with a hot sauce. Built from four simple elements—bread, a spread, a filling, and a garnish—sandwiches exemplify how a global approach to food can result in nearly endless variety.

The bread used for sandwiches runs a fairly wide gamut. Sliced white or wheat bread is often used to make cold sandwiches, but various other breads, buns, rolls, and wrappers can also be used.

Many sandwiches call for a spread to be applied directly to the bread. Spreads can be very subtly flavored, or they may themselves bring a special flavor and texture to the sandwich. A fat-based spread, such as mayonnaise or butter, provides a barrier to keep the bread from getting soggy. Other spreads can add moisture to a sandwich and help it hold together as it is eaten. Some sandwich fillings include the spread, such as a mayonnaise-dressed chicken or tuna salad.

The filling is the focus of any sandwich. The filling will determine how all the other elements of the sandwich are selected and prepared. Fillings may be substantial, like roasted meats or pan-fried fish, or minimal, like sliced cheese. It is as important to properly roast and slice turkey for club sandwiches as it is to be certain that the watercress for tea sandwiches is perfectly fresh and completely rinsed and dried.

Lettuce leaves, slices of tomato or onion, sprouts, marinated peppers, and olives are just a few of the many ingredients that can be used to garnish a sandwich. These garnishes become part of the sandwich's overall structure, so always consider the way they will complement or contrast the main filling. You may also choose to include a side garnish with a sandwich, such as sliced fruit, a pickle spear, or sprouts.

Basic Equipment for Sandwiches

SERRATED KNIFE. A sharp serrated knife is the perfect tool for slicing a loaf of bread for sandwiches. The serrated edge can cleanly slice a fine-grained bread without smashing or ripping it.

CHEF'S OR SLICING KNIFE. Depending on the type of sandwich, you may need to trim, chop, slice, or otherwise prepare a number of different types of vegetables or fruits as well as meat, poultry, fish, or seafood. Have a sharpened chef's or slicing knife ready to do these basic preparations.

MEASURING CUPS AND SPOONS. Accurate measuring is essential when preparing mayonnaise and other spreads for sandwiches.

EXPERT tips

WHEN ASSEMBLING sandwiches, everything should be at arm's reach. Slice bread, buns, or rolls and have any spreads prepared before you start.

GRILLED SANDWICHES can often be fully assembled in advance, held in the refrigerator, and then grilled when you're ready to serve them.

BY ADDING other flavoring ingredients or garnishes, a basic mayonnaise (see recipe page 316) can be transformed into a different sauce. Any of the following ingredients can be used:

  Capers

  Garlic

  Minced herbs

  Spices

  Crumbled cheese

  Prepared mustard

  Vegetable purée

  Worcestershire sauce

  Hot sauce

SOME SANDWICHES BENEFIT from being pressed, or weighted down, against the griddle as they cook, as shown below.

WHISK. A whisk is a necessary tool for preparing mayonnaise, vinaigrette, and some other sandwich spreads. The shape and motion of the whisk allow the fat and acidic ingredient to be combined into a homogenous mixture.

SPATULA. Use a spatula to evenly cover the entire surface of the bread with the sandwich spread.

GRILL OR BROILER. A grill or broiler may be used to cook an individual ingredient of a sandwich, such as grilled onions or broiled fish, or to heat the entire sandwich after it is assembled.

Chef's Lesson
MAKING MAYONNAISE

1. To make mayonnaise, whisk egg yolks with vinegar or lemon juice to loosen the yolks and prepare them to combine with oil.

2. Add oil to the egg yolks, a little at a time, while whisking constantly. The oil must be gradually whipped into the egg yolks so that it gets broken up into very fine droplets. If the oil is added too quickly, the droplets will be too large to emulsify properly, and the mayonnaise will look lumpy or broken.

3. The thickness and flavor of the mayonnaise can be adjusted by adding a bit more acid or water as you incorporate the oil. Add more lemon juice, vinegar, or water if the mayonnaise starts to get too thick. A properly made mayonnaise has a mild and balanced flavor, without any predominance of acidic or oily taste.

Wilted Spinach Salad with Warm Bacon Vinaigrette

VINAIGRETTE

4 bacon strips

2 tbsp minced shallot

1 tsp minced garlic

¼ cup packed brown sugar

3 tbsp apple cider vinegar

¼ cup plus 2 tbsp vegetable oil

Salt, as needed

Cracked black peppercorns, as needed

11 cups spinach

3 Hard-Cooked Eggs (page 330), **cut into small dice**

1⅓ cups sliced mushrooms

⅓ cup thinly sliced red onion

1½ cups croutons (see page 294)

1. To make the vinaigrette, cook the bacon in a medium pan over medium-low heat. When the bacon is crisp and the fat has rendered, remove the bacon from the pan and transfer to paper towels to drain and cool. When cool, dice the bacon and reserve.

2. In the same pan, add the shallots and garlic to the bacon fat and cook over low heat until soft and translucent. Stir in the brown sugar. Remove the pan from the heat. Add the vinegar and oil, and whisk thoroughly. Season with salt and cracked peppercorns.

3. In a large bowl, toss the spinach with the hard-cooked eggs, mushrooms, onion, croutons, and the reserved bacon. Slowly pour the warm vinaigrette over the salad, toss gently, and serve immediately.

BARLEY SALAD WITH CUCUMBER AND MINT

MAKES 5 SERVINGS

1 cup pearl barley

1 cup small-dice tomatoes

1 cup small-dice seeded cucumber

¾ cup roasted small-dice eggplant

1 cup chopped flat-leaf parsley

¼ cup chopped mint

½ cup thinly sliced green onions

1 tbsp grated lemon zest

¼ cup fresh lemon juice

1 tsp salt

½ tsp freshly ground black pepper

⅔ cup extra-virgin olive oil

1. Put the barley in a medium bowl, cover with cold water, and set aside to soak for 30 minutes.

2. Drain the barley well and transfer to a medium pot. Add enough salted water to cover the barley by 1 inch. Bring the barley and water to a boil over high heat, then reduce the heat to low and simmer until tender, 40 to 50 minutes.

3. Drain the barley and rinse with cold water. Drain well again and cool completely.

4. Combine the barley, tomatoes, cucumber, eggplant, parsley, mint, and green onions in a large bowl and toss until well mixed.

5. Combine the lemon zest, lemon juice, salt, and pepper in a small bowl. Whisking constantly, slowly pour the olive oil into the bowl.

6. Pour the dressing over the barley mixture and toss. Serve immediately or refrigerate for later use.

GERMAN-STYLE POTATO SALAD

5 cups cooked, peeled, and sliced waxy potatoes, warm

½ cup small-dice onion

3 tbsp red wine vinegar

½ cup Chicken Stock (page 38)

1½ tbsp prepared mustard, plus more as needed

1 tsp sugar, plus more as needed

Salt, as needed

Freshly ground black pepper, as needed

3 tbsp vegetable oil

5 bacon strips, cooked and cut into small dice

1 tbsp chopped flat-leaf parsley or chives

1. Place the warm potatoes in a large bowl.

2. In a medium pan over medium-high heat, combine the onion, vinegar, and stock and bring the mixture to a boil. Add the mustard and sugar, season with salt and pepper, and whisk until well combined. Adjust the seasoning as needed.

3. Reduce the heat to medium, slowly stir in the oil, and heat for 2 minutes. Immediately pour the hot dressing over the warm potato slices. Add the bacon and toss together.

4. Sprinkle the salad with the parsley or chives and toss gently. Let the salad stand for at least 1 hour before serving at room temperature, or refrigerate for later use.

ENDIVE SALAD WITH BLUE CHEESE AND WALNUTS

MAKES 5 SERVINGS

DRESSING

1 tbsp fresh lemon juice

1 tbsp hazelnut oil

1½ tsp chopped tarragon

Salt, as needed

Freshly ground black pepper, as needed

2 cups Belgian endive

⅓ cup roughly chopped toasted walnuts

½ cup crumbled blue cheese (such as Roquefort)

1. To make the dressing, combine the lemon juice, oil, and tarragon in a small bowl and whisk together to combine. Season with salt and pepper and let sit for 30 minutes.

2. Separate the endive by gently peeling off each leaf. Wash the leaves thoroughly under cold running water and pat dry with paper towels. Transfer to a large salad bowl. Add the walnuts and cheese and toss gently.

3. Add the dressing and toss until the endive, walnuts, and cheese are thoroughly coated. Serve immediately.

THAI SEAFOOD SALAD

DRESSING

2 tsp Thai chile paste (nam prik pao)

¼ cup fish sauce, plus more as needed

¼ cup fresh lime juice

1 tbsp sugar, plus more as needed

2 Thai bird chiles, minced

2 lemongrass stalks, white and light green parts only, very finely minced

2 shallots, halved lengthwise, cut into ⅛-inch slices

1 lb shrimp (26/30), peeled, deveined, and cut in half lengthwise

1 lb squid, cleaned and cut into bite-size pieces

4 red Fresno chiles, seeded and julienned

1 red bell pepper, seeded and julienned

¼ cup coarsely chopped cilantro

¼ cup coarsely chopped mint

Salt, as needed

1. To make the dressing, in a large bowl, whisk together the chile paste, fish sauce, lime juice, sugar, Thai bird chiles, and lemongrass until the sugar has dissolved. Stir in the shallots.

2. Place the shrimp and squid in a steamer insert over a pot of barely simmering water, and cook until the flesh loses its translucency and takes on an opaque appearance, about 4 minutes. Be very careful not to overcook. (See page 94 for more information on steaming.) Add the steamed shrimp and squid to the dressing and toss together while still warm. Let the mixture cool slightly.

3. Add the Fresno chiles and bell pepper and toss to coat with the dressing. Add the cilantro and mint. If necessary, adjust the seasoning with additional fish sauce, sugar, and salt. Cover and transfer to the refrigerator until chilled. Serve cold.

ONION AND CUCUMBER SALAD

3 cups medium-dice onion

1 seedless cucumber, cut into medium dice

1 cup seeded, medium-dice plum tomatoes

5 Thai bird chiles, chopped

2 tbsp chopped cilantro leaves and stems

Juice of 2 lemons

Salt, as needed

1. In a large salad bowl, combine the onion, cucumber, tomatoes, chiles, and cilantro. Refrigerate until needed.

2. Just before serving, strain any excess liquid that may have collected at the bottom of the bowl, season the salad with the lemon juice and salt, and toss gently. Serve immediately.

SHERRIED WATERCRESS AND APPLE SALAD

3 tbsp sherry vinegar

5 tsp minced shallots

1 tsp packed brown sugar

Salt, as needed

Freshly ground black pepper, as needed

⅓ cup vegetable oil

9½ cups watercress, cleaned and stemmed

1 cup peeled, cored, and julienned Golden Delicious apples

⅓ cup minced celery

¼ cup chopped, toasted walnuts

1. In a very large bowl, combine the vinegar, shallots, and sugar. Season with salt and pepper.

2. Gradually add the vegetable oil in a steady stream, whisking constantly until emulsified.

3. Add the watercress, apples, and celery to the bowl, and toss gently using a lifting motion until the greens are evenly coated.

4. Transfer to chilled plates, and garnish each salad with some of the walnuts.

Celeriac and Tart Apple Salad

2 tbsp fresh lemon juice

1 lb celeriac

Aciduated water, as needed (see Note)

DRESSING

3 tbsp Mayonnaise (page 316)

2 tbsp crème fraîche or sour cream

2 tbsp Dijon mustard

1 tbsp fresh lemon juice, plus more as needed

Salt, as needed

Freshly ground black pepper, as needed

2 cups peeled, cored, and diced Granny Smith apples

1. Bring a large pot of salted water to a boil and add the lemon juice. Prepare a bowl of ice water.

2. Peel the celeriac and cut it into long, thin strips or matchsticks. Place the cut celeriac into the aciduated water until ready to cook.

3. Boil the celeriac for about 3 minutes or until tender. Drain and plunge into the ice water. Drain again on paper towels to ensure that it is dry.

4. To make the dressing, in a small bowl, combine the mayonnaise, crème fraîche or sour cream, mustard, and lemon juice in a bowl and mix well. Season with salt and pepper.

5. Fold the celeriac and apples together in a large bowl, pour in the dressing, and gently toss.

6. Adjust the seasoning with additional salt, pepper, and lemon juice. Serve immediately, or refrigerate for later use.

NOTE *Celeriac discolors quickly once it is cut, so to prevent browning, place the cut celeriac into aciduated water (a mixture of water, flour, and an acid such as lemon juice) until ready to cook.*

Southwestern Slaw

1 lb green cabbage

Salt, as needed

2 tbsp fresh lime juice

2 tbsp honey

½ cup finely minced red onion

2 tsp seeded, finely minced jalapeño

¼ cup coarsely chopped cilantro

Freshly ground black pepper, as needed

1. Cut the cabbage into chunks and pulse it in a food processor until coarsely chopped.

2. In a large mixing bowl, thoroughly mix the chopped cabbage with 2 tablespoons of salt and allow the mixture to sit for about 15 minutes.

3. Rinse the cabbage and squeeze out the excess moisture. Combine the cabbage with the lime juice, honey, onion, jalapeño, and cilantro. Season with salt and pepper. Serve immediately.

Moroccan Carrot Salad

¼ cup fresh lemon juice

1 tbsp finely chopped cilantro

1½ tsp sugar

¼ cup extra-virgin olive oil

6 tbsp raisins, plumped and drained (see Note)

5 cups finely grated carrots

Salt, as needed

Freshly ground black pepper, as needed

1. In a medium bowl, combine the lemon juice, cilantro, and sugar. Whisking constantly, slowly pour the oil into the bowl in a thin, steady stream until completely emulsified.

2. Add the raisins and carrots to the dressing and toss until evenly coated. Season with salt and pepper. Serve immediately or refrigerate for later use.

NOTE *To plump raisins, cover them with water or a flavorful liquid such as apple cider or juice in a small bowl. Soak for 20 minutes, then drain.*

Sweet-and-Spicy Bulgur

MAKES 6 SERVINGS

1 tbsp olive oil, plus more as needed

2 cups cherry tomatoes

½ cup sun-dried tomatoes, minced

Salt, as needed

2 garlic cloves, minced

1½ cups bulgur wheat

2 cups water

¼ tsp red pepper flakes

2 tbsp fresh lemon juice

2 tsp honey

Freshly ground black pepper, as needed

1. Heat the oil in a large skillet over medium-high heat. Add the cherry tomatoes and sauté until softened, about 5 minutes.

2. Add the sun-dried tomatoes and continue cooking for 2 to 3 minutes more. Season with salt.

3. Reduce the heat to medium-low. Add the garlic and bulgur and sauté until fragrant, 1 to 2 minutes.

4. Add the water and bring to a boil over medium heat. Reduce the heat to low and simmer until the bulgur is tender, about 35 minutes.

5. Fluff the bulgur with a fork. Season with the red pepper flakes, lemon juice, honey, and black pepper. Serve warm.

NOTE *This dish can be made a little sweeter by adding more honey, but be careful not to add too much—some honeys have a very strong flavor. Taste along the way to achieve the right balance of sweet and spicy.*

MILLET À LA JARDINERA

MAKES 4 SERVINGS

1 cup millet

2 cups water, plus more as needed

2 tbsp butter

1 serrano, seeded and minced

1 cup small-dice green bell peppers

1 cup small-dice red bell peppers

1 shallot, minced

1½ tsp peeled, finely minced ginger

½ cup small-dice carrot

½ cup small-dice celery

Salt, as needed

Freshly ground black pepper, as needed

2 scallions, minced

1 tbsp chopped parsley

2 tsp chopped thyme

2 tbsp chopped oregano

1. Combine the millet with the water, bring to a simmer, and simmer until the millet is barely cooked, 4 to 5 minutes. Pour the cooked millet into a strainer and drain the excess water.

2. Transfer the millet to a large baking sheet, spread it out, and allow to cool. Using a fork, fluff the millet occasionally while cooling.

3. Melt the butter in a large sauté pan over medium heat. Add the chile, bell peppers, shallot, ginger, carrot, and celery. Season with salt and black pepper and sweat the vegetables until just beginning to soften.

4. Add the millet and continue to cook until heated through, adding water to help the reheating process, if needed.

5. Garnish with the scallions, parsley, thyme, and oregano, and serve.

NOTE *This flavorful side dish works well with nearly any grain—try it with couscous or wild rice. See the chart on page 262 for cooking times for other grains.*

GIARDINIERA

MAKES 4 PINTS

6 fresh serranos, thinly sliced

1 red bell pepper, seeded and sliced into strips

3 celery stalks, diced

2 carrots, cut into small dice or brunoise

½ head cauliflower, stems removed and chopped into small florets

½ cup kosher salt

3 garlic cloves, smashed

2 tsp dried oregano

1 tsp red pepper flakes

½ tsp celery seed

Pinch of freshly ground pepper

1 cup apple cider vinegar

1 cup olive oil

1. In a large bowl, toss together the serranos, bell pepper, celery, carrots, and cauliflower. Add the salt and toss to combine.

2. Pour enough water on top to cover the vegetables, cover with plastic wrap, and refrigerate overnight.

3. Drain the vegetables and rinse briefly. Pack the vegetables into pint jars or other airtight containers.

4. In a large bowl, combine the garlic, oregano, red pepper flakes, celery seed, pepper, and vinegar. Slowly whisk in the oil.

5. Pour the brine over the vegetables in the jars, cover, and let cool completely before serving. If not serving immediately, refrigerate up to 3 weeks.

CRACKED WHEAT AND TOMATO SALAD

MAKES 5 SERVINGS

1½ cups cracked wheat

3 cups peeled, seeded, medium-dice tomatoes

1¼ cups medium-dice red onion

⅓ cup small-dice fresh mozzarella

2 tbsp red wine vinegar

2 tbsp chopped oregano

2 tbsp chopped basil

2 tsp red pepper flakes

½ cup extra-virgin olive oil

1 tsp salt, plus more as needed

¼ tsp freshly ground black pepper

¼ cup grated Parmesan (optional)

1. Place the cracked wheat in a medium pot, cover with salted water, and bring to a simmer over medium heat. Continue to simmer until tender, 30 to 35 minutes. Remove from the heat and drain thoroughly. To ensure that all the water is gone, press gently to release any excess moisture. Set aside and allow the cracked wheat to cool at room temperature.

2. In a medium bowl, combine the tomatoes, onion, and mozzarella and mix gently.

3. In a large bowl, combine the vinegar, oregano, basil, and red pepper flakes. Gradually whisk in the oil. Season with salt and pepper. Add the tomato mixture and then the cooled cracked wheat. Toss gently.

4. Serve at room temperature or refrigerate until needed. If desired, garnish with the cheese before serving.

TABBOULEH

MAKES 5 SERVINGS

½ cup bulgur wheat

2 cups chopped parsley

½ cup chopped mint leaves

1 cup small-dice tomato

1 cup small-dice peeled cucumber

¼ cup olive oil

½ cup red wine vinegar or fresh lemon juice

½ cup chopped green onions

Salt, as needed

Freshly ground black pepper, as needed

1. Place the bulgur in a medium bowl. Bring 3 cups of water to a boil, pour over the bulgur, and cover the bowl with a lid or plate. Allow to stand for 30 minutes. Drain.

2. Combine the drained bulgur with all of the remaining ingredients and season with salt and pepper. Let the mixture chill in the refrigerator for at least 30 minutes before serving.

NOTE *For a slightly different flavor, replace the red wine vinegar with a combination of fresh lemon and orange juice, and add 2 teaspoons of finely grated lemon and orange zest.*

Red Wine Vinaigrette

1 cup red wine vinegar

2 tsp Dijon mustard (optional)

1 tbsp plus 2 tsp minced shallots

Salt, as needed

Freshly ground black pepper, as needed

2 tsp sugar, plus more as needed

3 cups olive oil or canola oil

2 tbsp minced herbs, such as chives, parsley, oregano, basil, or tarragon (optional)

1. In a medium bowl, combine the vinegar, mustard, if using, the shallots, salt, pepper, and sugar. Gradually whisk in the oil.

2. Stir in the herbs, if using, and adjust the seasoning with additional salt, pepper, and sugar. Use immediately or refrigerate for later use.

Wheat Berries with Oranges, Cherries, and Pecans

1½ cups orange segments and reserved juices

1 tsp chopped thyme

1 tsp chopped rosemary

½ tsp chopped sage

2 tbsp Champagne vinegar

2 tbsp extra-virgin olive oil

1½ tsp salt

½ tsp freshly ground black pepper

1¼ cups wheat berries, cooked

3 tbsp dried cherries, plus more as needed

⅓ cup pecans, toasted, plus more as needed

1. In a medium bowl, whisk together the orange juice, thyme, rosemary, sage, and vinegar. Gradually whisk in the oil. Whisk in the salt and pepper.

2. Add the wheat berries, cherries, pecans, and orange segments. Toss lightly, as these ingredients bruise easily.

3. Garnish with additional cherries and pecans, if desired. Serve immediately.

Panzanella

3 cups large-dice tomatoes

3 cups celery hearts, sliced thinly on the diagonal

2 cups stale or toasted Italian bread, torn into medium pieces

1½ cups medium-dice seeded cucumbers

1 cup medium-dice red bell peppers

1 cup medium-dice yellow bell peppers

20 anchovy fillets, thinly sliced (optional)

¼ cup chopped basil

3 tsp minced garlic

2 tbsp brined capers, drained and rinsed

1½ cups **Red Wine Vinaigrette** (page 309), plus more as needed

In a large bowl, combine the tomatoes, celery, bread, cucumbers, peppers, anchovies, if using, and the basil, garlic, and capers. Add the vinaigrette and toss to coat evenly, adding more dressing if needed. Serve the salad immediately or refrigerate for later use.

CROQUE MONSIEUR

10 slices Gruyère

5 thin slices ham

10 slices white Pullman bread

2 tbsp Dijon mustard

½ cup (8 tbsp/1 stick) butter, softened

1. Preheat the oven to 350°F.

2. For each sandwich, place 1 slice of the cheese and 1 slice of the ham on each of 5 slices of bread. Spread lightly with mustard. Place another slice of cheese on top and close with a second slice of bread. Lightly butter the top and bottom of each assembled sandwich.

3. Lightly butter a pan and place over medium heat. Cook the sandwiches, in batches as needed, until golden brown on both sides. If necessary, place the sandwiches on a baking sheet and continue cooking in the oven until the cheese has melted. Serve immediately.

Facing page: Croque Monsieur with Cream of Tomato Soup (page 53)

GRILLED VEGETABLE SANDWICH WITH MANCHEGO

MAKES 5 SERVINGS

1 medium chayote squash

Salt, as needed

2 eggplant, cut into ¼-inch slices

1 cup olive oil

1½ tbsp Dijon mustard

2½ tbsp minced garlic

1 tbsp seeded, minced serrano chile

2 tbsp chopped thyme

1 tbsp chopped oregano

Freshly ground black pepper, as needed

2 cups sliced red onion

2 cups roasted, peeled, halved, and seeded red bell peppers

1 cup roasted, peeled, halved, and seeded poblano chiles

10 portobello mushrooms, stems removed

5 hoagie rolls

1¼ cups Tapenade (page 83)

15 thin slices Manchego

1. In a medium pot over medium heat, simmer the squash in salted water until tender when pierced with a knife; the knife should slide out with little resistance. Drain and set aside to cool. When cool, cut the squash into ¼-inch slices. Discard the pits.

2. Lightly salt the eggplant slices on each side and drain in a colander for 30 minutes. Rinse the eggplant thoroughly under cold water, then blot dry on paper towels.

3. To make the marinade, in a small bowl mix together the oil, mustard, garlic, serrano, thyme, oregano, salt, and black pepper.

4. Place the chayote, eggplant, onion, bell peppers, chiles, and mushrooms in a large container.

5. Pour the marinade over the vegetable mixture and turn the vegetables until evenly coated. Cover and refrigerate for 2 hours or up to overnight.

6. Preheat the oven to 350°F. Preheat a grill to high heat.

7. Just before grilling, shake off the extra marinade from the vegetables to avoid flare-ups. Set aside the roasted peppers and chiles. Grill the chayote, eggplant, onion, and mushrooms on both sides over high heat. The vegetables should have visible grill marks and should not be mushy.

8. Transfer the vegetables, including the peppers and chiles, to a baking pan and bake in the oven for 10 minutes, or until the vegetables are soft to the touch. Reduce the oven temperature to 250°F.

9. Remove the mushrooms and slice them on the diagonal into ¼-inch-thick slices. Transfer all of the vegetables to a container and reserve at room temperature.

10. For each sandwich, slice open a roll. Spread a thin layer of tapenade on the cut surfaces. Layer with mushrooms, onion, poblanos, bell peppers, eggplant, and chayote. Top with 3 cheese slices. Top with the other half of the roll.

11. Place the sandwiches on a baking pan and warm them for 10 to 15 minutes in the oven. Serve immediately.

Mayonnaise

2 pasteurized egg yolks

1 tbsp water

1 tbsp white wine vinegar

1 tsp dry mustard or 2 tsp prepared mustard

¼ tsp sugar

1½ cups vegetable oil (see Note)

Salt, as needed

Ground white pepper, as needed

1 tbsp fresh lemon juice

1. Combine the egg yolks, water, vinegar, mustard, and sugar in a bowl. Mix well with a balloon whisk until the mixture is slightly foamy.

2. Gradually add the oil in a thin, steady stream, whisking constantly, until the oil is incorporated and the mayonnaise is emulsified, smooth, and thick.

3. Season with salt, white pepper, and the lemon juice.

4. Use the mayonnaise immediately, or refrigerate in a clean airtight container for later use.

NOTE *Olive oil or mild peanut oil may be substituted for some or all of the vegetable oil.*

ANCHOVY-CAPER MAYONNAISE *To the prepared mayonnaise, add 2 tbsp fresh lemon juice, 2 tsp Dijon mustard, 2 tbsp minced shallot, ¼ cup chopped flat-leaf parsley, ¼ cup minced, drained nonpareil capers, and 3 minced anchovy fillets. Adjust the seasoning with salt and pepper.*

TARTAR SAUCE *To 3 cups of prepared mayonnaise, add 1 cup drained sweet pickle relish, ¼ cup minced drained capers, and 1 small-dice Hard-Cooked Egg (page 330). Season with Worcestershire sauce, hot sauce, salt, and pepper.*

GREEN MAYONNAISE *Purée 1 cup spinach leaves and ¼ cup each chopped parsley, tarragon, chives, and dill in a blender. Mix the purée with the prepared mayonnaise and ¼ cup fresh lemon juice. Adjust the consistency with water, if necessary. Adjust the seasoning with salt and pepper.*

Falafel Sandwiches

1 cup dried chickpeas, soaked overnight (see page 257)

1 cup dried fava beans, soaked for 48 hours (see page 257)

1 bunch parsley, chopped

2 green onions, finely chopped

1 tsp cayenne pepper

1 tbsp ground cumin

1 tsp ground coriander

4 garlic cloves, crushed with salt to form a paste

2 tsp salt

1 tsp baking powder

½ cup sesame seeds

5 cups vegetable oil, plus more as needed

5 pita breads

10 leaves or one small head romaine lettuce, thinly sliced

2 cups thinly sliced green cabbage

1 medium cucumber, seeded and cut into 1-inch-thick slices

½ cup finely chopped red onion

½ cup roughly chopped Kalamata olives

¼ cup crumbled feta cheese

5 tbsp tahini

1. Drain the soaked chickpeas and beans. Rinse, drain, and blot dry between layers of paper towels.

2. In a food processor, process together the chickpeas, beans, parsley, green onions, cayenne, cumin, coriander, garlic, salt, and baking powder in batches until the mixture is thoroughly blended. Stir in the sesame seeds by hand.

3. Form the mixture into balls 1 inch in diameter. Slightly flatten the balls with the palm of your hand and set aside on a baking sheet lined with parchment paper.

4. In a large, deep pot or deep fryer, heat the oil until it registers 350°F on a deep-fry thermometer. Add the falafel, in batches if necessary, and deep fry until crisp and brown, about 4 minutes.

5. Using a slotted spoon or skimmer, transfer the falafel to paper towels to drain briefly.

6. Cut the top inch off of each pita bread. In a bowl, toss together the lettuce, cabbage, cucumber, red onion, olives, and feta cheese and divide the mixture evenly among the pita breads. Top each with about a tablespoon of tahini. Add a few falafel patties to each pocket and top with additional sauce as desired. Serve immediately.

COOKING EGGS

Eggs can be cooked in the shell, poached, fried, or scrambled, or prepared as omelets or custards. Using fresh eggs is important to ensure the best flavor and quality of the finished dish. The top grade of eggs, AA, indicates that the eggs are fresh. They should have a white that does not spread excessively once the egg is cracked and a yolk that rides high on the white's surface.

Basic Equipment for Cooking Eggs

POT. Choose an appropriate-size pot for cooking eggs in the shell and poaching eggs, as well as for baked and stirred custards, creams, and puddings.

PAN. Frying eggs, scrambling eggs, and making omelets require a small sauté pan. For flat omelets, use a larger, deeper ovenproof pan.

INSTANT-READ THERMOMETER. The water temperature is vital to successfully poaching eggs. Monitor the temperature with an instant-read thermometer.

CUPS OR BOWLS. In order to check for blood spots or other imperfections and to avoid breaks and spills, always crack raw eggs into a cup or bowl before adding them to the pot, pan, or other vessel.

SLOTTED SPOON OR SKIMMER. When poaching eggs, use a slotted spoon or skimmer to retrieve the cooked eggs from the pot of water.

SPATULA. A spatula is the perfect tool for turning fried eggs over in the pan and for transferring them to the plate.

WOODEN SPOON OR HEATPROOF RUBBER OR SILICONE SPATULA. When preparing scrambled eggs, a wooden spoon or heatproof rubber spatula should be used to stir the eggs as they cook. The flexibility of a heatproof rubber spatula makes it the perfect tool for making folded omelets.

FORK OR WHISK. A fork or small whisk can be used to beat eggs that will be used to prepare omelets, scrambled eggs, and custards.

PARING KNIFE. A paring knife can be used to trim any irregular edges off the whites of poached eggs.

RAMEKINS OR BAKING DISHES. Ramekins or other small baking dishes and pans are used to mold baked custards.

OFFSET METAL SPATULA. A small offset metal spatula is a helpful tool for cleanly unmolding baked custards for serving.

COOKING EGGS IN THE SHELL

EGGS ARE COOKED IN THE SHELL to make hard-cooked, soft-cooked, and coddled eggs. Although hard-cooked eggs are often called hard-boiled eggs, all eggs prepared in the shell should actually be cooked at a bare simmer for the best results. They may be served directly in the shell or they may be shelled and used to make another preparation, such as Deviled Eggs (page 331).

Check each egg carefully and discard any with cracked shells. Eggs should always be properly refrigerated until you are ready to cook them.

When cooking eggs in the shell, start timing the cooking only once the water reaches a simmer and cook to the desired doneness. For example, a 3-minute egg cooks for 3 minutes from the time the water returns to a simmer after the egg has been added to the water. If the timing is started when the water is cold, the egg will not be properly cooked. Simmer hard-cooked eggs for 10 to 12 minutes. Alternatively, the water and eggs can be brought to a simmer and then removed from the heat; the residual heat will cook the eggs.

The yolks of properly cooked soft-cooked eggs are warm but still runny, while those of medium-cooked eggs are partially coagulated. Properly hard-cooked eggs are completely and evenly coagulated, with firm but tender (not tough) whites and no unsightly green ring surrounding the yolk.

Hard-cooked eggs are easiest to peel while they are still warm. Place them under cold running water until they are cool enough to handle. Gently press down and roll the egg over a countertop to crack the shell before peeling. Peel the shell and membrane away with your fingers.

> **EXPERT tip**
>
> **THE GREEN RING** often found around the yolk of eggs cooked in the shell is the result of a chemical reaction between the iron and sulfur naturally present in eggs. Heat speeds up this reaction. The best way to prevent the green ring from forming is to watch the cooking time closely and not allow the eggs to cook longer than necessary. Quick cooling after cooking can also help keep the ring from forming.

1. Place the eggs in a pot with enough cold water to completely submerge them. It is common to have the water already at a simmer when preparing coddled and soft-cooked eggs. Hard-cooked eggs may be started in simmering or cold water.

2. Bring the water to a simmer. Do not allow it to boil rapidly. Water that is at or close to a simmer will allow the eggs to cook evenly without toughening the whites.

3. Start timing the cooking only once the water has returned to a simmer. Cook the eggs to the desired doneness.

POACHING EGGS

EGGS ARE MOST OFTEN POACHED IN WATER, though other liquids such as wine, stock, or cream can also be used. Add vinegar and salt to the water to encourage the egg protein to set faster. Otherwise, the egg whites can spread too much before they coagulate.

Poached eggs can be prepared in advance. To do this, slightly undercook the eggs, shock them in ice water to stop the cooking process, trim the edges of the whites, and hold them in cold water. When ready to serve, reheat the eggs by briefly submerging them in simmering water.

1

Chef's Lesson
POACHING EGGS

1. Fill a pan with water to a depth of a few inches and season it with a small amount of vinegar and salt to prevent the egg whites from spreading during cooking. The vinegar and salt should be barely perceptible, not enough that the poached egg tastes strongly of either.

Working in small batches is more efficient, since the more eggs added to the water, the more time it will take to properly poach them. To reduce the chance of breaking an egg in the poaching liquid, break the eggs into cups. Discard any eggs that have blood spots on the yolks. Gently pour the egg from the cup into the poaching liquid.

2. Once added, the egg will sink to the bottom of the pot, then float back to the top. The white will set around the yolk to create a teardrop shape.

It generally takes 3 to 4 minutes to poach an egg properly, depending on its size. The more eggs added to the water at a time, the longer it will take for the eggs to poach properly.

3. Use a slotted spoon or skimmer to gently lift the poached egg from the water. Blot the egg on paper towels to remove as much excess water as possible.

4. A properly poached egg should have a fully coagulated egg white and a warm center that is only partially set, and should be tender with a compact oval shape.

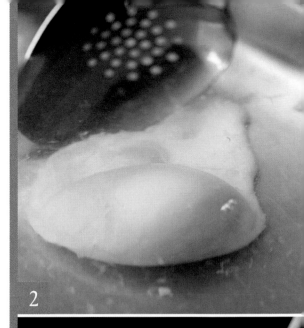

EXPERT tips

THE SHAPE OF THE POACHED EGG can be affected by its handling prior to and during the cooking process. For the perfect shape, handle the eggs carefully when removing them from the shell, when dropping them into the water, and when removing the finished poached eggs from the pot. This will lessen the chances for the yolk to break prior to the cooking process, as well as prevent an undesirable or messy appearance.

IF THE OUTER EDGES OF THE POACHED EGG WHITE look irregular or messy, use a paring knife to gently trim the edges before serving.

FRYING EGGS

TO PREPARE EGGS FOR FRYING, break them into clean cups. Any eggs with broken yolks can be reserved for another use. Refrigerate the shelled eggs. (This may be done up to 1 hour before cooking.)

Using very fresh eggs is the only way to ensure a rich flavor and good appearance in the final product. When the egg is fried, the white should hold together in a neat shape and the yolk is more likely to stay intact.

Use oils, butter, or rendered bacon fat for frying, even if using a nonstick pan or griddle. These cooking fats not only lubricate the pan, but they can also add their own distinct flavor. For the best flavor, eggs should be seasoned with salt and pepper as they cook.

If the heat is too low, the egg will stick; if it is too high, the edges of the white may blister and brown before the rest of the egg is properly cooked. Eggs are done once the whites have coagulated; the yolks may be soft and runny or set, depending on personal preference.

OVER-EASY EGGS

Cooking over-easy eggs can be an intimidating task for some cooks, but it is actually a very simple method. First, break the egg into a cup. Heat the fat in a pan over medium-high heat until it is very hot but not smoking. Slide or pour the egg into the pan, and immediately reduce the heat to medium-low. Fry the egg, shaking the pan occasionally to keep it from sticking, until the white becomes opaque. Carefully turn the egg over using a heatproof or metal spatula and cook for about 30 seconds on the second side.

Fried eggs should be served with the yolks intact. If you are worried about breaking the yolk, instead of flipping the egg over, use a spoon to baste the egg with the hot fat in order to set the top side.

Chef's Lesson
FRYING EGGS

1. Place a frying pan over medium heat. Add the fat and continue to heat until the fat is hot.

2. Slide or pour the cracked egg out of the cup and into the pan.

3. For eggs cooked over easy or over hard, flip the egg over using a spatula halfway through cooking. Alternatively, for sunny-side-up eggs, baste the egg with the hot fat to set the top.

SCRAMBLING EGGS

FOR SCRAMBLING, CHOOSE EGGS THAT ARE FRESH, WITH SHELLS INTACT. Scrambled eggs can be seasoned with salt and pepper and flavored or garnished with fresh herbs, cheese, sautéed vegetables, smoked fish, or truffles. Adding a small amount of water or stock (about 2 teaspoons per egg) to the beaten eggs will make them puffier as the water turns to steam during cooking. Milk or cream may also be used to enrich the eggs before scrambling.

Eggs can be scrambled in a sauté pan or on a griddle. Nonstick surfaces make it easy to prepare scrambled eggs with a minimum amount of added fat. Black steel pans are appropriate, as long as they are properly maintained and seasoned. If possible, reserve pans used for eggs for that use only. A heatproof rubber spatula, wooden spoon, or spatula can be used to stir the eggs as they cook.

Properly prepared scrambled eggs have a moist texture, creamy consistency, and delicate flavor. Moisture weeping from the eggs indicates that they were overcooked.

LIQUID CAN BE USED to modify the texture of scrambled eggs. Liquids to consider include:

> Water
>
> Stock
>
> Milk
>
> Heavy cream

GARNISHING SCRAMBLED EGGS is a great way to introduce flavor and texture. Depending on the desired result, any of the following can be added:

> Spices
>
> Fresh herbs
>
> Grated cheese
>
> Cooked bacon, ham, or sausage
>
> Prepared vegetables

Chef's Lesson
SCRAMBLING EGGS

1. Crack the eggs and stir them with a fork or whisk until the yolks and whites are combined into a smooth, homogenous mixture. Add liquid, if using, and seasonings.

2. Heat the pan and the cooking fat over medium heat.

3. Pour the eggs into the pan; they should begin to coagulate almost immediately. Reduce the heat to low. Using the back of a wooden spoon or heatproof rubber spatula, stir the eggs as they cook. Keep both the pan and the spoon in motion to produce small, softly set curds. The lower the heat and the more constant the agitation, the creamier the finished scrambled eggs will be. In fact, they may be prepared by stirring them constantly over a water bath to prevent browning altogether.

4. Once the eggs are almost completely set, add garnishes, cheeses, or flavoring ingredients. Fold these ingredients in over low heat, just until incorporated. Remove the eggs from the heat when slightly underdone; they will continue to cook slightly from the heat they retain.

MAKING OMELETS

THE ROLLED (FRENCH-STYLE) OMELET starts out like scrambled eggs, but when the eggs start to set, they are rolled over. A folded (American-style) omelet is prepared in much the same way, but instead of being rolled, it is simply folded in half. Known variously as farmer-style omelets, frittatas (Italian), or tortillas (Spanish), flat omelets are a baked version that is denser and easier to slice into servings.

When making any type of omelet, choose eggs that are fresh, with shells intact. Season omelets with salt, pepper, and herbs. Butter is the most common cooking fat, although vegetable oils also work well.

Omelets may be filled or garnished with cheese, sautéed vegetables, cooked potatoes, meats, and smoked fish, among other things. These fillings and garnishes must be incorporated at the appropriate point to be certain that they are fully cooked and hot when the eggs have finished cooking. Grated or crumbled cheeses will melt sufficiently from the heat of the eggs and are often added just before an omelet is rolled or folded.

Chef's Lesson
MAKING OMELETS

1. Consider the size of the pan in relation to the size of the omelet you are making. A pan that is too large or too small with have an ill effect on the end result. Ensure that there is enough fat in the pan to keep the omelet from sticking but not so much that the omelet will not set.

Crack the eggs for an omelet into a bowl. Using a fork or whisk, blend the eggs until the whites and yolks are combined. Add a liquid, if using, and season as desired.

Add the fat to the pan and allow it to heat over high heat. Before adding the eggs, the fat should appear lightly hazy but should not be smoking.

Add the eggs to the pan. At the beginning of cooking, stir the eggs constantly with a spatula to encourage even cooking. As the eggs become set, gently shake the pan to evenly spread the eggs or use a spatula to spread them out flat on the bottom of the pan. Make sure that the omelet is of a uniform thickness or it will cook unevenly.

2. Add the desired garnishes.

EXPERT tip

GARNISHING AN OMELET is a way to introduce flavor and texture. Any of the following can be added:

Spices

Fresh herbs

Grated cheese

Cooked bacon, ham, or sausage

Prepared vegetables

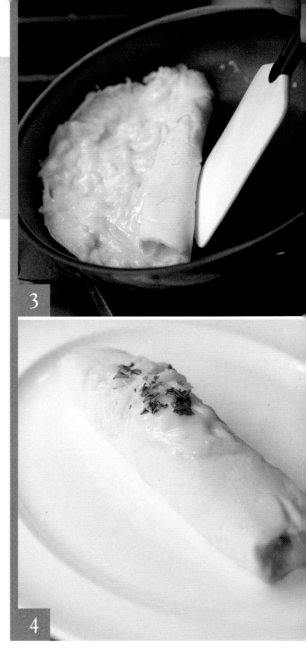

3

4

3. For a rolled omelet, use a spatula to roll one side of the omelet toward the center. To finish a rolled omelet, hold the pan near the plate and roll the omelet onto the plate. For an American-style omelet, fold one half of the omelet up and over the garnish items to create a half-circle shape. Transfer the folded omelet from the pan to a plate using the spatula.

4. A finished omelet should be golden yellow in color, with a creamy, moist interior.

Chef's Lesson
MAKING FRITTATAS

1. Prepare any vegetables or other flavoring ingredients for the frittata and reserve. Crack the eggs into a bowl and use a fork or whisk to blend the eggs until the whites and yolks are combined.

2. Heat a small amount of fat in an appropriate-size sauté pan. Ladle or pour the eggs into the pan. As soon as they begin to coagulate, top the eggs with the flavoring ingredients.

3. Once the eggs begin to set and brown slightly, place the pan in a 400°F oven and bake until the eggs are set.

MAKING CUSTARDS

THERE ARE SEVERAL DIFFERENT TYPES OF CUSTARDS, including baked custards, stirred custards, creams, and puddings.

BAKED CUSTARDS

EXPERT tips

IT IS ESPECIALLY IMPORTANT to have all the necessary equipment assembled before you begin preparing a stirred custard, cream, or pudding.

USING A HOT WATER BATH when baking custard keeps the heat constant and gentle, resulting in a smooth texture in the finished product.

A simple baked custard calls for blending eggs and a liquid such as milk or cream (known as the custard base) and then baking in the oven until the mixture is set. Cream cheese or other soft fresh cheese may be substituted for part of the milk or cream for a richer, firmer result, such as for cheesecake. The proportion of eggs also may be varied, as may the choice of whole eggs or yolks only, or a combination of the two, according to a specific recipe. Baked custards can be savory or sweet, and a wide variety of ingredients can be incorporated into either type of custard. There are two basic methods for combining the ingredients to make a baked custard: cold and warm.

COLD METHOD. For the cold method of mixing a custard base, the ingredients are simply stirred together, then poured into molds and baked. Typically, this method will be effective for the size of the batches you'll be making at home.

WARM METHOD. Larger batches of baked custard benefit from the warm method of mixing. To mix a custard base using the warm method, heat the milk or cream and some of the sugar, if using, and stir with a wooden spoon. Add the flavorings at this point and allow them to steep off the stovetop, covered, if necessary, long enough for them to give the liquid a rich, full flavor. Blend the eggs and the remaining sugar, if using, to make a liaison (see page 30 for more information about using a liaison) and bring the milk or cream to a boil. Whisking constantly, slowly add about one-third of the hot milk, a few ladlefuls at a time, to the liaison to temper it. Once the liaison is tempered, you can add the rest of the hot milk more rapidly without scrambling the egg mixture.

1. Stir the custard base, eggs, and any remaining ingredients together until well combined. (This is known as the cold method of combining the ingredients. For information on the warm method, see opposite page.)

2. Ladle the custard into ramekins. Coat the ramekins lightly with softened butter before filling if you intend to unmold the finished custard. Arrange the ramekins about 1 inch apart inside a baking dish with high sides; add enough hot or boiling water to the dish to come about two-thirds up the sides of the ramekins. Be very careful not to splash or pour any of the water into the custards. Very gently place the baking dish into the oven. To check the custard for doneness, shake the ramekin gently; when the ripples on the surface move back and forth, rather than in concentric rings, the custard is properly baked.

3. Carefully remove the ramekins from the water bath and wipe them dry. Place them on a cool sheet pan, allow them to cool, and then place them in the refrigerator. Some baked custards are traditionally unmolded before serving, but many are simply served inside the baking dish; consult the specific recipe for instructions.

STIRRED CUSTARDS, CREAMS, AND PUDDINGS

Stirred custards are custards that are prepared on the stovetop and must be stirred constantly during cooking. Creams and puddings are stirred custards that are thickened with starch and cooked on the stovetop; they must be stirred constantly until they come to a full boil, both so the starch is heated enough to thicken the mixture and to remove the unpleasant flavor and texture of uncooked starch. Crème anglaise, or vanilla sauce, pastry cream, and chocolate pudding are basic preparations that fall into this category.

Some recipes for stirred custards, creams, and puddings include whole milk, while others call for heavy cream, light cream, or a combination. Some recipes use only egg yolks, while others use whole eggs or a blend of whole eggs and yolks.

HARD-COOKED EGGS

10 eggs

1. Place the eggs in a large pot. Fill the pot with enough cold water to cover the eggs by 2 inches.

2. Bring the water to a simmer over medium heat and immediately lower the temperature to maintain a simmer. Begin timing the cooking at this point. Cook small eggs for 10 minutes, medium eggs for 11 minutes, large eggs for 12 to 13 minutes, and extra-large eggs for 14 minutes.

3. After cooking, quickly submerge the eggs in cold water and peel as soon as possible. Serve the eggs immediately, or refrigerate until needed.

NOTES *Cracking the eggs just after cooking will allow the trapped gases inside to escape, thus reducing the amount of green discoloration around the yolk. Additionally, the eggs will peel easier if peeled as soon as they are cool enough to handle. If allowed to cool completely, the membrane under the skin tends to stick to the hard-cooked egg white, making them difficult to peel.*

An alternative method for hard cooking eggs is to remove the pot holding the eggs from the heat when the water reaches a simmer. Cover the pot and let the eggs stand in the hot water for 12 to 15 minutes.

CODDLED EGGS *Lower cold eggs into simmering water and simmer for 30 seconds.*

PICKLED EGGS

5 Hard-Cooked Eggs (above)
1 tsp dry mustard powder
1 tsp cornstarch
1 tbsp cold water
1¾ cups white wine vinegar
1 tsp sugar
1 tsp turmeric or curry powder

1. Place the eggs in a stainless steel bowl and set aside.

2. In a small saucepan, dilute the mustard and cornstarch in the cold water. Add the vinegar, sugar, and turmeric or curry powder. Bring the mixture to a boil over medium heat and simmer for 10 minutes.

3. Pour the mixture over the eggs. Cool the eggs and the pickling solution to room temperature, then refrigerate overnight.

RED PICKLED EGGS *Replace 1 cup of the vinegar with beet juice.*

DEVILED EGGS

5 Hard-Cooked Eggs (opposite), **cold**

6 tbsp mayonnaise

2 tsp prepared mustard

Salt, as needed

Freshly ground black pepper, as needed

1. Slice the eggs in half lengthwise. Carefully separate the yolks from the whites. Set aside the whites until ready to fill.

2. Rub the yolks through a sieve into a bowl or place them in a food processor and process until smooth.

3. Add the mayonnaise, mustard, salt, and pepper to the bowl or food processor. Mix or process the ingredients into a smooth paste.

4. Pipe or spoon the yolk mixture into the egg whites, garnish as desired, and serve immediately.

NOTES *The eggs can be separated and the filling mixed in advance, but if the eggs are not to be served immediately, the whites and the yolks should be held separately and assembled just before serving.*

Garnishes may include chopped parsley, snipped chives, sliced green onion tops, dill sprigs, pimiento strips, chopped olives, caviar, shredded carrots, ground cumin, dried oregano, cayenne pepper, or crushed red pepper flakes.

Substitutions for all or part of the mayonnaise include soft butter, sour cream, puréed cottage cheese, softened cream cheese, yogurt, or crème fraîche.

DEVILED EGGS WITH TOMATO *Add ¼ cup sautéed chopped tomato, ½ tsp dried herbs (basil, oregano, sage, thyme), and/or ½ tsp sautéed minced garlic or shallots to the yolk mixture.*

DEVILED EGGS WITH GREENS *Add ¼ cup blanched and puréed spinach, watercress, sorrel, lettuce, or other greens to the yolk mixture.*

DEVILED EGGS WITH VEGETABLES *Add small-dice cooked, raw, or marinated vegetables, such as celery, carrots, red onions, bell peppers, fennel, mushrooms, tomatoes, green beans, peas, corn, or eggplant to the yolk mixture.*

DEVILED EGGS WITH PEPPERS *Add ¼ cup puréed roasted red or green bell peppers to the yolk mixture.*

DEVILED EGGS WITH CHEESE *Add ¼ cup grated hard cheese (such as Parmesan or Gruyère) or ½ cup soft cheese (such as fresh goat) to the yolk mixture.*

Eggs Benedict

10 poached eggs (see page 332)

5 English muffins, split, buttered, and toasted

10 slices Canadian bacon, heated through

1¼ cups Hollandaise Sauce (page 74), warm

1. If the eggs have been poached in advance, reheat them in simmering water until warmed through. Blot with paper towels to remove excess water.

2. Top each muffin half with a slice of the Canadian bacon and an egg.

3. Ladle 2 tablespoons of the warm hollandaise sauce over each egg. Serve immediately.

EGGS FLORENTINE *Replace each slice of Canadian bacon with ¼ cup sautéed spinach.*

POACHED EGGS AMERICAN STYLE *Replace each slice of Canadian bacon with 1 sautéed sliced, peeled tomato and replace the hollandaise with Cheddar Cheese Sauce (page 72). Garnish with chopped, cooked bacon and parsley.*

POACHED EGGS WITH SMOKED SALMON *Replace the English muffin with a toasted bagel and replace each slice of Canadian bacon with 1 slice smoked salmon. Garnish with chopped chives.*

Poached Eggs Mornay

MAKES 5 SERVINGS

10 toast rounds or ovals

4 tbsp butter, melted

10 poached eggs (see page 322)

1 cup Mornay Sauce (page 72), warm

½ cup grated Gruyère

1. Preheat the oven to 400°F.

2. Brush each round of toast with butter and top with a poached egg. Coat with the sauce and sprinkle with the grated Gruyère.

3. Brown lightly in the oven and serve immediately.

POACHED EGGS FARMER STYLE *Top each round of toast with peeled tomato slices, boiled ham slices, creamed mushrooms, and a poached egg.*

Eggs Florentine

Huevos Rancheros

Eight 6-inch corn tortillas

2 cups Refried Beans (page 286)

4 tbsp butter or vegetable oil

16 eggs

Salt, as needed

Freshly ground black pepper, as needed

1 cup grated Monterey Jack

2 avocados

4 tsp fresh lime juice

1 cup Salsa Fresca (page 82)

½ cup sour cream, as needed

8 cilantro sprigs

1. Preheat the broiler.

2. Heat the tortillas by toasting them one at a time in a dry, cast-iron skillet or directly over a gas flame until lightly toasted. Transfer to a baking sheet, spread each tortilla with ¼ cup of the refried beans, and cover to keep warm.

3. Working in batches as needed, heat the butter in a large skillet over medium-high heat until it is very hot but not smoking and the foaming has subsided. Crack the eggs directly into the hot butter and reduce the heat to medium-low or low. Fry the eggs, shaking the pan occasionally to keep the eggs from sticking. Season the eggs with salt and pepper. Fry about 2 minutes for sunny-side-up eggs, 3 minutes for medium yolks, and 3½ to 4 minutes for hard yolks.

4. Top each prepared tortilla with 2 fried eggs and 2 tablespoons of the cheese. Slide the tortillas under the broiler to melt the cheese, but be careful not to overcook the eggs.

5. Meanwhile, dice the avocados and toss with the lime juice to prevent discoloration. Divide the diced avocados evenly among the tortillas. Top each serving with 2 tablespoons of salsa and 2 tablespoons of sour cream and garnish with a sprig of cilantro.

SCRAMBLED EGGS

15 eggs

1 tbsp salt

1 tsp ground white pepper

3 tbsp water or milk (optional)

2 tbsp clarified butter, canola oil, or vegetable oil

1. Crack the eggs into a medium bowl and stir well with a whisk. Season with salt and pepper, add the water or milk, if using, and whisk to combine.

2. Heat a large omelet pan or skillet over medium heat and add the butter or oil, tilting the pan to coat the entire surface. The pan should be hot, but not smoking.

3. Pour the egg mixture into the pan and cook over low heat, stirring frequently with the back of a fork or a wooden spoon, until the eggs are soft and creamy. Remove the eggs from the heat when fully cooked but still moist and serve immediately on heated plates.

SCRAMBLED EGGS GRATINÉE *For each portion, top the scrambled eggs with Mornay Sauce (page 72), sprinkle with grated Gruyère, and brown lightly under the broiler.*

FRENCH TOAST

MAKES 5 SERVINGS

15 slices challah bread, cut ¼ to ½ inch thick

2 cups whole milk

4 eggs

2 tbsp sugar

Pinch salt

Pinch ground cinnamon (optional)

Pinch freshly grated nutmeg (optional)

1 tbsp butter, plus more as needed

1. Dry the bread slices on a baking sheet overnight or in a 200°F oven for 1 hour.

2. Combine the milk, eggs, sugar, salt, and cinnamon and nutmeg, if using, in a medium bowl and whisk until smooth. Cover and refrigerate until needed.

3. Preheat the oven to 150°F.

4. In a large skillet, melt 1 tablespoon butter over medium heat.

5. Dip 5 slices of the bread into the batter, coating the slices evenly. Fry the slices on one side until evenly browned, then flip and brown the opposite side. Repeat the process with the remaining slices of bread, adding more butter to the pan as needed. Keep the French toast warm in the oven while cooking the remaining batches.

6. Serve the immediately on heated plates.

NOTE *Serve the French toast with butter and maple syrup or honey. Garnishing options include confectioners' sugar, cinnamon sugar, toasted nuts, or fresh or dried fruit.*

PLAIN ROLLED OMELET

MAKES 5 SERVINGS

15 eggs

1 tbsp salt

1 tsp ground white pepper

⅓ cup water, stock, milk, or heavy cream (optional)

Clarified butter or vegetable oil, as needed

1. For each portion, crack 3 eggs into a medium bowl and beat well with a whisk. Season with salt and pepper, add 1 tablespoon of the liquid, if using, and whisk to combine.

2. Heat a nonstick omelet pan over high heat and add the butter or oil. When properly heated, the butter should foam or the oil should flow freely like water. Tilt the pan to coat the entire surface.

3. Pour the egg mixture into the pan and scramble it with the back of a fork. Swirl the pan on the burner in one direction and stir the egg mixture in the

opposite direction with a heatproof rubber spatula until the egg mixture has cooked slightly. Stir until the eggs have lost their glossy appearance and small curds appear, but the mixture still is runny. Smooth the eggs into an even layer by gently pressing down with the spatula.

4. Reduce the heat to medium and let the egg mixture finish cooking without stirring for 15 to 20 seconds.

5. Tilt the pan and slide a fork or spoon around the lip of the pan and under the omelet to make sure it is not sticking. Slide the omelet to the front of the pan and, using a fork or a wooden spoon, fold it inside to the center.

6. Tilting the pan in one hand and holding the plate in the other, roll the omelet onto the plate. The finished omelet should be oval shaped.

NOTE *A precooked filling may be added to the eggs after they have been smoothed into an even layer and before the omelet is rolled. Alternatively, the rolled omelet can be slit open at the top, and a precooked, heated filling or sauce can be spooned into the pocket. To give the omelet an attractive sheen, brush the surface lightly with softened butter.*

SPANISH OMELET *Fill each omelet with ½ cup diced tomatoes or tomato sauce and ¼ cup each sautéed, diced onions and green bell peppers.*

SOUFFLÉD CHEDDAR OMELET

MAKES 5 SERVINGS

15 eggs
2½ tsp salt
1¼ tsp ground white pepper
¾ cup grated sharp cheddar
1 tsp minced chives

1. Preheat the oven to 400°F.

2. For each serving, separate 3 eggs. In a bowl, beat the yolks and season with ½ teaspoon of salt and ¼ teaspoon of white pepper. Divide the cheese and chives among the beaten yolks.

3. In a separate clean bowl, beat the egg whites to medium peaks. Divide and fold them into the yolks.

4. Pour each portion of eggs into a preheated, well-buttered or -oiled, small cast-iron or nonstick skillet. When the sides and bottom have set, finish each omelet in the oven until fully set and golden on top. Serve immediately.

Frittata

MAKES 6 SERVINGS

1 tbsp olive oil

1 onion, cut into small dice

1 potato, cut into medium dice and boiled until tender

6 eggs, lightly beaten

½ cup whole milk

1 tsp salt

½ tsp freshly ground black pepper

½ cup shredded cheddar (optional)

1. Preheat the oven to 350°F.

2. Heat the oil in a medium skillet over medium heat. Add the onion and sauté until translucent, 4 to 5 minutes.

3. Add the potato and sauté until golden, 3 to 5 minutes more.

4. In a medium bowl, whisk the eggs, milk, salt, and pepper to combine. Add the egg mixture to the hot skillet, and reduce the heat to low. Cook for a few minutes, until the edges begin to set.

5. Sprinkle the top of the frittata with the cheese, if using, and transfer the skillet to the oven. Bake until the eggs are just set, 7 to 9 minutes more. Serve warm.

BACON AND CHEDDAR QUICHE

MAKES 10 SERVINGS

½ recipe Pie Dough (page 370)

8 oz diced slab bacon

2 tbsp butter or vegetable oil

¾ cup heavy cream

¾ cup whole milk

3 eggs

1 tsp salt

¼ tsp freshly ground black pepper

Pinch freshly grated nutmeg

4 oz grated Emmentaler

1. Preheat the oven to 350°F.

2. On a lightly floured work surface, roll the dough to a thickness of ⅛ inch and fit into a 9-inch pie or quiche pan. Line the pie shell with parchment paper and fill with dry beans or pie weights. Trim any overhanging dough from the edge. Blind bake the pie shell until very light golden brown, about 15 minutes. Remove the beans and parchment paper and continue to bake to a golden brown, about 5 minutes more. Cool the pie shell completely.

3. In a medium sauté pan, cook the bacon in the butter or oil until browned. Using a slotted spoon, transfer the bacon to paper towels to drain. Discard the rendered fat or save for another use.

4. Whisk together the cream, milk, and eggs. Season with the salt, pepper, and nutmeg.

5. Scatter the bacon and cheese evenly over the pie crust. Add the egg mixture gradually, stirring it gently with the back of a fork to distribute the filling ingredients evenly.

6. Set the pan on a baking sheet and bake until a knife blade inserted in the center comes out clean, 40 to 45 minutes. Serve hot or at room temperature.

NOTE *Quiche may also be baked without a pastry crust. Butter a shallow casserole or 9-inch baking dish. Sprinkle it with grated Parmesan, if desired. Spread the filling ingredients over the casserole bottom. Pour the egg mixture on top. Place the baking dish in a roasting pan with enough water to come two-thirds of the way up the sides and bake until a knife inserted near the center comes out clean, about 1 hour. Quiche may also be baked in tartlet shells, timbale molds, or custard cups.*

BROCCOLI AND CHEDDAR QUICHE *Substitute 5 oz broccoli florets, sautéed in olive oil until tender, for all or part of the bacon. Substitute cheddar for the Emmentaler.*

Broccoli and Cheddar Quiche

SPINACH SOUFFLÉ

MAKES 5 SERVINGS

SOUFFLÉ BASE

2 tbsp butter

⅓ cup all-purpose flour

1½ cups whole milk

Salt, as needed

Freshly ground black pepper, as needed

7 eggs

Butter, softened, as needed

½ cup grated Parmesan, plus more as needed

1½ cups blanched chopped spinach

Salt, as needed

Freshly ground black pepper, as needed

1. Preheat the oven to 425°F.

2. To make the soufflé base, melt the butter in a medium saucepan over medium heat and stir in the flour. Cook over low to medium heat for 5 to 6 minutes, stirring frequently, to make a blond roux.

3. Add the milk and whisk well. Season with salt and pepper. Simmer over low heat, stirring constantly, for 15 to 20 minutes until very thick and smooth.

4. Separate the eggs, reserving 5 of the whites. Lightly whisk the egg yolks in a bowl. Ladle a small amount of the soufflé base into the yolks and continue whisking. Return the tempered yolks to the milk mixture and continue to simmer over very low heat for 3 to 4 minutes.

5. Adjust the seasoning with additional salt and pepper and strain through a sieve if necessary.

6. Prepare five 6-ounce soufflé molds by brushing them liberally with softened butter. Lightly dust the interior of each mold with grated cheese and tap out any excess that doesn't stick to the mold.

7. Stir together the soufflé base, spinach, cheese, salt, and pepper until the spinach is evenly distributed. In a clean mixing bowl, beat the reserved 5 egg whites to soft peaks. Fold about one-third of the beaten whites into the base. Add the remaining whites in one or two additions.

8. Spoon the soufflé batter into the prepared molds to within ½ inch of the rim. Wipe the rim carefully to remove any batter, which would interfere with the rising of the soufflé. Tap the soufflés gently on the countertop to settle the batter. Sprinkle the soufflé tops with the additional cheese, about 1 teaspoon for each mold.

9. Place the soufflés on a baking sheet, transfer to the oven, and bake, undisturbed, until puffy, 16 to 18 minutes; a skewer or cake tester should come out relatively clean. Serve immediately.

WARM GOAT CHEESE CUSTARD

⅓ cup cream cheese, at room temperature

½ cup goat cheese, at room temperature

½ tsp freshly ground black pepper, plus more as needed

5 eggs

1½ cups heavy cream

2 tbsp sliced chives

1 tbsp salt, plus more as needed

20 seedless green grapes

1. Preheat the oven to 325°F. Butter five 2-ounce timbale molds.

2. In a food processor, combine the cream cheese with ¼ cup goat cheese, reserving the remainder for garnish. Season with the pepper and process until the mixture is very smooth.

3. Add the eggs, ½ cup of the cream, 1 tablespoon of the chives, and the salt. Pulse the processor until the ingredients are just blended. Divide the mixture among the molds and cover with buttered parchment paper. Place the on a baking sheet.

4. Bake in the oven until a knife inserted near the center of a custard comes away clean.

5. In a medium saucepan over medium heat, reduce the remaining cream by half and season with salt and pepper. Add the remaining 1 tablespoon chives and the grapes to the cream just before serving.

6. Unmold the custards and coat with the sauce. Garnish with the reserved goat cheese and serve immediately.

NOTE *You can replace the goat cheese with another soft cheese, such as Boursin, Brillat-Savarin, Camembert, or Brie.*

BREADS AND DESSERTS

Although they share many similarities, baking and cooking are fundamentally different activities. While a soup, stew, or even a sauté can be assessed and changed at virtually any stage of preparation, the quality of baked items cannot be assessed until they are mixed and baked. Try to approach baking in a systematic way. Before you begin, gather all the equipment and ingredients, and read the recipe carefully before you start measuring and mixing. Baking is a process that invites you to slow down, think, and enjoy the process of creating food.

YEAST DOUGHS

YEAST DOUGHS ARE DIVIDED INTO TWO CATEGORIES: lean doughs and enriched doughs. Lean doughs are produced with only flour, yeast, salt, and water. Other ingredients, such as spices, herbs, dried fruits, and nuts, can be added to vary this dough, but they will not greatly change the basic texture. Breads made from lean dough tend to have a chewier texture, more bite, and a crisp crust. Hard rolls, French- and Italian-style breads, and whole wheat and rye breads are considered lean.

An enriched dough is made by adding ingredients such as sugar or syrup, butter or oil, eggs or egg yolks, and milk or heavy cream to the dough. When fats are introduced, they change the dough's texture, yielding a softer, more tender bread. Enriched breads may be golden in color because of the use of eggs and butter, and the crust is soft rather than crisp. Soft rolls, brioche, and challah are considered enriched.

Basic Equipment for Yeast Breads

STAND MIXER. Yeast breads are mixed with the dough hook attachment of a stand mixer.

BOWL AND KITCHEN TOWEL. Many yeast breads can be proofed inside a large bowl that is loosely covered with a clean kitchen towel.

BAKING SHEET. Many yeast breads are formed by hand and baked on a baking sheet.

PANS OR BASKETS. Specialty baking pans or baskets may be used to shape certain breads.

EXPERT tips

COOLING BREADS MADE WITH A LEAN DOUGH on wire racks will maintain air circulation, prevent moisture from collecting on the bread as it cools, and preserve the crisp crust.

GARNISHING THE TOP of loaves or rolls adds flavor as well as visual appeal. Most garnishes are applied after the dough has been shaped. Use a bit of water to adhere the garnish if the dough is not moist enough on its own to make it stick. Garnishes include:

   Fresh herbs

   Coarse salt

   Sliced or chopped olives

   Seeds

   Grated cheese

Chef's Lesson
MIXING BREAD DOUGH

1. Mix the dough according to the specific recipe. During the mixing, the gluten (the protein contained in flour) begins to develop elasticity. Dough that has reached the proper level of gluten development will look smooth and will not tear when it is stretched. To check for gluten development, chefs use what is referred to as the gluten window (see photo). Hold a piece of dough in both hands, and gently stretch it until the dough has formed a thin membrane that you can see through.

2. After mixing, the dough must be rested in order for the yeast to do the leavening; this process is known as proofing. Typically the dough is covered and left in a warm place until it has risen to the appropriate volume, usually when it has doubled in size.

3. Lean doughs are baked in a hot oven (400° to 450°F), and enriched doughs are baked at a slightly lower temperature (about 375°F). The type of oven, temperature, size and shape of the bread, and the desired crust and color development will affect the baking time, so refer to the specific recipe for instructions.

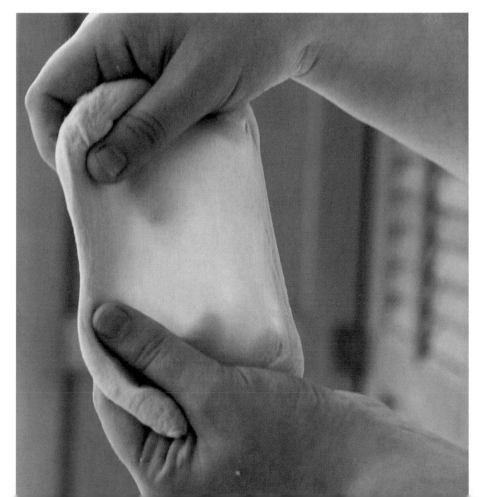

The gluten window test can be used to check for the proper gluten development when mixing yeast dough. If the dough has not been mixed enough, it will not be able to form a thin membrane without ripping; if the dough is overmixed, it will be too wet and sticky to form the membrane.

Rubbed Doughs

BISCUITS, SCONES, AND PIE CRUSTS can be prepared using the rubbed-dough, or cutting-in, method. The ingredients are not blended into a smooth batter; instead, the fat is chilled and then rubbed into the flour to create flakes that will yield a tender, flaky product.

Flour, a solid fat such as butter or shortening, and a very cold liquid are the basic components of most rubbed doughs.

Butter and shortening are the most common fats used for this method, and they should be broken or cut into pieces and kept cool. Rubbed-dough recipes typically call for a relatively small amount of liquid, and the liquid, like the fat, should be very cold. Water, milk, and buttermilk are all common liquid ingredients. Combine the liquid with the other ingredients just enough to allow the moisture to be absorbed by the flour and just until the ingredients come together, at which point the dough should be allowed to rest in the refrigerator.

There are a few special considerations when preparing a rubbed dough. The dry ingredients should be sifted together prior to adding the fat to ensure that all ingredients are evenly distributed. Rubbing the fat into the dry ingredients is not enough to adequately mix them together. Also, work the dough only as much as needed to achieve the desired result. It is crucial that the dough is not overworked, because overworking will promote the development of gluten and will make the dough tough, making it difficult to roll out and have an unpleasantly hard texture after it is baked.

FLAKY AND MEALY DOUGHS

The two basic types of rubbed doughs are flaky and mealy. Flaky pie dough is achieved by leaving the flakes of fat larger before the liquid is added. If the flakes of butter or shortening are rubbed into the dough so that they remain visible, the result will be what is often referred to as a flaky dough. If the butter or shortening is more thoroughly worked into the dough until the mixture resembles coarse meal, the result will be a mealy dough.

Flaky dough is best for pies and tarts that are filled with a fruit filling and baked. Mealy dough is best suited for pies and tarts that require a fully baked shell that is filled after cooling and chilled until the filling is set, and for pies with custard or other liquid fillings that are baked until set.

Basic Equipment for Rubbed Doughs

ROLLING PIN. The dough for pie and tart crusts is rolled into a thin, even sheet with a rolling pin.

WORK SURFACE. The surface for rolling out the dough should give you ample space to roll out the dough and be room temperature or slightly cool to the touch to keep the fat cool.

SPATULA OR BENCH SCRAPER. When dough is rolled out, it can be difficult to move. Either of these tools will help to lift, rotate, or otherwise move the dough without tearing it.

Chef's Lesson
MAKING RUBBED DOUGH

1. Sift or blend the dry ingredients well. Make sure that the fat is very cold so that it is solid enough to be worked into the dry ingredients without blending the mixture into a smooth dough. Add the fat to the dry ingredients all at once. Rub the fat into the dry ingredients, being careful not to work it too thoroughly.

2. Work the fat into the dry ingredients until the mixture forms small clumps, ranging from the size of peas to the size of small walnuts. Make a well in the center and add the cold liquid. Slowly mix the flour and fat mixture together with the liquid, starting on the inside of the well and working toward the outside.

3. Do not overwork the dough once the liquid is added; vigorous or prolonged mixing will result in a tough product.

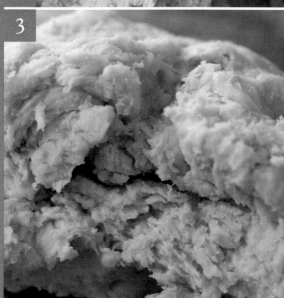

Cookies

Cookies are prepared in many different ways: dropped, rolled and cut, molded and sliced, and piped, just to name a few. Some cookies must be shaped and baked as soon as the batter or dough is prepared. Others need to be chilled before they are shaped. Prepare the dough or batter as directed in the recipe.

Cookies contain a high percentage of sugar, so the oven temperature must be carefully regulated during baking. Convection ovens, which bake more evenly than conventional ovens, are especially good for baking cookies.

DROP COOKIES

Drop cookies, which are dropped by the spoonful onto the baking sheet, must be arranged in even rows for baking. These cookies have a tendency to spread as they bake, so allow enough room for them to expand without touching each other. Bake drop cookies until the bottoms are golden brown and the cookies are baked through but still moist. Cool them on wire racks and store in airtight containers at room temperature or freeze for longer storage.

The dough for most drop cookies can also be portioned by slicing rather than scooping. For sliced cookies, roll the finished cookie dough into a log and wrap it in parchment paper or plastic wrap. Refrigerate or freeze until firm. When ready to bake, simply cut the log into uniform slices using a chef's knife. Neatly arrange the slices in even rows on a baking sheet, leaving enough room for them to spread during baking.

ROLLED AND CUT COOKIES

Rolled and cut cookies are made from stiff doughs that are often chilled before rolling. Roll out the dough on a lightly floured surface; for some rolled cookies, the surface and rolling pin are dusted with confectioners' sugar. When finished rolling, the dough should be even and generally no more than ⅛ to ⅙ inch thick. Cutters of various shapes and sizes may be used, or the dough can simply be cut into pieces using a knife. Bake rolled and cut cookies until the edges just start to turn golden. Immediately transfer them to a wire rack to cool.

Rolled and cut cookies are often glazed or iced. These coatings should be applied after the cookies are completely cool. If the cookies are to be frozen for longer storage, freeze them plain and decorate or ice them after they have been thawed.

MOLDED AND SLICED COOKIES

Biscotti, or twice-baked cookies, are a type of molded and sliced cookie. They are made into a half-moon-shaped log, and once baked, the log is sliced into individual cookies. The cookies are then returned to the oven on a baking sheet, to lightly toast and dry.

PIPED COOKIES

Piped cookies are shaped as soon as the batter is made, so you should assemble all of the necessary equipment before starting to mix the batter. Pastry bags and tips are used to pipe the batter onto the baking sheet in the desired shape and size. Arrange the cookies in neat, even rows, and leave some room for them to spread as they bake.

Basic Equipment for Cookies

BAKING SHEET. Cookies are baked in the oven on a baking sheet. The baking sheet may be used ungreased, prepared with fat, or lined with parchment paper or a silicone mat.

ROLLING PIN. The dough for rolled and cut cookies is rolled into a thin, even sheet with a rolling pin.

COOKIE CUTTERS. Cookie cutters are available in a wide variety of sizes and shapes.

PARCHMENT PAPER. Parchment paper is a heat-resistant paper that is often used to line baking pans.

PASTRY BAG AND TIPS. A pastry bag is a canvas or plastic bag that is made to be fitted with a decorative tip and used to pipe out batters and icings.

CAKES

There are many options for assembling and finishing a cake. You can use a variety of cakes, fillings, and frostings, such as the Devil's Food Cake on page 370 and the Italian Buttercream on page 385. All cakes should be allowed to cool completely before you begin any assembly. For the best results, use a cake-decorating turntable and a knife with a long, thin, serrated blade for cutting and trimming cake layers.

Any fillings or frostings should complement and enhance the flavor and texture of the cake. Fillings spread between cake layers should generally be less than ½ inch thick. Cake layers may also be moistened with a variety of syrups, from plain simple syrup to those infused with spices or a liqueur. To do this, brush the syrup evenly over the cut surface of each layer before it is assembled; the layers should be moistened but not soggy.

Chef's Lesson
ICING A CAKE

1. The domed tops of baked cake layers are sometimes trimmed to create a flat surface for frosting and layering. Layers are also sometimes sliced horizontally to make thinner layers for a finished cake. Place the cake on a turntable. Use a long, serrated knife to make guide marks on the side of the cake. Cut through the cake layer using a gentle back-and-forth motion, with the opposite hand resting on top of the cake to keep the knife level and layer even, and use this hand to slowly turn the table as you continue slicing into the cake, until the top is completely separated from the rest of the cake. Brush away crumbs with a pastry brush.

2. The best tools for spreading cake filling are offset spatulas or palette knives. To fill a cake, spoon some filling in the center of the layer. The amount of filling depends on the type: for jams, a thin, even layer is ideal, but for creamy fillings, such as a buttercream, the layer will be thicker. Use an offset spatula to spread the filling from the center out, rotating the turntable to help ensure an even coating.

3. When the next layer is placed, make sure to press it down gently, to ensure level layers. If the layers are uneven, use extra filling to compensate.

4. To frost the cake, spoon a generous amount of icing onto the cake's top. Remember that some will be removed as you go. Using a large offset spatula, spread the icing from the center, creating an even layer that extends over the edge of the cake, rotating the turntable as you go. Scoop up some icing with the spatula and, holding it vertically, generously coat the sides of the cake. Rotate the turntable, and use a back-and-forth motion to apply an even layer, picking up more icing as needed. Once the cake is coated, clean off the spatula with a clean, damp towel and hold it vertically against the side of the cake at a 45-degree angle. Rotate the turntable and gently press the spatula against the cake to smooth the sides.

5. To smooth the edges and top of the cake, clean the offset spatula with a damp towel. Holding the knife horizontally, at a 45-degree angle to the top of the cake, draw the icing toward the center. Repeat around the entire cake, cleaning the knife each time to ensure a smooth layer. To finish, hold the clean spatula at a 45-degree angle to the top of the cake and, in one motion, smooth from one end of the cake to the other for a clean, even top surface. If desired, pipe a border or other design onto the cake.

6. Slice the finished cake in even portions with a sharp knife that has been dipped in warm water and dried. Clean the knife in between each cut to help ensure clean slices.

Basic Equipment for Cakes

TURNTABLE. A cake-decorating turntable is very helpful when cutting and assembling cake layers and frosting the assembled cake.

SERRATED KNIFE. Use a long, thin, serrated knife to trim and cut cake layers.

PASTRY BRUSH. A pastry brush is used to apply syrups to moisten cut cake layers before they are assembled.

OFFSET METAL SPATULA. An offset metal spatula is an essential tool used to help move and arrange cake layers, spread fillings, and apply frostings and other cake decorations.

CRÊPE BATTER CAN BE USED TO CREATE both savory and sweet dishes. Crêpes can be served rolled or folded around a filling or used in other desserts, such as Crêpes Suzette (page 375). To prepare crêpes:

- Heat a buttered crêpe or sauté pan over medium heat. Ladle the crêpe batter into the pan and swirl to coat the entire surface of the pan evenly. Be sure that the crêpe is of a uniform thickness or it will cook unevenly.

- As soon as the crêpe has set and the edges are golden brown, gently turn it over using a long, offset spatula and cook on the second side.

CUSTARDS, PUDDINGS, AND CREAMS

WHEN YOU HEAT A BASIC CUSTARD, whether you bake it or stir it over direct heat, the eggs in the mixture are what thickens it. When you make a pudding or a pastry cream, you may replace the thickening effect of the eggs—all of the eggs or just some of them—with a starch such as flour or cornstarch.

Pudding is a delightful dessert served on its own or topped with whipped cream. Pastry cream is used as a filling or as a building block, or base, to create a hot dessert soufflé.

SOUFFLÉS

A SOUFFLÉ IS MADE by folding beaten egg whites into pastry cream. When the mixture cooks in a hot oven, the egg white foam expands and the pastry cream bakes into a network that just barely supports the soufflé as it rises above the rim of the ramekin.

You can add flavor and color to soufflés by blending ingredients into the pastry cream, such as fruit purées, liqueurs, melted chocolate, or extracts. A soufflé requires some planning; when it comes out of the oven, it must be served immediately.

FROZEN DESSERTS

WHEN YOU MAKE A CRÈME ANGLAISE, or vanilla sauce, and then stir or agitate it as it freezes, the result is ice cream. The same freezing method produces sorbet, but the base mixture contains no milk or cream—it is made of fruit purées, juices, or other flavored liquids that are sweetened with the right amount of sugar to produce a smooth and sweet frozen treat. The base mixture of a granita, or granité, is basically the same as for sorbet, but rather than being churned in an ice cream freezer, the mixture is frozen in a pan and stirred only as the frozen crystals begin to develop.

CHALLAH WITH GOLDEN RAISINS

MAKES TWO 24-OUNCE LOAVES

SPONGE

½ cup plus 1 tbsp bread flour

1 tbsp instant dry yeast

⅓ cup warm water, 90°F

DOUGH

¾ cup warm water, 92°F

¼ cup vegetable oil

2 tbsp honey

5 eggs

2 egg yolks

4½ cups bread flour

2 tsp salt

⅔ cup sugar

1½ cups golden raisins

Egg wash: 1 egg whisked with 2 tbsp cold milk or water

1. To make the sponge, combine the flour with the yeast in a bowl and add the warm water. Mix the sponge together by hand for 2 minutes; you will develop some gluten structure. Make sure all of the ingredients are combined into a homogenous mass. Cover the bowl with plastic wrap and place in a warm area. Allow the sponge to ferment for 30 minutes.

2. To make the dough, in the bowl of a stand mixer fitted with the dough hook, combine the water, oil, honey, eggs, egg yolks, and sponge. Mix for 1 minute on low speed to break up the sponge (the sponge can also be broken up by hand a little if needed). Next, add the flour, salt, and sugar and mix for 8 minutes on medium speed, making sure to scrape down the sides of the bowl and flip the dough over in the bowl at least 3 times during this mixing process. The dough should now have very good gluten development. Add the raisins and mix for 2 minutes on low speed, making sure to scrape down the sides of the bowl and flip the dough over. Remove the dough from the mixer and transfer it to a lightly oiled bowl, and then cover the bowl with plastic wrap. Allow the dough to rest and ferment in a warm place for 45 to 60 minutes.

3. Divide the dough into eight 6-ounce pieces for two 4-strand braids. Preshape each piece of the dough into a 3-inch oblong loaf. To accomplish this, bring the left and right ends of the dough to the center and then pull the top of the dough over one-half of the way. Roll the dough down to enclose the edges, and seal the seam well. Keep the pieces covered with plastic wrap.

4. For a 4-strand braid: Roll each piece of dough out to a length of 16 inches. If needed, rest the dough again and then continue to roll it out in order to achieve the 16-inch length. Arrange the strands side by side and pinch one end of all the strands together. Take the pinched strands and lightly flour them, then place the pinched end at the top.

5. Follow these steps to form the braid:

   STEP 1: With your right hand, hold the outer right strand and with your left hand, hold the second strand from the left (this should leave one strand to the left of each of your hands). Take the right hand and go under the two left-hand strands, then place the left-hand strand where the right hand was, so that the pieces have now switched positions, and the right strand is now under the left-hand strand.

STEP 2: With your left hand, hold the outer strand on the left, and with your right hand, hold the second strand from the right (this should leave one strand to the right of each of your hands). Take the left hand and go under the two right-hand strands, then place the right-hand strand where the left-hand strand was. The strands should have switched exact positions so that the left-hand strand is under the right hand.

REPEAT STEPS 1 AND 2 until no more dough is left. Make sure to lay the strands tightly together, but do not pull on them. An easy way to remember the steps is: step 1, right hand under left hand, step 2, left hand under right hand.

FINISH THE BRAID and pinch off any excess dough, then place the top of the braid parallel to you. Place each hand at the end with your small finger pressing the dough into the table and roll the dough back and forth to close off the ends. The braid should be about 11 to 12 inches long. Repeat with the remaining dough to make a second loaf.

6. Place the two loaves on a baking sheet lined with parchment paper. Brush the loaves with egg wash and cover lightly with plastic wrap. Allow to rest and ferment in a warm place, such as on top of the refrigerator or on top of the stove while the oven warms up, for 45 minutes. Brush the loaves with egg wash again, cover, and allow them to ferment 45 to 60 minutes more.

7. Preheat the oven to 400°F.

8. Brush the loaves with egg wash again. Place the loaves in oven and reduce the oven temperature to 375°F. Bake for 15 minutes, then rotate the baking sheet, reduce the oven temperature to 350°F, and bake for 10 to 15 minutes more. Transfer the baking sheet to a wire rack and allow the bread to cool before cutting and serving.

PARKER HOUSE ROLLS

½ cup room-temperature water

2 tsp active dry yeast

2 tbsp sugar

¾ cup whole or low-fat milk, boiled and cooled to room temperature

3 tbsp melted butter, plus more as needed

2 eggs, lightly beaten

2½ to 3 cups bread flour, plus more as needed

1 tsp salt

Egg wash: 1 egg whisked with 2 tbsp cold milk or water

Sesame seeds or poppy seeds, as needed (optional)

1. Combine the water, yeast, and sugar in a large bowl. Let sit until frothy, 2 to 3 minutes. Add the cooled milk, the 3 tablespoons of butter, the eggs, 1 cup of the flour, and the salt. Stir until the dough begins to form long elastic strands, 5 to 6 minutes. Gradually add more flour until the dough is too heavy to stir.

2. Turn the dough out onto a floured work surface and knead for about 10 minutes, adding only enough flour to prevent the dough from sticking. The dough should be moist, smooth, and springy when it is properly kneaded. Transfer the dough to a lightly oiled bowl, turn to coat with the oil, cover with a clean, damp cloth, and let rise in a warm place until doubled in size, 1 to 2 hours. Fold the dough over and let rest for 10 minutes.

3. Lightly grease two 9 x 13-inch baking pans with oil. Turn the dough out onto a lightly floured surface. Cut the dough into 24 equal pieces. Cover and let rest until relaxed, 15 to 20 minutes. Use a rolling pin to roll each piece into a 2 x 5-inch oval. Press the dull edge of a table knife in the center of each oval lengthwise to make a crease.

4. Brush each roll with a thin coat of melted butter and fold each in half so that the butter is on the inside. Place the rolls in the prepared pans seam side up; they should be close, but not touching one another. Cover the rolls with a damp cloth and let rise until nearly doubled in size.

5. Preheat the oven to 350°F.

6. Brush the rolls lightly with the egg wash. If desired, sprinkle with sesame seeds or poppy seeds. Bake until golden brown, 15 to 20 minutes. Let the rolls cool slightly before serving.

Cinnamon-Raisin Bread

MAKES 2 LOAVES

4½ cups bread flour, plus more as needed

2 tsp active dry yeast

2 cups whole or low-fat milk, boiled and cooled to room temperature

½ cup (8 tbsp/1 stick) butter, at room temperature

¼ cup sugar

2 eggs

2 tsp salt

1 cup dark raisins

1 tbsp ground cinnamon

Egg wash: 1 egg whisked with 2 tbsp cold milk or water

Cinnamon-Sugar: ½ tsp ground cinnamon mixed with ⅓ cup sugar

1. Combine the flour and yeast in the bowl of a stand mixer fitted with the dough hook. Add the milk, butter, sugar, eggs, and salt and mix on low speed for 4 minutes. Increase the speed to medium and knead for 4 minutes. Add the raisins during the last minute of kneading. Then add the cinnamon during the last 30 seconds, kneading just long enough to create a swirl. The dough should be slightly soft.

2. Transfer the dough to a lightly oiled bowl, turn to coat with the oil, cover with plastic wrap or a damp towel, and let rise in a warm place until nearly doubled in size, about 1 hour. Fold the dough over gently.

3. Allow the dough to rest for 15 minutes more before transferring it to a lightly floured work surface. Divide the dough into two equal pieces and round each into a smooth ball, pulling the outer layer taut and pinching together the excess dough at the base of the ball. Place, seam side down, on a lightly floured surface, cover, and let rest, 15 to 20 minutes.

4. On a lightly floured work surface, stretch each piece of dough into an 8 x 12-inch rectangle. Brush the dough lightly with egg wash and sprinkle with the cinnamon-sugar. Fold each short end of the rectangle in about 1 inch. Roll the long top end of the dough toward the center and press the seam closed with your fingertips. Continue to roll the dough into a cylinder and seal the seam with the palm of your hand. Gently roll the cylinder back and forth until it is about 11 inches long and of even thickness.

5. Place each cylinder of dough, seam side down, into a lightly oiled loaf pan. Brush each loaf lightly with egg wash. Let the loaves rise in a warm place, uncovered, until the dough fills the pan and springs back slowly to the touch but does not collapse, 1 to 2 hours.

6. Preheat the oven to 425°F.

7. Gently brush the dough with egg wash again before baking. Bake until the loaves have a brown crust and the sides retain their structure when pressed, 25 to 30 minutes. Immediately remove the bread from the pans and transfer to wire racks to cool completely before slicing and serving.

Bran Muffins

2½ cups all-purpose flour

1 tbsp plus 1½ tsp baking powder

½ cup (8 tbsp/1 stick) butter

1 cup sugar

½ tsp salt

4 eggs

1 cup whole milk

⅓ cup honey

⅓ cup molasses

4 cups unprocessed wheat bran

1. Preheat the oven to 375°F.

2. Lightly butter two 12-cup muffin pans, or use paper liners.

3. Sift together the flour and baking powder into a bowl.

4. In the bowl of a stand mixer fitted with the paddle attachment, cream together the butter, sugar, and salt on medium speed until light and fluffy, about 3 minutes.

5. Combine the eggs and milk in a bowl, then add to the butter mixture in three additions, mixing until fully incorporated after each addition and scraping down the bowl as needed. Add the honey and molasses and blend until just incorporated.

6. Add the sifted dry ingredients and the bran and mix on low speed until evenly moistened.

7. Scoop the batter into the prepared muffin pans, filling them three-quarters full. Gently tap the filled pans on the countertop to release any air bubbles.

8. Bake for 30 minutes, or until a skewer inserted near the center of a muffin comes out clean.

9. Cool the muffins in the pans for a few minutes, then transfer to wire racks to cool completely.

LEMON-POPPY SEED MUFFINS

2¾ cups pastry flour

2½ cups bread flour

1 tbsp plus 1½ tsp baking powder

2 cups (32 tbsp/4 sticks) butter

2⅔ cups granulated sugar

½ tsp salt

1 cup crème fraîche or sour cream

7 eggs

¼ cup fresh lemon juice

1½ tsp lemon extract

½ cup vegetable oil

2 tbsp lemon zest

⅓ cup poppy seeds

¼ cup coarse sugar

1. Preheat the oven to 375°F.

2. Lightly butter two 12-cup muffin pans, or use paper liners.

3. Sift together the pastry flour, bread flour, and baking powder into a medium bowl.

4. In the bowl of a stand mixer fitted with the paddle attachment, cream together the butter, granulated sugar, and salt on medium speed until light and fluffy, about 3 minutes. Scrape down the bowl as needed.

5. In a medium bowl, whisk together the crème fraîche or sour cream, eggs, lemon juice, lemon extract, and oil. Add to the butter mixture in two to three additions, mixing until fully incorporated after each addition and scraping down the bowl as needed. Stir in the lemon zest and poppy seeds.

6. Add the sifted dry ingredients and mix on low speed until evenly moistened.

7. Scoop the batter into the prepared muffin pans, filling them three-quarters of the way full. Gently tap the filled pans on the countertop to release any air bubbles. Sprinkle with the coarse sugar.

8. Bake for 30 minutes, or until a skewer inserted near the center of a muffin comes out clean.

9. Cool the muffins in the pans for a few minutes, then transfer to wire racks to cool completely.

CRANBERRY-ORANGE MUFFINS

MAKES 1 DOZEN MUFFINS

3 cups all-purpose flour

2 tsp baking powder

5 tbsp butter, soft

⅔ cup granulated sugar

1½ tsp salt

3 eggs

½ cup buttermilk

1 tbsp pure vanilla extract

¼ cup plus 1 tbsp vegetable oil

1½ cups fresh or frozen cranberries

1 tbsp grated orange zest

¼ cup coarse sugar

1. Preheat the oven to 375°F.

2. Lightly butter one 12-cup muffin pan, or use paper liners.

3. Sift together the flour and baking powder into a medium bowl.

4. In the bowl of a stand mixer fitted with the paddle attachment, cream together the butter, granulated sugar, and salt on medium speed, scraping down the bowl periodically, until light and fluffy, about 5 minutes.

5. In a separate bowl, whisk together the eggs, buttermilk, vanilla, and oil. Add to the butter mixture in two to three additions, mixing until fully incorporated after each addition and scraping down the bowl as needed.

6. Add the sifted dry ingredients and mix on low speed until evenly moistened. Fold in the cranberries and orange zest.

7. Scoop the batter into the prepared muffin pans, filling them three-quarters full. Gently tap the filled pans on the countertop to release any air bubbles. Sprinkle with the coarse sugar.

8. Bake for 30 minutes, or until a skewer inserted near the center of a muffin comes out clean.

9. Cool the muffins in the pans for a few minutes, then transfer to wire racks to cool completely.

BASIC COOKIE DOUGH

MAKES 2 POUNDS DOUGH

1 cup (16 tbsp/2 sticks) butter, soft

¾ cup sugar

1 tsp pure vanilla extract

2 eggs

4 cups cake flour, sifted

1. In the bowl of a stand mixer fitted with the paddle attachment, cream together the butter, sugar, and vanilla on medium speed, scraping down the bowl periodically, until smooth and light in color. Add the eggs one at a time, scraping down the bowl and blending until smooth after each addition. Add the flour all at once and mix on low speed just until combined.

2. Wrap the dough tightly in plastic wrap and refrigerate for at least 1 hour before using. (The dough can also be refrigerated or frozen for future use.)

NOTE *This dough can be used to line tart pans or as a base for bar cookies, as well as for rolled and cut cookies. Bake it at 350°F.*

ROLLED-OUT SUGAR COOKIES

½ cup (8 tbsp/1 stick) butter

1¾ cups sugar

¼ tsp salt

2 tsp pure vanilla extract

2 eggs

4 cups all-purpose flour

½ tsp baking soda

½ tsp cream of tartar

1. In the bowl of a stand mixer fitted with the paddle attachment, cream the butter, sugar, and salt on medium speed until light and fluffy, 3 to 4 minutes.

2. Reduce the mixer speed to low. Add the vanilla, then the eggs, one at a time, scraping down the bowl after each addition.

3. Sift the flour, baking soda, and cream of tartar together into a medium bowl. Add to the butter mixture and mix on low speed just until combined. Scrape down the bowl as needed.

4. Wrap the dough tightly in plastic wrap and refrigerate until chilled, 15 to 20 minutes.

5. While the dough is chilling, preheat the oven to 350°F. Line two baking sheets with parchment paper.

6. On a lightly floured surface, roll out the dough to a thickness of ¼ inch. Cut as desired with floured cookie cutters. Transfer the cookies to the prepared baking sheets, spacing them about 1½ inches apart. As you are working, reserve the scraps so they can be rolled again and cut.

7. Bake the cookies until lightly golden around the edges, 6 to 8 minutes. Rotate and switch the baking sheets as necessary for even baking.

8. Let the cookies cool for 1 minute on the baking sheets, then, using a spatula, transfer them to a wire rack to cool completely.

9. Store the cookies in an airtight container.

CHERRY-CHOCOLATE CHUNK COOKIES

½ cup (8 tbsp/1 stick) butter, soft

⅔ cup granulated sugar

½ cup packed light brown sugar

1 tsp salt

2 tsp pure vanilla extract

2 eggs

2 tsp baking soda

2½ cups all-purpose flour

1 cup dried cherries

3 cups semisweet chocolate chunks or very coarsely chopped semisweet chocolate

1. Preheat the oven to 350°F. Line two baking sheets with parchment paper.

2. In the bowl of a stand mixer fitted with the paddle attachment, gently mix the butter, granulated sugar, brown sugar, salt, and vanilla on medium speed until combined, about 2 minutes.

3. Add the eggs, one at a time, scraping down the bowl after each addition.

4. In a medium bowl, whisk to combine the baking soda and flour. Add to the butter mixture and mix on low speed just until combined.

5. Using a rubber spatula, fold in the cherries and chocolate. Scoop the dough onto the prepared baking sheets using a #40 scoop (about a heaping tablespoon), placing them about 1½ inches apart.

6. Bake the cookies until golden around the edges but still light in the center, 8 to 10 minutes. Rotate and switch the baking sheets as necessary for even baking.

7. Let the cookies cool for 1 minute on the baking sheets, then, using a spatula, transfer them to a wire rack to cool completely.

8. Store the cookies in an airtight container.

PISTACHIO-ORANGE BISCOTTI

MAKES ABOUT 5 DOZEN BISCOTTI

1¼ cups (20 tbsp/2½ sticks) butter, soft

1½ cups sugar

¼ cup grated orange zest

¼ tsp salt

3 eggs

1½ tsp pure vanilla extract

3¼ cups all-purpose flour

2 tsp baking powder

1½ cups unsalted shelled pistachios

1. Preheat the oven to 325°F. Line two baking sheets with parchment paper.

2. In the bowl of a stand mixer fitted with the paddle attachment, mix the butter, sugar, orange zest, and salt on medium speed for 2 minutes. Scrape down the bowl as needed.

3. Add the eggs one at a time, scraping down the bowl after each addition. Mix in the vanilla. Reduce the mixer speed to low.

4. Sift together the flour and baking powder into a medium bowl. Add to the butter mixture and mix on low speed just until combined. Using a rubber spatula, gently fold in the pistachios.

5. Divide the dough into two equal pieces. Shape each piece into a log about 10 inches long. Transfer the logs to the prepared baking sheets.

6. Bake until evenly golden brown and firm, 30 to 35 minutes. Rotate and switch the baking sheets as necessary for even baking. Remove the logs from the oven and reduce the oven temperature to 250°F.

7. Let the logs cool until easy to handle. Using a sharp, serrated knife, slice the logs diagonally into pieces ½ inch thick. Lay the slices flat on the baking sheets.

8. Return the biscotti to the oven and bake until crisp, 10 to 15 minutes. Rotate and switch the baking sheets as necessary for even baking. Flip the biscotti halfway through to ensure even browning.

9. Let the biscotti cool for 1 minute on the baking sheets, then, using a spatula, transfer to a wire rack to cool completely.

10. Store the biscotti in an airtight container.

PECAN DIAMONDS

MAKES ONE 12 × 16-INCH PAN PECAN DIAMONDS

COOKIE CRUST

1⅓ cups (21 tbsp/2½ sticks plus 1 tbsp) butter, soft

¾ cup sugar

1 tsp pure vanilla extract

1 egg

4 cups cake flour, sifted

FILLING

2½ cups packed light brown sugar

½ cup granulated sugar

2 cups (32 tbsp/4 sticks) butter

1 cup honey

Pinch salt

½ cup heavy cream

1 tsp pure vanilla extract

9 cups pecan halves, coarsely chopped

1. Preheat the oven to 350°F. Line a 12 x 16-inch baking sheet with parchment paper.

2. To make the crust, in the bowl of a stand mixer fitted with the paddle attachment, cream the butter, sugar, and vanilla on medium speed until light and fluffy, about 3 minutes. Add the egg, scraping down the bowl as needed.

3. Add the flour all at once and mix on low speed just until combined. Wrap the finished dough in plastic wrap and refrigerate for at least 1 hour before rolling.

4. On a floured surface, roll out the chilled dough to a thickness of about ¼ inch. Transfer the dough to the prepared baking sheet. Make sure the dough covers the base and sides of the pan. Prick holes in the dough all over using the tines of a fork.

5. Bake the crust until it is firm and just beginning to color (see Note). Remove from the oven and reserve.

6. To make the filling, in a large, heavy-bottomed pot, combine the sugars, butter, honey, salt, and cream. Bring the mixture to a boil, stirring constantly.

7. Once the mixture comes to a boil, stop stirring and continue to cook until the mixture registers 240°F on a candy thermometer. Wash down the sides of the pot with a pastry brush dipped in water as needed during cooking to prevent crystallization.

8. Remove the pot from the heat and stir in the vanilla and pecans. Spread the finished nut mixture into the prebaked crust.

9. Place the baking sheet onto another, larger sheet to catch any mixture if it boils over. Bake until the filling bubbles evenly across the surface and the crust is golden brown, 25 to 30 minutes. Cool thoroughly before cutting into 1-inch diamonds.

NOTE *Be sure to parbake the crust before beginning to prepare the filling. The filling must be used immediately once it is prepared, so the crust needs to be ready.*

FUDGY BROWNIES

1½ cups (24 tbsp/3 sticks) butter

8 oz unsweetened chocolate, finely chopped

3⅓ cups sugar

5 eggs

2 tsp pure vanilla extract

¼ tsp salt

2 cups cake flour, sifted

1. Preheat the oven to 350°F. Lightly grease a 9 x 13-inch baking pan and line it with parchment paper or aluminum foil, letting the ends hang over.

2. Fill the bottom of a double boiler or a saucepan with a couple of inches of water and bring to a simmer over medium heat. Put the butter and the chocolate in the top of the double boiler or in a medium heatproof bowl and place over the simmering water. Stir occasionally until the chocolate and butter are melted. Remove from the heat and set aside.

3. Put the sugar and eggs in the bowl of a stand mixer. Place the bowl over the simmering water and heat, stirring constantly, until all of the sugar is melted and the mixture is warm to the touch or registers 110°F on a candy thermometer.

4. Attach the bowl of sugar and egg mixture to the mixer, and fit with the whisk attachment. Add the vanilla and salt to the egg mixture and whip on medium speed for 5 minutes.

5. Reduce the speed to low. Drizzle in the melted chocolate and butter mixture and mix until combined. Scrape down the bowl as needed. Mix in the sifted flour.

6. Pour the batter into the prepared pan and spread with a spatula to level.

7. Bake until the brownies just begin to puff, 35 to 40 minutes.

8. Allow to cool completely in the pan before cutting.

POUND CAKE

MAKES ONE 9-INCH LOAF CAKE

1½ cups cake flour

3 tbsp cornstarch

2 tsp baking powder

Scant ⅔ cup (10 tbsp/1 stick plus 2 tbsp) butter

¾ cup sugar

Grated zest of 1 lemon

¼ tsp salt

4 eggs

1. Preheat the oven to 375°F. Lightly grease a 9-inch loaf pan and line it with parchment paper.

2. Sift together the flour, cornstarch, and baking powder into a medium bowl.

3. In a stand mixer fitted with the paddle attachment, cream together the butter, sugar, lemon zest, and salt on medium speed, scraping down the bowl as needed, until smooth and light in color.

4. With the mixer on low speed, add the eggs, one at a time, alternately with three additions of the sifted dry ingredients.

5. Pour the batter into the prepared pan.

6. Bake until a skewer inserted near the center of the cake comes out clean, about 45 minutes.

7. Allow the cake to cool to the touch in the pan. Remove the cake from the pan and transfer to a wire rack to cool completely.

Devil's Food Cake

1½ cups sugar

1½ cups cake flour

¼ tsp baking soda

2½ tsp baking powder

¾ cup unsweetened cocoa powder, sifted

2 eggs

½ cup butter (8 tbsp/1 stick), melted and kept warm

1 cup warm water

1 tsp pure vanilla extract

1. Preheat the oven to 350°F.

2. Lightly grease an 8-inch cake pan and line with a parchment paper circle.

3. Sift together the sugar, flour, baking soda, baking powder, and cocoa powder into a medium bowl.

4. In the bowl of a stand mixer fitted with the paddle attachment, combine the eggs, butter, water, and vanilla and mix on medium speed. Blend in the sifted dry ingredients, scraping down the bowl periodically, until a smooth batter forms.

5. Pour the batter into the prepared pan.

6. Bake until a skewer inserted near the center of the cake comes out clean, about 45 minutes.

7. Cool the cake in the pan for a few minutes, then unmold onto a wire rack to cool completely.

Pie Dough

MAKES ENOUGH DOUGH FOR TWO 9-INCH PIE CRUSTS, OR ONE DOUBLE-CRUST PIE

2½ cups all-purpose flour

2 tsp salt

1 cup (16 tbsp/2 sticks) butter, cold, cut into ½-inch cubes

½ cup cold water

1. Combine the flour and salt in the bowl of a food processor and pulse for 3 seconds to combine.

2. Add half of the cold butter. Pulse for 3 to 5 seconds, or until the butter is the size of peas.

3. Add the remaining butter and pulse for 3 seconds.

4. Add the water, a few tablespoons at a time, until a dough ball begins to form.

5. Wrap and chill the dough in the refrigerator for at least 1 hour before using, or freeze for future use.

Apple Pie

Pie Dough (opposite)

1 lb 8 oz Golden Delicious apples, peeled, cored, and sliced

¾ cup sugar

2 tbsp plus ½ tsp cornstarch

2 tbsp tapioca starch

½ tsp salt

½ tsp ground cinnamon

½ tsp freshly grated nutmeg

1 tbsp fresh lemon juice

2 tbsp butter, melted

1. Preheat the oven to 375°F.

2. Divide the pie dough into two equal pieces. Roll out half of the dough to a thickness of ⅛ inch and transfer it to a pie pan. Reserve the other half, wrapped tightly in plastic wrap and refrigerated.

3. In a large bowl, toss the apples with the sugar, cornstarch, tapioca starch, salt, cinnamon, nutmeg, lemon juice, and butter. Fill the pie shell with the apple mixture.

4. Roll out the remaining dough to a thickness of ⅛ inch and place it over the filling.

5. Crimp the edges to seal and cut several vents in the top of the pie.

6. Bake the pie until the filling is bubbling, 45 minutes to 1 hour.

7. Let cool completely before slicing and serving.

Pecan Pie

MAKES ONE 9-INCH PIE

½ recipe Pie Dough (opposite)

1¼ cup pecans

2 tbsp sugar

¼ cup bread flour

1½ tbsp corn syrup

3 eggs

1 tsp salt

2 tsp pure vanilla extract

2 tbsp melted butter

1. Roll out the dough to a thickness of ⅛ inch and transfer it to a pie pan.

2. Preheat the oven to 400°F. Spread the pecans in an even layer in the bottom of the unbaked pie crust.

3. Place the sugar and flour in a large stainless steel bowl and whisk to combine. Add the corn syrup and blend.

4. Add the eggs, salt, and vanilla and stir until they are fully combined. Stir in the butter.

5. Pour the filling into the pie shell.

6. Bake the pie until the filling has set and the crust is a golden brown, about 40 minutes.

7. Let cool completely before slicing and serving.

Coconut Cream Pie

½ recipe Pie Dough (page 370)

3 cups whole milk

1¼ cups sweetened shredded coconut, plus ¼ cup, toasted

1 cup sugar

1 vanilla bean, split lengthwise, seeds scraped

⅓ cup cornstarch

2 eggs

3 egg yolks

2 tbsp butter

1 cup Whipped Cream (page 387)

1. Preheat the oven to 350°F.

2. On a lightly dusted work surface, roll out the dough to a thickness of ⅛ inch and transfer it to a pie pan. Line the pie shell with parchment paper and fill with dry beans or pie weights. Blind bake the pie shell until very light golden brown, about 15 minutes. Remove the beans and parchment paper and continue to bake to a golden brown, about 5 minutes more. Cool the pie shell completely.

3. Combine 2¼ cups of the milk with the coconut and ¾ cup of the sugar in a saucepan. Add the vanilla bean seeds and pod. Bring the mixture to a boil, and stir to dissolve the sugar.

4. Meanwhile, combine the remaining ¼ cup sugar with the cornstarch, and stir together with a whisk. Add the remaining ¾ cup milk, the eggs, and egg yolks and whisk to blend.

5. Temper the egg mixture by gradually adding one-third of the hot milk mixture, whisking constantly. Return the tempered egg mixture to the remaining milk mixture in the saucepan and cook, stirring constantly, just until it reaches a boil. Cook, stirring constantly, for 2 minutes more.

6. Remove the pan from the heat and whisk in the butter. Strain the filling through a fine-mesh sieve.

7. Pour the hot filling into the prebaked pie shell. Cover with plastic wrap pressed directly on the surface of the cream to prevent a skin from forming. Cool to room temperature.

8. Refrigerate overnight. Just before serving, pipe a border of whipped cream onto the pie and garnish with the toasted coconut.

CRÊPES SUZETTE

10 tablespoons sugar

1½ cups (24 tbsp/3 sticks) butter, cubed

1 tbsp orange zest

¾ cup fresh orange juice

30 Dessert Crêpes (page 376)

¾ cup Grand Marnier

¾ cup brandy or cognac

Whipped Cream (page 387), as needed

1. Sprinkle the sugar evenly across the bottom of a preheated large sauté pan. Allow the sugar to melt and start to caramelize.

2. As the sugar begins to caramelize, add approximately 2 tablespoons of the butter to the outside edges of the pan and gently shake the pan. This will allow the butter to evenly temper and blend with the sugar. Add the remaining butter over low heat and swirl the sauce together.

3. Add the orange zest and shake the pan gently until all of the ingredients have blended together and become a light-orange caramel color.

4. Slowly pour the orange juice around the outer edges of the pan, allowing it to temper and blend with the melted sugar.

5. Shake the pan gently to incorporate all of the ingredients and allow the sauce to thicken.

6. Carefully pick up one crêpe and place it into the sauce. Flip the crêpe over to coat the opposite side. Set it aside on a baking sheet lined with parchment paper.

7. Repeat with the remaining crêpes, moving quickly so the sauce does not become too thick.

8. Remove the pan from the heat and add the Grand Marnier. Return the pan to the heat and shake gently. Do not ignite it.

9. Slide the pan back and forth over the burner to allow the pan to get hot again.

10. Remove the pan, add the brandy or cognac, and tip the pan slightly to ignite. Shake the pan until the flame burns out.

11. Plate 3 crêpes per portion on individual dessert plates, overlapping one over the other, and coat with the sauce. Garnish with whipped cream and serve immediately.

Dessert Crêpes

4 eggs

2 cups heavy cream

1 cup whole milk

1 tbsp vegetable oil

2 cups all-purpose flour

½ cup confectioners' sugar

1 tsp salt

1½ tsp pure vanilla extract

1. Combine the eggs, cream, milk, and oil in a large bowl and beat just until blended.

2. Sift together the flour, sugar, and salt into a large bowl.

3. Add the wet ingredients and mix until smooth, scraping down the bowl as necessary. Add the vanilla. Stir just until the ingredients are blended into a relatively smooth batter. (The batter may be prepared to this point and refrigerated for up to 12 hours. Strain the batter if necessary before cooking the crêpes.)

4. Ladle a small amount of batter into a preheated, buttered crêpe pan over medium heat, swirling the pan to coat the bottom with batter.

5. When the crêpe has set, using a long, offset spatula, turn it over and finish cooking on the opposite side.

6. Fill as desired, roll or fold, or use in other desserts (see Crêpes Suzette, page 375).

NOTE *The cooked crêpes may be cooled, stacked between parchment paper, wrapped, and refrigerated or frozen. Thaw frozen crêpes before filling and folding.*

CRÈME CARAMEL

MAKES 5 SERVINGS

CARAMEL

½ cup sugar

CUSTARD

1 cup plus 3 tbsp whole milk

¼ cup plus 2 tbsp sugar

1 tsp pure vanilla extract

2 eggs, lightly beaten

2 egg yolks

1. Preheat the oven to 325°F.

2. To make the caramel, add a small amount of the sugar to a small pan set over medium heat. Allow the sugar to melt.

3. Add the remaining sugar in small increments, allowing it to melt before each new addition. Continue this process until all the sugar has been added. Cook the caramel to a deep amber color.

4. Divide the caramel equally among five 4-ounce ramekins, swirling to coat the bottoms. Place the ramekins into a deep baking dish and reserve.

5. To prepare the custard, combine the milk and 3 tablespoons sugar in a small saucepan and bring to a simmer over medium heat, stirring gently with a wooden spoon. Remove from the heat and add the vanilla.

6. In a small bowl, combine the eggs, egg yolks, and remaining 3 tablespoons sugar. Temper the egg mixture by gradually adding about one-third of the hot milk mixture, whisking constantly. Return the tempered egg mixture to the remaining milk mixture in the saucepan.

7. Strain the custard through a fine-mesh sieve into a bowl and then ladle it into the caramel-coated ramekins, filling them three-quarters full. Pour enough water into the baking pan to come halfway up the sides of the ramekins to make a water bath. Be careful not to splash any water into the custard. Bake the ramekins until fully set, about 1 hour.

8. Remove the custards from the water bath and wipe the ramekins dry. Allow the custards to cool.

9. Wrap each custard individually and refrigerate them for at least 24 hours before unmolding and serving.

10. To unmold the custards, run a small sharp knife between the custard and the side of the ramekin, invert each one onto an individual serving plate, and tap it lightly to release.

CRÈME BRÛLÉE

2 cups heavy cream

Pinch salt

½ vanilla bean

3 egg yolks, beaten

1¼ cup plus 2 tbsp granulated sugar, plus more as needed

1. Preheat the oven to 325°F.

2. In a saucepan, combine the cream and salt and bring to a simmer over medium heat, stirring gently with a wooden spoon. Remove the pan from the heat. Split the vanilla bean lengthwise, scrape the seeds from the pod, and add both the scraped seeds and the pod to the cream. Allow to infuse for 10 minutes.

3. Return the saucepan to the heat and bring the heavy cream mixture to a boil.

4. In a bowl, whisk together the egg yolks and sugar. Temper the egg mixture by gradually adding about one-third of the hot cream mixture, whisking constantly. Return the tempered egg mixture to the remaining cream mixture in the saucepan. Strain the custard through a fine-mesh sieve into a bowl and then ladle it into five 6-ounce crème brûlée ramekins, filling them halfway to three-quarters full.

5. Place the custards in a baking pan and pour enough water into the pan to come halfway up the sides of the ramekins to make a water bath. Be careful not to splash any water into the custard. Bake until just set, 20 to 25 minutes.

6. Remove the custards from the water bath and wipe the ramekins dry. Wrap each custard in plastic wrap and refrigerate until fully chilled.

7. To finish the crèmes brûlée, evenly coat the surface of each custard with a thin layer (¹⁄₁₆ inch) of sugar. Use a propane torch to melt and caramelize the sugar.

Bread and Butter Pudding

½ cup raisins

½ cup rum

Six 1-inch-thick slices homemade or store-bought Challah (page 356)

6 tbsp butter, melted

4 cups whole milk

¾ cup sugar

6 eggs, beaten

4 egg yolks, beaten

½ tsp pure vanilla extract

½ tsp ground cinnamon

½ tsp salt

1. Preheat the oven to 350°F.

2. Place the raisins in a small bowl and add the rum. Set them aside to plump for 20 minutes, then drain.

3. Cut the bread into ½-inch cubes. Place the cubes on a baking sheet and drizzle with the butter. Toast in the oven, stirring once or twice, until golden brown.

4. Combine the milk and half the sugar in a saucepan and bring to a boil.

5. Meanwhile, whisk together the eggs, egg yolks, vanilla, and the remaining sugar in a medium bowl. Gradually add about one-third of the hot milk mixture, whisking constantly. Add the remaining hot milk and strain the custard into a bowl.

6. Fill a bowl that is larger than the custard bowl halfway with ice water.

7. Add the bread mixture, cinnamon, salt, and drained raisins to the custard. Soak over the ice bath for at least 1 hour to allow the mixture to absorb the custard. Lightly brush ten 6-ounce ramekins with softened butter.

8. Ladle the mixture into the prepared ramekins, filling them three-quarters full. Place the ramekins in a large roasting pan and add enough water to the pan to come halfway up the sides of the ramekins, being careful not to splash any water into the custard. Bake until just set, 45 to 50 minutes.

9. Remove the custards from the water bath and wipe the ramekins dry. Refrigerate until fully chilled before serving.

RICE PUDDING

4 cups whole milk

½ cup sugar

1 cinnamon stick

1 orange slice

½ cup long-grain white rice, rinsed

1 tbsp cornstarch

2 eggs

1 tsp pure vanilla extract

1. Combine the milk, ¼ cup of the sugar, the cinnamon stick, and the orange slice in a nonreactive saucepan and bring to a boil. Add the rice and simmer over low heat until tender, about 30 minutes.

2. Meanwhile, just as the rice is finished cooking, combine the cornstarch with the remaining ¼ cup sugar in a bowl. Add the eggs and whisk until the mixture is completely smooth.

3. Remove the orange slice and cinnamon stick from the rice. Temper the egg mixture by adding about one-third of the hot milk and rice mixture, whisking constantly. Return the tempered egg mixture to the remaining hot milk in the saucepan. Continue cooking, whisking constantly, until the pudding comes to a boil. Remove from the heat and stir in the vanilla.

4. Pour the pudding into serving dishes. Cover and refrigerate until fully chilled.

CHOCOLATE SOUFFLÉ

MAKES 10 SERVINGS

¾ cup sugar, plus more as needed

PASTRY CREAM

2 cups milk

½ cup sugar

⅔ cups all-purpose flour

1 egg

2 egg yolks

6 tbsp (¾ stick) butter, soft

10 oz bittersweet chocolate, coarsely chopped

3 egg yolks

12 egg whites

1. Preheat the oven to 350°F. Prepare an ice-water bath.

2. Coat the inside of ten 4-ounce ramekins with softened butter, making sure to coat the rims as well as the insides, and dust with sugar.

3. To make the pastry cream, combine ¼ cup of the milk with ¼ cup of the sugar in a small saucepan and bring to a boil, stirring gently with a wooden spoon.

4. Meanwhile, in a medium bowl, combine the flour with the remaining ¼ cup sugar. Whisk in the remaining 1¾ cups milk. Add the egg and egg yolks and whisk until the mixture is completely smooth.

5. Temper the egg mixture by gradually adding about one-third of the hot milk mixture, whisking constantly. Return the tempered egg mixture to the remaining milk mixture in the saucepan. Cook over medium heat, whisking, until the pastry cream comes to a boil and is thick enough that the whisk leaves a trail when stirred. Transfer the pastry cream to a bowl and set over the ice bath to cool completely. (If desired, the pastry cream may be made ahead of time and refrigerated, covered, until ready to use.)

6. Melt the butter and chocolate together in a bowl set over a pan of barely simmering water, gently stirring to blend. Blend the chocolate mixture into the pastry cream. Whisk in the egg yolks and set aside.

7. In a stand mixer fitted with the whisk attachment, beat the egg whites to soft peaks.

8. While continuing to beat, gradually sprinkle in the ¾ cup sugar, then beat the meringue to medium peaks.

9. Gently blend approximately one-third of the meringue into the chocolate base. Fold in the remaining meringue, thoroughly incorporating it.

10. Divide the soufflé mixture among the prepared ramekins.

11. Bake until fully risen, about 20 minutes. Serve immediately.

CHOCOLATE MOUSSE

5 oz bittersweet chocolate, coarsely chopped

2 tbsp butter

3 eggs, separated

1 tbsp water

2 tbsp sugar

½ cup heavy cream, whipped

1. Combine the chocolate and butter in a heatproof bowl and set over a pot of simmering water, or use a double boiler. Cook, stirring, until chocolate is melted.

2. Fit a stand mixer with the whisk attachment. In the mixer bowl, combine the egg yolks with the water and 1 tablespoon of the sugar and whisk over a hot water bath until the temperature holds at 145°F for 15 seconds. Remove from the heat and transfer to the stand mixer. Beat until cool.

3. In a clean mixing bowl, combine the egg whites with the remaining sugar and whisk over a hot water bath to 145°F. Remove the whites from the heat and beat to full volume. Continue beating until cool.

4. Using a large rubber spatula, fold the chocolate mixture into the egg yolks.

5. Fold the egg white mixture into the egg yolk and chocolate mixture.

6. Fold in the whipped cream.

7. To serve, spoon or pipe the mousse into 5 small bowls or into a larger serving dish.

RASPBERRY MOUSSE

2½ tsp gelatin

6 tbsp water

½ cup heavy cream

1 cup raspberry purée

3 egg whites

5 tbsp sugar

1. In a small bowl, sprinkle the gelatin over the water and allow to bloom. Set aside.

2. In the bowl of a stand mixer fitted with the whisk attachment, whip the heavy cream to medium peaks. Cover and refrigerate the whipped cream.

3. Warm ½ cup of the fruit purée in a saucepan over medium heat. Remove from the heat and set aside. Melt the bloomed gelatin in a heatproof bowl set over a pan of barely simmering water. Add the melted gelatin to the purée and stir to incorporate. Mix in the remaining ½ cup purée.

4. Combine the egg whites and sugar in a heatproof bowl set over a pan of barely simmering water. Heat the mixture, stirring constantly with a wire whisk, until it registers 145°F on a candy thermometer. Transfer the mixture to the bowl of a stand mixer fitted with the whisk attachment and whip on high speed until stiff peaks form. Continue beating until the meringue has completely cooled.

5. Cool the raspberry mixture to 70°F.

6. Using a spatula, gently blend approximately one-third of the cooled meringue into the raspberry mixture to lighten it. Fold in the remaining meringue, thoroughly incorporating it. Fold in the reserved whipped cream.

7. Immediately pipe or ladle the mousse into serving dishes.

CREAM CHEESE ICING

MAKES 5 CUPS ICING

1 lb cream cheese
2 cups (32 tbsp/4 sticks) butter, soft
¾ cup confectioners' sugar, sifted
1 tbsp pure vanilla extract

1. In the bowl of a stand mixer fitted with the paddle attachment, beat the cream cheese on low speed until smooth.

2. Add the butter, a little at a time, and beat well. Add the sugar and blend on low speed until fully incorporated. Beat on high speed until light and fluffy, about 5 minutes. Add the vanilla and mix until combined.

3. Cover and refrigerate until ready to use.

ITALIAN BUTTERCREAM

MAKES ABOUT 6 CUPS BUTTERCREAM

¾ cup sugar
5 egg whites
¼ cup water
2 cups (32 tbsp/4 sticks) butter, cut into 1-inch cubes, at room temperature
1½ tsp pure vanilla extract

1. Combine ½ cup of the sugar with the egg whites in the bowl of a stand mixer fitted with the whisk attachment.

2. Combine the water with the remaining ¼ cup sugar in a small saucepan. Cook the mixture over medium heat, without stirring, until it reaches the soft ball stage, 240°F on a candy thermometer.

3. When the sugar syrup reaches 230°F, begin whipping the egg whites on medium speed. The egg whites should reach soft peaks at the same time the sugar reaches the desired temperature.

4. With the mixer running, stream the hot sugar into the egg whites and continue whipping until cooled to room temperature.

5. Once the meringue is cool, switch to the paddle attachment and gradually add the butter on medium speed. Add the vanilla and beat until smooth and light.

6. Cover and refrigerate until ready to use.

LEMON CURD

1¼ cups (20 tbsp/2½ sticks) butter, cubed

1¼ cups sugar

1 tbsp lemon zest

1 cup fresh lemon juice

12 egg yolks

1. Combine the butter, half of the sugar, and the lemon zest and juice in a medium pot and bring to a boil over medium heat, stirring gently to dissolve the sugar.

2. Meanwhile, in a medium bowl, blend the egg yolks with the remaining sugar. Temper the egg-yolk mixture by gradually adding about one-third of the lemon juice mixture, whisking constantly. Return the tempered egg-yolk mixture to the lemon juice mixture in the pan and continue cooking, whisking constantly, until the mixture comes to a boil.

3. Strain the curd into a large shallow container or bowl. Cover with plastic wrap pressed directly on the surface to prevent a skin from forming. Set over an ice water bath to cool. Cover and refrigerate until ready to use.

CLASSIC CARAMEL SAUCE

MAKES 4 CUPS SAUCE

3 cups heavy cream

2 cups sugar

¾ cup corn syrup

5 tbsp butter, cubed, soft

1. Place the heavy cream in a saucepan over medium heat and bring to a boil. Reduce the heat to low and keep warm.

2. Prepare an ice bath. Combine the sugar and corn syrup in a heavy-bottomed saucepan and cook over medium heat, stirring constantly, until all the sugar has dissolved. Stop stirring and continue to cook to a golden caramel. Remove from the heat and shock the bottom of the saucepan in the ice bath to stop the cooking.

3. Remove the pan from the ice bath and stir in the butter. Carefully stir in the hot cream and mix until fully blended. Serve the sauce warm or chilled.

CHOCOLATE SAUCE

1¼ cups sugar

2 cups water

⅓ cup corn syrup

1¼ cups cocoa powder, sifted

1 lb bittersweet chocolate, melted

1. Combine the sugar, water, and corn syrup in a heavy-bottomed saucepan and bring to a boil over medium-high heat. Remove from the heat.

2. Put the cocoa in a bowl and add enough of the hot sugar syrup to make a paste, stirring until smooth. Gradually add the remaining syrup and mix until fully incorporated.

3. Add the chocolate and blend until fully incorporated.

4. Strain the sauce through a fine-mesh sieve. Serve warm or chilled.

WHIPPED CREAM

MAKES ABOUT 2 CUPS

1 cup heavy cream

3 tbsp confectioners' sugar, plus more as needed

½ tsp pure vanilla extract

In the bowl of a stand mixer fitted with the whisk attachment, beat the cream until soft peaks form. Beat in the sugar and vanilla. Taste and add more sugar if desired. Continue beating until soft to stiff peaks form.

Vanilla Ice Cream

2 cups whole milk

2 cups heavy cream

1 vanilla bean, split lengthwise and scraped

1 cup sugar

3 tbsp corn syrup

¼ tsp salt

15 egg yolks

1. Combine the milk, heavy cream, vanilla bean pod and seeds, ½ cup of the sugar, the corn syrup, and salt in a saucepan.

2. Bring the mixture to a simmer over medium heat, stirring constantly, 7 to 10 minutes.

3. Remove the saucepan from the heat, cover the pan, and allow it to infuse for 5 minutes.

4. Meanwhile, in a bowl, blend the egg yolks with the remaining ½ cup sugar.

5. Remove the vanilla pod from the milk mixture and return the mixture to a simmer.

6. Temper the egg yolk mixture by gradually adding about one-third of the hot milk mixture, whisking constantly. Return the tempered egg-yolk mixture to the saucepan with the remaining hot milk mixture, stirring constantly over medium heat until the mixture is thick enough to coat the back of a spoon, 3 to 5 minutes.

7. Strain the ice cream base into a metal container over an ice bath and stir occasionally until the base registers below 40°F on an instant-read thermometer, about 1 hour. Cover and refrigerate the base for a minimum of 12 hours.

8. Process the base in an ice-cream machine according to the manufacturer's directions.

9. Pack the ice cream in storage containers or molds as desired and freeze for several hours or overnight before serving.

COFFEE ICE CREAM *Substitute ½ cup coarsely ground coffee for the vanilla bean. Strain the infused milk before proceeding with the recipe.*

CHOCOLATE ICE CREAM *Before straining the ice cream base, stir 6 oz melted bittersweet chocolate into the mixture.*

RASPBERRY GRANITA

MAKES 6 CUPS GRANITA

3 cups raspberry purée

3 cups water

1 cup sugar

1 tbsp fresh lemon juice

1. Place a 9 x 13-inch pan in the freezer to chill.

2. In a large bowl, combine the purée, water, sugar, and lemon juice. Stir until blended and the sugar has dissolved.

3. Pour into the chilled pan and place in the freezer. Scrape with a fork every 15 to 20 minutes until it resembles crushed ice.

4. Cover tightly and freeze until ready to serve.

MANGO GRANITA

MAKES 4 CUPS GRANITA

1 cup mango purée

2¾ cups water

½ cup sugar

3 tbsp dark rum

3 tbsp fresh lemon juice

1. Place a 9 x 13-inch pan in the freezer to chill.

2. In a medium bowl, combine the purée, water, sugar, rum, and lemon juice.

3. Pour into the chilled pan and place in the freezer. Scrape with a fork every 15 to 20 minutes until it resembles crushed ice.

4. Cover tightly and freeze until ready to serve.

RASPBERRY COULIS

MAKES 3 CUPS COULIS

7½ cups (about 2 lb) raspberries, fresh or frozen

1 cup sugar, plus more as needed

1 tbsp fresh lemon juice, plus more as needed

1. Combine the raspberries, sugar, and lemon juice in a medium saucepan over medium heat. Simmer, stirring, until the sugar has dissolved, about 10 minutes.

2. Strain the coulis through a fine-mesh sieve.

3. Adjust the flavor with additional sugar and lemon juice, if necessary. Serve immediately, or cover and refrigerate until ready to serve.

THICK HOT CHOCOLATE

MAKES 10 CUPS HOT CHOCOLATE

1 lb 13 oz dark chocolate (64%), chopped

5 cups whole milk

1¾ cups heavy cream

½ tsp fleur de sel

1. Put the chocolate in a medium heatproof bowl.

2. In a medium saucepan over medium heat, bring the milk and heavy cream to a boil and pour it over the chocolate.

3. Using an immersion blender, blend the milk and cream mixture with the chocolate. Add the salt and continue to blend until you obtain a uniform mixture.

4. Strain and serve hot.

THIN HOT CHOCOLATE

1 lb 8 oz dark chocolate (64%), chopped
3½ qt whole milk
½ tsp fleur de sel

1. Put the chocolate in a medium heatproof bowl.

2. In a medium saucepan over medium heat, bring the milk to a boil and pour it over the chocolate.

3. Using an immersion blender, blend the milk with the chocolate. Add the salt and continue to blend until you obtain a uniform mixture.

4. Strain and serve hot.

Conversions and Equivalents

Experienced home cooks have traditionally relied on pinches, dashes, and a little of this or that. They know when a food is done cooking by touch or feel. They can accomplish this feat because they have become accustomed over time to the way foods look when they are done, what their hands and fingertips can hold, how fast salt pours from their shaker, and how full their pans and bowls typically look when making a particular dish.

However, you may want to follow the measurements given in a recipe exactly the first time you make it, then make adjustments to suit your taste. If you are reading and using these recipes in a kitchen outside the United States, you will most likely need to convert to metric measurements for weight, volume, and temperature. The unit of measure for oven temperatures in some areas also differs from those in the United States; "gas marks" are used instead of a Fahrenheit or Celsius temperature. The information in the following charts allows you to make a variety of conversions—pounds to kilograms, ounces to grams, cups to milliliters and liters, Fahrenheit to Celsius, and volume to weight.

WEIGHT CONVERSIONS

U.S. MEASURE	METRIC (rounded)
½ oz	15 g
1 oz	30 g
2 oz	55 g
3 oz	85 g
4 oz (¼ lb)	115 g
8 oz (½ lb)	225 g
1 lb (16 oz)	455 g
5 lb	2.25 kg
10 lb	4.5 kg

VOLUME CONVERSIONS

VOLUME MEASURE	U.S. VOLUME	METRIC (rounded)
1 tsp	⅙ fl oz	5 ml
1 Tbsp (3 tsp)	½ fl oz	15 ml
⅛ cup (2 Tbsp)	1 fl oz	30 ml
¼ cup	2 fl oz	60 ml
⅓ cup	2⅔ fl oz	80 ml
½ cup	4 fl oz	120 ml
⅔ cup	5⅓ fl oz	160 ml
¾ cup	6 fl oz	180 ml
1 cup	8 fl oz	240 ml
¾ pt (1½ cups)	12 fl oz	360 ml
1 pt (2 cups)	16 fl oz	480 ml
1 qt (2 pt)	32 fl oz	950 ml (1 L)
1 gal (4 qt; 16 cups)	128 fl oz	3.75 L

TEMPERATURE CONVERSIONS

GAS MARK	FAHRENHEIT	CELSIUS	DESCRIPTION
1	275	120	very slow oven
2	300	150	slow oven
3	325	160	slow oven
4	350	180	moderate oven
5	375	190	moderate oven
6	400	200	hot oven
7	450	230	very hot oven
8	475	250	very hot oven

TO CONVERT OUNCES AND POUNDS TO GRAMS
Multiply ounces by 28.35 to determine grams; divide pounds by 2.2 to determine kilograms.

TO CONVERT GRAMS TO OUNCES OR POUNDS
Divide grams by 28.35 to determine ounces; divide grams by 453.59 to determine pounds.

TO CONVERT FLUID OUNCES TO MILLILITERS
Multiply fluid ounces by 30 to determine milliliters.

TO CONVERT MILLILITERS TO FLUID OUNCES
Divide milliliters by 30 to determine fluid ounces.

GLOSSARY

ALBUMEN: The egg white. Makes up about 70 percent of the egg and contains most of the protein in the egg.

AL DENTE: Literally, "to the tooth"; refers to an item, such as pasta or vegetables, cooked until it is tender but still firm.

ARBORIO: A high-starch, short-grain rice traditionally used in the preparation of risotto.

AROMATICS: Ingredients, such as herbs, spices, vegetables, citrus fruits, wines, and vinegars, used to enhance the flavor and fragrance of food.

ARROWROOT: A powdered starch made from the root of a tropical plant of the same name. Used primarily as a thickener. Remains clear when cooked.

BAIN-MARIE: The French term for a water bath used to cook foods gently by surrounding the cooking vessel with simmering water.

BAKE: To cook food by surrounding it with dry heat in a closed environment, as in an oven.

BARBECUE: To cook food by grilling it over a wood or charcoal fire. Usually some sort of marinade or sauce is brushed on the item during cooking. Also, meat that is cooked in this way.

BÂTONNET: Items cut into pieces somewhat larger than julienne; ¼ x ¼ x 1 to 2 inches. French for "stick" or "small stick."

BLANCH: To cook an item briefly in boiling water or hot fat before finishing or storing it. Preserves the color, lessens strong flavors, and helps remove the peels of some fruits and vegetables.

BLEND: A mixture of two or more flavors combined to achieve a particular flavor or quality. Also, to mix two or more ingredients together until combined.

BOIL: TO cook items are by immersing in liquid at or above the boiling point (212°F).

BOUQUET GARNI: A small bundle of herbs tied with string. It is used to flavor stocks, braises, and other preparations. Usually contains bay leaf, parsley, thyme, and possibly other aromatics wrapped in leek leaves.

BRAISE: A cooking method in which the main item, usually meat, is seared in fat, then simmered at a low temperature in a small amount of stock or another liquid (usually halfway up the meat item) in a covered vessel for a long time. The cooking liquid is then reduced and used as the base of a sauce.

BRAN: The outer layer of a cereal grain and the part highest in fiber.

BRINE: A solution of salt, water, and seasonings used to preserve or moisten foods.

BROIL: To cook by means of a radiant heat source placed above the food.

BROILER: The piece of equipment used to broil foods; can be found as a setting on most ovens.

BROTH: A flavorful, aromatic liquid made by simmering water or stock with meat, vegetables, and/or spices and herbs.

BROWN SAUCE: A sauce made from a brown stock and aromatics and thickened by roux, a pure starch slurry, and/or a reduction; includes demi-glace, jus de veau lié, and pan sauces.

BROWN STOCK: An amber liquid produced by simmering browned bones and meat (usually veal or beef) with vegetables and aromatics (including caramelized mirepoix and tomato purée).

BRUISE: To partially crush a food item in order to release its flavor.

BRUNOISE: Dice cut of ⅛-in cubes. For a brunoise cut, items are first cut in julienne, then cut crosswise. For a fine brunoise of 1/16-in cubes, cut items first in fine julienne.

BUTTERFLY: To cut an item (usually meat or seafood) and open out the edges like a book or the wings of a butterfly.

BUTTERMILK: A dairy beverage with a slightly sour flavor similar to that of yogurt. Traditionally, the liquid by-product of butter churning, now usually made by culturing skim milk.

CANDY THERMOMETER: A thermometer used to measure the temperature of sugar and other ingredients when making caramel, confections, and meringues. Can also be used as a deep-fry thermometer.

CARAMELIZATION: The process of browning sugar in the presence of heat. Occurs from 320° to 360°F.

CARRY-OVER COOKING: Heat retained in cooked foods that allows them to continue cooking even after removal from the cooking medium. Especially important to roasted foods.

CEPHALOPOD: Marine creatures whose tentacles and arms are attached directly to their heads, such as squid and octopus.

CHIFFONADE: Leafy vegetables or herbs cut into fine shreds; often used as a garnish.

CHILE: The fruit of certain types of capsicum peppers (not related to black pepper), used fresh or dried as a seasoning. Chiles come in many types (e.g., jalapeño, serrano, poblano) and varying degrees of spiciness.

CHILI POWDER: Dried chiles that have been ground or crushed, often with other ground spices and herbs added.

CHOP: To cut into pieces of roughly the same size. Also, a small cut of meat including part of the rib.

CHOWDER: A thick soup that may be made from a variety of ingredients but usually contains potatoes.

COAGULATION: The curdling or clumping of proteins, usually due to the application of heat or acid.

COARSE CHOP: A type of preparation in which food is cut into pieces of roughly the same size. Used for items such as mirepoix, where appearance is not important.

COCOA: The pods of the cacao tree, processed to remove the cocoa butter and ground into powder. Used as a flavoring.

COLLAGEN: A fibrous protein found in the connective tissue of animals, used to make glue and gelatin. Breaks down into gelatin when cooked in a moist environment for an extended period of time.

COMBINATION METHOD: A cooking method that involves the application of both dry and moist heat to the main item (e.g., meats seared in fat then simmered in a sauce for braising or stewing).

COMPOSED SALAD: A salad in which the items are carefully arranged separately on a plate, rather than tossed together.

CONDIMENT: An aromatic mixture, such as pickles, chutney, and some sauces and relishes, which accompanies food.

CONVECTION: A method of heat transfer in which heat is transmitted through the circulation of air or water.

CONVECTION OVEN: An oven that employs convection currents by forcing hot air through fans so it circulates around food, cooking it quickly and evenly.

CORNSTARCH: A fine, white powder milled from dried corn; used primarily as a thickener for sauce and occasionally as an ingredient in batters.

COULIS: A thick purée of vegetables or fruit, served hot or cold. Traditionally refers to the thickened juices of cooked meat, fish, shellfish purée, or certain thick soups.

COUSCOUS: Pellets of semolina or cracked wheat usually cooked by steaming, traditionally in a couscoussière. Also, the stew with which this grain is traditionally served.

COUSCOUSSIÈRE: A set of nesting pots, similar to a steamer, used to cook couscous.

CRUSTACEAN: A class of hard-shelled arthropods with elongated bodies, primarily aquatic, which include edible species such as lobster, crab, shrimp, and crayfish.

CURRY: A mixture of spices, used primarily in Indian, Jamaican, and Thai cuisine. May include turmeric, coriander, cumin, cayenne or other chiles, cardamom, cinnamon, clove, fennel, fenugreek, ginger, and garlic. May be dry or a paste. Also, the name for the stew-like dish seasoned with curry.

DEBEARD: To remove the shaggy, inedible fibers from a mussel. These fibers anchor the mussel to its mooring.

DEEP FRY: To cook food by immersion in hot fat; deep-fried foods are often coated with bread crumbs or batter before being cooked.

DEEP-POACH: To cook food gently in enough simmering liquid to completely submerge the food.

DEGLAZE: To use a liquid, such as wine, water, or stock, to dissolve food particles and/or caramelized drippings left in a pan after roasting or sautéing. The resulting mix then becomes the base for the accompanying sauce.

DEGREASE: To skim the fat off the surface of a liquid, such as a stock or sauce.

DICE: To cut ingredients into evenly sized small cubes (¼ inch for small, ½ inch for medium, and ¾ inch for large is the standard).

DIRECT HEAT: A method of heat transfer in which heat waves radiate from a source (e.g., an open burner or grill) and travel directly to the item being heated with no conductor between heat source and food. Examples are grilling, broiling, and toasting. Also known as radiant heat.

DREDGE: To coat food with a dry ingredient such as flour or bread crumbs prior to frying or sautéing.

DURUM: A very hard wheat typically milled into semolina, which is primarily used in the making of pasta.

DUSTING: Distributing a film of flour, sugar, cocoa powder, or other such ingredients on pans or work surfaces, or on finished products as a garnish.

DUTCH OVEN: A kettle, usually of cast iron, used for stewing and braising on the stovetop or in the oven.

EGG WASH: A mixture of beaten eggs (whole eggs, yolks, or whites) and a liquid, usually milk or water, used to coat baked goods to give them a sheen.

EMULSION: A mixture of two or more liquids, one of which is a fat or oil and the other is water based, so that tiny globules of one are suspended in the other. This may involve the use of stabilizers, such as egg or mustard. Emulsions may be temporary, permanent, or semipermanent.

ENDOSPERM: The largest portion of the inside of the seed of a flowering plant, such as wheat; composed primarily of starch and protein. This is the portion used primarily in milled grain products.

FIBER, DIETARY FIBER: The structural component of plants that is necessary to the human diet and is indigestible. Also referred to as roughage.

FILÉ: A thickener made from ground dried sassafras leaves; used primarily in gumbos.

FINES HERBES: A mixture of herbs, usually parsley, chervil, tarragon, and chives, which lose their flavor quickly. They are generally added to the dish just prior to serving.

FOLD: To gently mix together two items, usually a light, airy mixture with a denser mixture.

FOND: The French term for stock. Also describes the pan drippings remaining after sautéing or roasting food. It is often deglazed and used as a base for sauces.

FOOD MILL: A strainer with a crank-operated, curved blade. Used to purée soft foods while straining.

FOOD PROCESSOR: A machine with interchangeable blades and disks and a removable bowl and lid separate from the motor housing. It can be used for a variety of tasks, including chopping, grinding, puréeing, emulsifying, kneading, slicing, shredding, and cutting into julienne.

FORK-TENDER: Degree of doneness in braised foods and vegetables; fork-tender foods are easily pierced or cut by a fork, or should slide readily from a fork when lifted.

FRENCHING: The process of cutting and scraping meat from rib bones before cooking.

GARNISH: An edible decoration or accompaniment to a dish or item.

GAZPACHO: A cold soup made from vegetables, typically tomatoes, cucumbers, peppers, and onions.

GELATIN: A protein-based substance found in animal bones and connective tissue. When dissolved in hot liquid and then cooled, it can be used as a thickener and stabilizer.

GELATINIZATION: A phase in the process of thickening a liquid with starch in which the starch molecules swell to form a network that traps water molecules.

GLUTEN: A protein present in wheat flour that develops through hydration and mixing to form elastic strands that build structure and aid in leavening.

GRIDDLE: A heavy metal cooking surface, which may be either fitted with handles, built into a stove, or heated by its own gas or electric element. Cooking is done directly on the griddle.

GRILL: A cooking technique in which foods are cooked by a radiant heat source placed below the food. Also, the piece of equipment on which grilling is done. Grills may be fueled by gas, electricity, charcoal, or wood.

GRILL PAN: A skillet with ridges that is used on the stovetop to simulate grilling.

GUMBO: A Creole soup/stew thickened with filé or okra, flavored with a variety of meats and fishes and dark roux.

INFUSION: Steeping an aromatic or other item in liquid to extract its flavor. Also, the liquid resulting from this process.

INSTANT-READ THERMOMETER: A thermometer used to measure the internal temperature of foods. The stem is inserted in the food, producing an instant temperature read-out.

JULIENNE: Vegetables, potatoes, or other items cut into thin strips; ⅛ x ⅛ x 1 to 2 inches is standard. Fine julienne is ¹⁄₁₆ x ¹⁄₁₆ x 1 to 2 inches.

JUS: Juice. Refers to fruit and vegetable juices as well as juices from meats. Jus de viande is meat gravy. Meat served "au jus" is served with its own juice or jus lié.

JUS LIÉ: Meat juice thickened lightly with arrowroot or cornstarch.

KOSHER SALT: Pure, refined salt used for pickling. Because it does not contain magnesium carbonate, it does not cloud brine solutions. Also known as coarse salt or pickling salt.

LEGUME: The seeds of certain pod plants, including beans and peas, which are eaten for their earthy flavors and high nutritional value. Also, the French word for vegetable.

LIAISON: A mixture of egg yolks and cream used to thicken and enrich sauces.

LIQUEUR: A spirit flavored with fruit, spices, nuts, herbs, and/or seeds and usually sweetened. Also known as cordials, liqueurs often have a high alcohol content, a viscous body, and a slightly sticky feel.

MANDOLINE: A slicing device of stainless steel with carbon steel blades. The blades may be adjusted to cut items into various shapes and thicknesses.

MARBLING: The intramuscular fat found in meat that makes it tender and juicy.

MARINADE: A mixture used before cooking to flavor and moisten foods; may be liquid or dry. Liquid marinades are usually based on an acidic ingredient, such as wine or vinegar; dry marinades are usually salt based.

MEDALLION: A small, round scallop of meat.

MERINGUE: Egg whites beaten with sugar until they stiffen. Types include regular or common, Italian, and Swiss.

MILLET: A small, round, glutenless grain that may be boiled or ground into flour.

MILLING: The process by which grain is separated into germ/husk, bran, and endosperm and ground into flour or meal.

MINCE: To chop into very small pieces.

MINESTRONE: A hearty vegetable soup that typically includes dried beans and pasta.

MIREPOIX: A combination of chopped aromatic vegetables—usually two parts onion, one part carrot, and one part celery—used to flavor stocks, soups, braises, and stews.

MISE EN PLACE: Literally "put in place." The preparation and assembly of ingredients, pans, utensils, and plates or serving pieces needed for a particular dish or service period.

MOLLUSK: Any of a number of invertebrate animals with soft, unsegmented bodies usually enclosed in a hard shell; mollusks include gastropods (univalves), bivalves, and cephalopods. Examples include clams, oysters, snails, octopus, and squid.

NUTRIENT: A basic component of food used by the body for growth, repair, restoration, and energy. Includes carbohydrates, fats, proteins, water, vitamins, and minerals.

PAILLARD: A scallop of meat pounded until thin; usually grilled or sautéed.

PAN FRYING: To cook food by partial immersion in hot fat, usually in a shallow pan such as a skillet or sauté pan.

PAN STEAMING: A method of cooking foods in a very small amount of liquid in a covered pan over direct heat.

PAPILLOTE, EN: A moist-heat cooking method similar to steaming, in which items are enclosed in parchment and cooked in the oven.

PARCHMENT: Heat-resistant paper used in cooking for such preparations as lining baking pans, cooking items en papillote, and covering items during the process of shallow poaching.

PARCOOK: To partially cook an item before storing or finishing.

PASTRY BAG: A bag—usually made of plastic, canvas, or nylon—that can be fitted with plain or decorative tips and used to pipe out icings and puréed foods.

PESTO: A thick, puréed mixture of an herb, traditionally basil and oil. Used as a sauce for pasta and other foods and as a garnish for soup. Pesto may also contain grated cheese, nuts or seeds, and other seasonings.

PILAF: A technique for cooking grains in which the grain is sautéed briefly in butter then simmered in stock or water with various seasonings until the liquid is absorbed.

POACH: To cook gently in simmering liquid that is 160° to 185°F.

POLENTA: Cornmeal cooked in simmering liquid until the grains soften and the liquid absorbs. Polenta can be eaten hot or cold, firm or soft.

PRAWN: A crustacean that closely resembles shrimp; often used as a general term for large shrimp.

PULSE: The edible seed of a leguminous plant, such as a bean, lentil, or pea. Often referred to simply as legume. Also, the action of turning a food processor or blender on and off to control mixing speed and time.

PURÉE: To process food by mashing, straining, or chopping it very finely in order to make it a smooth paste. Also, a product produced using this technique.

RAGOÛT: A stew of meat and/or vegetables.

RAMEKIN: A small, ovenproof dish, usually ceramic.

REDUCE: To decrease the volume of a liquid by simmering or boiling; used to provide a thicker consistency and/or concentrated flavors.

RISOTTO: Rice that is sautéed briefly in fat with onions and possibly other aromatics, then combined with stock, which is added in several additions and stirred constantly, producing a creamy texture with grains that are still al dente.

ROAST: A dry-heat cooking method where the item is cooked in an oven or on a spit over a fire.

ROUX: A mixture containing equal parts of flour and fat (usually butter) used to thicken liquids. Roux is cooked to varying degrees (white, blond, or brown), depending on its intended use. The darker the roux, the less thickening power it has, but the fuller the taste.

SACHET D'ÉPICES: Literally, "bag of spices." Aromatic ingredients, encased in cheesecloth, that are used to flavor stocks and other liquids. A standard sachet contains parsley stems, cracked peppercorns, dried thyme, and a bay leaf.

SAUCE: A liquid accompaniment to food, used to enhance the flavor of the food.

SAUTÉ: To cook quickly in a small amount of fat in a pan on the range top.

SAVORY: Not sweet. Also, a family of herbs (including summer and winter savory) that taste like a cross between thyme and mint.

SCALD: To heat a liquid, usually milk or cream, to just below the boiling point. May also refer to blanching fruits and vegetables.

SCALE: To measure ingredients by weighing, or to divide dough or batter into portions by weight. Also, to remove the scales from fish.

SCALLOP: A bivalve whose adductor muscle (the muscle that keeps its shells closed) and roe are eaten. Also, a small, boneless piece of meat or fish of uniform thickness. Also, a side dish where an item is layered with cream or sauce and topped with bread crumbs prior to baking.

SCORE: To cut the surface of an item at regular intervals to allow it to cook evenly, allow excess fat to drain, or help the food absorb marinades or for decorative purposes.

SEAR: To brown the surface of food in fat over high heat before finishing by another method (e.g., braising or roasting) in order to add flavor.

SEA SALT: Salt produced by evaporating seawater. Available refined or unrefined, crystallized or ground. Also known as sel gris (French for "gray salt").

SEASONING: Adding an ingredient to give foods a particular flavor using salt, pepper, herbs, spices, and/or condiments. Also, the process by which a protective coating is built up on the interior of a pan.

SEMOLINA: The coarsely milled hard durum wheat endosperm used for gnocchi, some pasta, and couscous. Semolina has a high gluten content.

SHALLOW POACH: To cook gently in a shallow pan of simmering liquid. The liquid is often reduced and used as the base of a sauce.

SHELLFISH: Various types of marine life consumed as food, including mollusks such as univalves, bivalves, cephalopods, and crustaceans.

SIEVE: A container made of a perforated material, such as wire mesh, used to drain, rice, or purée foods.

SIMMER: To maintain the temperature of a liquid just below boiling. Also, to cook in simmering liquid. The temperature range for simmering is 185° to 200°F.

SKIM: To remove impurities from the surface of a liquid, such as stock or soup, during cooking.

SLURRY: A starch such as arrowroot, cornstarch, or potato starch dispersed in cold liquid to prevent it from forming lumps when added to hot liquid as a thickener.

SMOKE POINT: The temperature at which a fat begins to break (and smoke) when heated.

SOUFFLÉ: Literally "puffed." A preparation made with a sauce base (usually béchamel for savory soufflés, pastry cream for sweet ones), whipped egg whites, and flavorings. The egg whites cause the soufflé to puff during cooking.

SPÄTZLE: A soft noodle or small dumpling made by dropping bits of a prepared batter into simmering liquid.

SPICE: An aromatic vegetable substance from numerous plant parts, usually dried and used as seasoning.

SPIDER: A long-handled skimmer used to remove items from hot liquid or fat and to skim the surface of liquids.

STANDARD BREADING PROCEDURE: The assembly-line procedure in which items are dredged in flour, dipped in beaten egg, then coated with crumbs before being pan fried or deep-fried.

STEAMER: A set of stacked pots with perforations in the bottom of each pot. They fit over a larger pot that is filled with boiling or simmering water. Also, a perforated insert made of metal or bamboo that can be used in a pot to steam foods.

STEAMING: A cooking method in which items are cooked in a vapor bath created by boiling water or other liquids.

STEEP: To allow an ingredient to sit in warm or hot liquid to extract flavor or impurities, or to soften the item.

STEW: A cooking method nearly identical to braising but generally involving smaller pieces of meat and hence a shorter cooking time. Stewed items also may be blanched, rather than seared, to give the finished product a pale color. Also, a dish prepared by using the stewing method.

STIR-FRYING: A cooking method similar to sautéing in which items are cooked over very high heat using little fat. Usually this is done in a wok, and the food is kept moving constantly.

STOCK: A flavorful liquid prepared by simmering meat bones, poultry bones, seafood bones, and/or vegetables in water with aromatics until their flavor is extracted. It is used as a base for soups, sauces, and other preparations.

STOCKPOT: A large, straight-sided pot that is taller than it is wide. Used for making stocks and soups. Some have spigots. Also called a marmite.

STRAIN: To pass a liquid through a sieve or screen to remove particles.

SWEAT: To cook an item, usually vegetables, in a covered pan in a small amount of fat until it softens and releases moisture but does not brown.

TABLE SALT: Refined, granulated salt. May be fortified with iodine and treated with magnesium carbonate to prevent clumping.

TEMPER: To heat gently and gradually. May refer to the process of incorporating hot liquid into a liaison to gradually raise its temperature.

THICKENER: An ingredient used to give additional body to liquids. Arrowroot, cornstarch, gelatin, and roux are examples of thickeners.

TRUSS: To tie up meat or poultry with string before cooking it in order to give it a compact shape for more even cooking and better appearance.

WHIP/WHISK: To beat an item, such as cream or egg whites, to incorporate air. Also, a special tool for whipping, made of looped wire attached to a handle.

WHITE MIREPOIX: Mirepoix that does not include carrots and may include chopped mushrooms or mushroom trimmings and parsnips. It is used for pale or white sauces and stocks.

WHOLE GRAIN: An unmilled or unprocessed grain.

WHOLE WHEAT FLOUR: Flour milled from the whole grain, including the bran, germ, and endosperm.

WOK: A round-bottomed pan, usually made of rolled steel, which is used for nearly all cooking methods in Chinese cuisine. Its shape allows for even heat distribution and easy tossing of ingredients.

YEAST: Microscopic fungus whose metabolic processes are responsible for fermentation. It is used for leavening bread and in the making of cheese, beer, and wine.

YOGURT: Milk cultured with bacteria to give it a slightly thick consistency and sour flavor.

ZEST: The thin, brightly colored outer part of citrus rind. It contains volatile oils, making it ideal for use as a flavoring.

INDEX

Page numbers in *italics* indicate recipe illustrations